# TEN-GALLON WAR

## ALSO BY JOHN EISENBERG

*The Longest Shot: Lil E. Tee and the Kentucky Derby*

*Cotton Bowl Days: Growing Up with Dallas
and the Cowboys in the 1960s*

*From 33rd Street to Camden Yards:
An Oral History of the Baltimore Orioles*

*Native Dancer: Hero of a Golden Age*

*The Great Match Race: When North Met South
in America's First Sports Spectacle*

*My Guy Barbaro: A Jockey's Journey Through Love,
Triumph, and Heartbreak with America's Favorite Horse*
(with Edgar Prado)

*That First Season: How Vince Lombardi Took the Worst
Team in the NFL and Set It on the Path to Glory*

# TEN-GALLON WAR

The NFL's Cowboys, the AFL's Texans,
and the Feud for Dallas's Pro Football Future

## John Eisenberg

Houghton Mifflin Harcourt
BOSTON   NEW YORK
2012

www.hmhbooks.com

*Library of Congress Cataloging-in-Publication Data*
Eisenberg, John, date.
Ten-gallon war : the NFL's Cowboys, the AFL's Texans,
and the feud for Dallas's pro football future / John Eisenberg.
p. cm.
Includes index.
ISBN 978-0-547-43550-3
1. Dallas Cowboys (Football team)—History.
2. Houston Texans (Football team)—History. I. Title.
GV956.D3E58 20012
796.332'6409764—dc23
2012016241

Book design by Brian Moore

Printed in the United States of America
DOC 10 9 8 7 6 5 4 3 2 1

*For Mary Wynne, with love*

# CONTENTS

———— ☆ ————

## PART IV

## PART V

# PROLOGUE

THE SELLOUT CROWD crammed into Arrowhead Stadium in Kansas City, Missouri, on October 11, 2009, was taken aback when the Dallas Cowboys and Kansas City Chiefs took the field wearing "throwback" uniforms from a half-century earlier, when they represented the same city, played in rival leagues, and fought bitterly for the hearts and minds of the same fans.

What was this? Putting aside their famous metallic-blue colors for a day, the Cowboys wore dark blue jerseys with white numerals, white pants, and white helmets with dark blue stars on the sides — their uniform from the early sixties, when they were a pitiful expansion team rather than one of the most popular sports franchises on the planet. The Chiefs wore white pants, bright red jerseys, and bright red helmets with the state of Texas outlined on either side — their attire from when they were known as the Dallas Texans of the American Football League.

Their surprising apparel was part of the National Football League's yearlong celebration of the fiftieth anniversary of the AFL's birth — an ironic commemoration in a way, considering the AFL had been the NFL's fierce adversary at first, an upstart seeking to muscle in on the established league's turf. The two had stabbed each other in the back, told lies, fought over players, gone to court, and practically pushed each other to bankruptcy before agreeing to merge. But all that was ancient history now. They had long ago joined hands to become America's preeminent sports league.

A half-century later, the NFL readily admitted that the AFL had contributed enthusiasm, bright ideas, and some damn good football teams to the merger and willingly commemorated its birth. During the 2009 season, former AFL teams such as the Oakland Raiders, San Diego Chargers, and Buffalo Bills were donning replicas of their old uniforms to play each other in what were being called "AFL Legacy Games." The Cowboys, now an iconic franchise known as "America's Team," were the only pre-merger NFL team playing in such a game, the league having decided it simply couldn't pass up an opportunity to pit the franchises that had once fought over Dallas.

The Cowboys and Texans had shared a home stadium for three years in the early sixties, playing on alternate Sundays at the Cotton Bowl, the concrete colossus then known as one of college football's grandest stages. Both teams drew meager crowds, sometimes giving away as many tickets as they sold. They never faced each other on the field, but they battled in every other way, resorting to trickery and lawsuits to try to gain an edge, fighting over players, and stealing each other's ideas as they sought to elbow the other out of town. Both franchises were owned by young men from oil-rich families unaccustomed to failure.

Spotting the AFL Legacy Game on their 2009 schedule, the Chiefs had run with the idea, selling it as "The Game That Never Was," a reprise of the Cowboys-Texans battle. Sadly, most of the frontline warriors from those rollicking days were gone. Lamar Hunt, the sports pioneer who founded the AFL and owned the Texans, had died, as had Clint Murchison Jr., the Cowboys' original owner. Both coaches, the Cowboys' Tom Landry and the Texans' Hank Stram, were gone. So was Tex Schramm, the Cowboys' general manager, who had battled as fiercely as anyone.

Much of the bitterness from those days was gone too. The franchises had operated in different cities for more than four decades, dulling the distrust and dislike that boiled over back in the day. When Lamar Hunt was alive, he lived near Cowboys owner Jerry Jones on Preston Road in Dallas, and when their teams played, they lightheartedly competed for the "Preston Road Trophy." Their teams had played a handful of regular-season games against each other over the years as part of the NFL's regular schedule rotation.

But while games between the Cowboys and Chiefs had become routine to most people, there were exceptions — old lions from the early sixties who, like southerners who still pledged allegiance to Dixie, swore they would "never forget."

Sitting in his den in Dallas on that October afternoon in 2009, a seventy-two-year-old car salesman named Jack Spikes watched on television as his former team took on the Cowboys in the uniform he had worn when he was a hard-hitting fullback for the Texans in the early sixties. He worked at a BMW dealership now, occasionally selling expensive cars to Cowboy players, some of whom he liked. But his dislike for their high-and-mighty franchise, which dated to when he played for the other team in town, had never abated. He didn't like the Cowboys one bit.

*I hope to hell the Chiefs beat the crap out of them,* Spikes thought, *just like we would have back then.*

The sight of the teams in their old uniforms startled Mike Rhyner, a well-known sports radio talk-show host in Dallas, who was ten years old when the Cowboys and Texans started up a half-century earlier. Rhyner had sided with the Texans at first, mostly because his father demanded it, but later switched to the Cowboys. Having lived through those days, he knew this wasn't just any game from a historical standpoint.

*Wow. Too bad they never played like this, in those uniforms, all those years ago,* he thought. *That would have been some war.*

Watching the game in person, from a private box at Arrowhead, Chris Burford had the same thought. Like Spikes, he had played for the Texans and continued with the franchise when it moved to Kansas City. He had been a pass-catching fiend in those days, a wily receiver whose meticulous routes and sure hands befuddled opponents. Now seventy-one, a spry and sharp Bay Area lawyer, he had put football behind him, but he enjoyed coming back and mingling with other former Chiefs at the franchise's annual alumni weekend. That occasion had brought him to Arrowhead on this Sunday.

To most of the other former Kansas City players in the box, a game against the Cowboys carried no extra significance. But Burford felt a tingling in his stomach. The smug preeminence of the Cowboys and their fans irritated him, as it did Spikes and the other former Texans who had fought the Cowboys long ago.

*The game that never was? Sheee-it.*

This one, in 2009, wasn't a fair fight, Burford thought. The struggling Chiefs were 0-4. The Cowboys were perennial playoff contenders.

But that wasn't the case when they shared Dallas in the early sixties and everyone had wanted them to settle their differences on the field.

"'The game that never was' . . . what a bunch of horse crap," Burford snorted later when asked about sitting at Arrowhead that day. "We would have kicked the shit out of the Cowboys back then. I would have loved to have played them every week. We were the better team. No one thought so, but we would have whipped them."

Hell, yeah, he remembered those days.

# PART I

# 1

---
☆
---

# "Would you be interested in starting up a new league?"

L AMAR HUNT WAS AT 30,000 feet, his head literally in the clouds, when the idea of starting a new professional football league came to him. "The lightbulb just came on," he would say later. That it did so in the sky, on an American Airlines flight, seemed entirely appropriate, for the idea was, if anything, a flight of fancy.

As Hunt flew from Miami to his hometown of Dallas on a February evening in 1959, the National Football League had never been more popular. After grinding along for almost four decades in the shadow of Major League Baseball, the NFL was suddenly taking off like a Russian rocket. Six weeks earlier, a television audience of 40 million had watched NBC's broadcast of the league's championship game, a thriller between the Baltimore Colts and New York Giants decided in sudden-death overtime.

Even though Hunt, as the son of one of the world's wealthiest men, oilman Haroldson Lafayette "H.L." Hunt, had been brought up to think Texas big, he understood it was a long-odds proposition to take on the NFL and survive. Three leagues had tried and failed over the years, most recently the All-America Football Conference, a late-forties start-up that folded after spewing red ink for four years. The NFL's feisty old guard, led by the Chicago Bears' George Halas, had fended off that challenge and celebrated by annexing the dying league's best teams.

Less than a decade later, as Lamar sat in his seat in the plane's first-class cabin and contemplated what he thought was a bright idea, he quickly concocted a list of major questions a new league would face. Why would anyone buy in as the owner of a franchise knowing that he would probably lose millions in the early years? Why would any decent players bypass the NFL to play in the league? Why would any fans care about teams with no history or tradition?

Lamar was just twenty-six, barely removed from his callow days as a fun-loving Kappa Sigma fraternity brother at Southern Methodist University in Dallas. His idea was easily dismissed as a fantasy, the idle stirring of a young man with more money than sense. In the coming years, many people in the NFL would view his new league as just that, a folly.

But they would discover that it was a mistake to underestimate Lamar Hunt.

Yes, he was young, but he had a realistic vision for his new league from the moment he conceived it. His enthusiasm for football, and sports in general, was unmatched. And oh, he was determined. His goal — his sole motivation, at least at the outset — was to bring pro football to Dallas, his oil-rich hometown, of which he was so proud. But as he had learned very quickly, the NFL was not inclined to help.

A year earlier, Hunt had called the NFL's commissioner, Bert Bell, to see about buying his way into the established league, which had been in operation since shortly after World War I. It had seen dozens of teams come and go over the years — the Canton (Ohio) Bulldogs, the Pottstown (Pennsylvania) Maroons — but it had been stable for almost a decade with an even dozen franchises: the Chicago Bears, Baltimore Colts, New York Giants, Cleveland Browns, Pittsburgh Steelers, Washington Redskins, Philadelphia Eagles, Chicago Cardinals, Detroit Lions, Green Bay Packers, Los Angeles Rams, and San Francisco 49ers.

Bell told Lamar to call Walter and Violet Wolfner, who owned the lamentable Cardinals, a losing team perpetually overshadowed in the Windy City by Halas's more successful Bears. Representatives from a half-dozen cities without NFL teams, including Minneapolis, Atlanta, Seattle, and New Orleans, had already approached the Wolfners about buying and relocating the franchise. The Wolfners had turned them all down.

Lamar met with the Wolfners in Chicago. The older couple enjoyed his company. He listened intently, spoke deliberately, and kept notes. With his black-frame glasses, neatly parted chestnut hair, business attire, and southern manners, he seemed older than he was.

When the Wolfners turned him down, he offered to take a minority stake, believing he would eventually gain control and move the Cardinals to Dallas. The Wolfners were intrigued by his persistence and especially his money, but ultimately offered him just a 20 percent stake in the team, with no hope of a move to Dallas.

Around the same time, Lamar also joined a group from Dallas and Fort Worth seeking a baseball franchise in a proposed third major league being organized by Branch Rickey, the legendary executive who had integrated the major leagues with Jackie Robinson a decade earlier. Lamar traveled to New York for a meeting led by Rickey. Insightful and forward-thinking at age seventy, Rickey explained that a new league could work because baseball hadn't added a franchise in more than fifty years, stubbornly sticking with two eight-team circuits because the owners distrusted change and didn't want to cut up their revenues any more. Numerous large cities had been frozen out, and yet they were more than capable of supporting teams, Rickey said. He cited Milwaukee, where attendance records had been set since the Braves moved there from Boston in the early fifties.

Lamar was impressed with Rickey, but he preferred football. On the last Sunday of 1958, he sat at home in Dallas and watched the NFL championship game between the Colts and Giants. The Colts, led by a brilliant young quarterback, Johnny Unitas, jumped out to a 14–3 lead and appeared to have the game wrapped up, but the Giants rallied in the fourth quarter to take a three-point lead as a sellout crowd cheered so loudly that Yankee Stadium seemed to vibrate. But Unitas, exhibiting remarkable poise, led a drive that resulted in a last-second field goal, forcing the game into overtime — a first for the NFL. Unitas then led another long drive, which ended with Colts fullback Alan Ameche diving into the end zone for the winning touchdown. On the drives, Unitas connected repeatedly with Raymond Berry, a star receiver with whom Lamar had played college ball at SMU.

As he shut off his television, Lamar was exhilarated. What a sporting event! The game had featured brilliant performances, dramatic momentum swings, breathtaking moments, last-second heroics, and larger-than-life figures — Unitas was as cocksure as any western gunslinger. And NBC had effectively captured it all, bringing the drama right into his den.

Watching the game had a profound effect on Lamar. He saw that pro football, long overshadowed by the college version of the sport as well as by baseball, was becoming quite a spectacle and that television, though barely a decade old as a popular medium, could deliver it magnificently to massive audiences. *Pro football just might be the sport of the future,* he thought. When he read that millions had watched the game, drawn to their black-and-white sets by the drama, he was convinced the nation's appetite for pro football was growing.

Redoubling his efforts to buy into the NFL, Lamar flew to Miami for another meeting with the Wolfners, this time at their winter home. But the trip was fruitless. The Wolfners simply weren't selling.

As they parted, Walter Wolfner mentioned offhandedly that another young Texan from an oil family had come to Miami to discuss purchasing the Cardinals. Kenneth S. "Bud" Adams, the son of the president of Phillips Petroleum, had wanted to move the franchise to Houston. Like Hunt, he had been turned down.

Digesting this news, Lamar took a taxi to the airport, boarded his American Airlines flight to Dallas, and took stock. He had been trying to secure an NFL team for a year, but the Wolfners weren't selling, and Bert Bell had told him the league wouldn't expand anytime soon, at least not until the Cardinals relocated. Yet a whole group of wealthy people from major cities wanted teams, starting with himself and Bud Adams.

Branch Rickey had said a new baseball major league could work because there was a hunger for the game in so many cities without teams. Was the same not true for professional football?

Lamar asked a stewardess for stationery, took out a pen, and jotted down some ideas for a new league under the heading "Original 6:

First Year's Operations." There would be six teams. Each would play three exhibitions and fifteen regular-season games and own territorial draft picks, enabling them to add popular local college players. The home team at every game would receive 60 percent of the "gate" — the proceeds from ticket sales — with the visitors receiving 40 percent or $35,000, whichever was higher. Lamar knew about the game's finances because the Wolfners had let him see their books.

When he finished, Lamar sat back and appraised the in-flight stationery with his writing on it. He smiled. *This really could work*, he thought. Maybe the idea of a new pro football league wasn't a flight of fancy after all.

H. L. Hunt loved to gamble. There were rumors about the old man betting as much as $50,000 a weekend on college football.

Years earlier, before he entered the oil business, Lamar's father had run a professional card table in Arkansas. After he came to Texas in the twenties, drawn by rumors of vast oil riches, he wagered his future on oil reserves — the profits from crude *expected* to spew out of the ground. If the wells had come up dry, he would have been sunk.

But the wells were not dry. He backed enough winners to stay afloat and then in 1930 entered negotiations with one Columbus Marion "Dad" Joiner, a former Tennessee legislator turned Oklahoma wildcatter, who had struck oil on the East Texas farm of a widow named Daisy Bradford. Joiner was in a familiar pinch, having oversold shares in his wells to finance more drilling. He needed a bailout. H.L. spent several days with him in a hotel suite trying to strike a deal. Joiner, who was seventy, finally sold his leases to the younger man for $1.5 million. The wells turned out to be worth infinitely more. Within a year it became clear that a vast and unimaginably fertile oil field, perhaps forty-five miles long, lay beneath the red soil and piney hills of the widow Bradford's farm and the properties surrounding it.

By 1932, H.L.'s production company had nine hundred wells in operation in East Texas. Targeted by dozens of lawsuits in the wake of his deal with Joiner, H.L. settled them all and moved on. The owner of the world's largest oil field could afford good lawyers.

Life for the Hunt family changed in a hurry. H.L. and his wife had three teenage children and two other youngsters when Lamar, their sixth child, was born in El Dorado, Arkansas, in 1932. They soon moved into a mansion in Tyler, Texas, a fast-developing oil town, and then on to Dallas, where H.L. purchased a ten-acre estate on White Rock Lake that featured a house modeled after Mount Vernon, George Washington's home.

Growing up with five siblings in the sprawling mansion, Lamar quickly exhibited a taste for sports. One of his first memories was his trip to the Cotton Bowl to see a college football game on January 1, 1937. He pored over baseball box scores in the newspapers, listened to college football games on the radio, memorized statistics, and shot baskets in his driveway for hours. He was so infatuated with sports that his brothers and sisters called him "Games."

By the late forties, H.L.'s Hunt Oil was producing 65,000 barrels of crude a day, generating around $1 million a week in gross income. But while his children knew they were fortunate, they did not grasp the extent of their father's staggering income. It was never mentioned in the media, which H.L. loathed. He did not buy cars or yachts. The subject of money seldom came up at dinner. A servant occasionally drove Lamar to school, which embarrassed him. He just wanted to be a normal kid, and for the most part he was.

For his high school years, he was packed off to the Hill School, an exclusive prep institution in Pennsylvania, which his older brothers, Bunker and Herbert, had also attended. Not surprisingly, the young man known as "Games" focused on football as much as his studies. He had dreamed of being a hero on the field, and as a slender quarterback at Hill, he emulated his idol, Doak Walker, a Heisman Trophy–winning halfback for his beloved SMU Mustangs in Dallas. Wearing Walker's uniform number 37, Lamar sparkled on cool autumn Fridays in the leafy Northeast, ducking prep school tacklers, breaking long runs, and leading his team to a title.

For college, he thought about attending Washington and Lee in Virginia, where Herbert had gone, but he missed Texas, missed football, and ended up returning to Dallas and enrolling at SMU. He was expected to traipse faithfully down a predestined path, study geology, and join Herbert and Bunker at Penrod Drilling, the oil company their father had set up for them.

But all Lamar really wanted to do was keep playing football. Although he had been born into a silver-spoon existence, he was a jock at heart, bored by the cold corridors of business. Attending SMU would give him the opportunity to try to live out his dream. SMU's athletic director, Matty Bell, a former football coach who had directed the Mustangs to a national title in the thirties, was happy to let H. L. Hunt's boy join the program.

The situation was potentially disastrous. The Mustangs competed in the prestigious Southwest Conference against national powers such as Texas, Arkansas, Rice, and Texas Christian. They had a prominent place in the chronicle of Texas college football history thanks to the exploits of Doak Walker and others, and every year they brought in a new group of blue-chip recruits with the talent to continue the saga. The five-foot-eleven, 180-pound Lamar might be out of his league.

Lamar suited up for SMU's freshman team in the fall of 1951. To train, he jogged on the streets alongside a car driven by Bunker. When practice began, he surprisingly held his own. He could take a hit. The coaches rewarded him with playing time. As the team rolled through a five-game schedule without a defeat, Lamar scored a touchdown, carried the ball on ten rushes, and caught eight passes to finish third on the team in that statistic, behind Doyle Nix and Ed Bernet, a pair of future pros. It was enough to earn a letter.

He was listed among the backs on the Mustangs' 1952 varsity roster, but his lack of size and ability finally caught up with him when he found himself on the practice field with Forrest Gregg, Bill Forester, and other rugged upperclassmen destined for long careers in the NFL — real football players. His dream of emulating Doak Walker abruptly ended. Relegated to the bench as a third-string end, he stood forlornly among the other subs during home games, wearing uniform number 80, and didn't make road trips because the "traveling squad" was limited to players who might actually participate.

Yet while his place on the end of the bench appeared irrevocable, he never stopped believing his prospects might change if he worked hard enough and did what his coaches asked. And whether or not he played, he really wanted just to blend in, be a typical college athlete. He hoarded pennies, drove a battered car, and stole socks from the athletic department like everyone else. He never brought up his family's wealth, and the subject seldom came up in conversation. Many of his teammates had no idea he was, in fact, one of *those* Hunts.

While taking extra geology classes (and escaping the Texas summer heat) in Colorado in the summer of 1954, he became friends with Buzz Kemble, a teammate from Fort Worth who was taking the same classes. They bet on dog races at night and took their girlfriends to a water park that Lamar's family owned. Kemble never realized his quiet friend was H.L.'s son. One evening Lamar had to borrow a dollar to pay for a toll as they drove home from dinner.

Inevitably, word spread. One day in practice at SMU, a younger end outweighing him by fifty pounds literally knocked him off the field and onto a curb, then taunted, "Poor boy, you better get Popsie to cover that curb with foam rubber." Day after day, Lamar absorbed practice-field beatings that left him bruised and sore.

But Lamar was rewarded for his patience and determination. In 1954 he finally made it onto the traveling squad, and then onto the field for the Mustangs in early-season wins over nonconference opponents Kansas and Missouri. Kemble, a fellow third-stringer, carried the ball. Lamar blocked. His limited playing time wasn't enough to earn a varsity letter.

After that season, Kemble quit football to concentrate on swimming, and Lamar decided to hang up his cleats, even though he was eligible to play one more season. He had married a girl named Rosemary Carr, whom he had known since high school. They were considering starting a family. He would be twenty-three in the fall of 1955. It was time to move on.

Seeking other outlets for his passion, he opened his first sports business venture — a baseball batting-cage operation called Zima Bat, located on Dallas's North Central Expressway. Operating it with a friend, Lamar charged customers a quarter to hit ten balls. When business soared, he added a pitching mound so they could throw, and he erected a miniature golf course and snowball stand as well. Zima Bat was a hit.

When he was a college senior, Lamar and Rosemary were invited to an uncle's dinner party where he found himself sitting beside another guest named Clint Murchison Jr. They had a lot in common. Both were the sons of oil millionaires. Both were from Dallas. Both loved football.

Although Murchison was nine years older and had been too small to play the game, he followed the local college scene as avidly as Lamar and also kept up with the pros.

They spent an enjoyable evening together, never imagining they would end up locked in a football feud, owning rival teams in their hometown. "It was the only time," Murchison commented later, "that Lamar and I would meet before we declared war on each other."

After graduating from SMU, Lamar went to work at Penrod Drilling. His older brothers, having already turned the company into a thriving concern, tried to find something for him to do. Lamar was named a managing partner. He traveled around to branch offices and wells, attended meetings, and learned the ropes. But his heart wasn't in it. Penrod's chief financial officer, Jack Steadman, never saw Lamar more excited than on Monday mornings when he came in and reviewed the football games he had attended or watched over the weekend.

Drifting away from the family business, he used his fortunate circumstances to explore the business of sports instead. He traveled around the country to events that interested him — a tennis tournament in California, a car race in the South, pro and college basketball games, pro and college football contests — and took notes on their inner workings, how they were financed and staged.

In the spring of 1957, he phoned a former college classmate and teammate, Don McIlhenny. They had much in common. They had pledged Kappa Sig together, run with the same crowd, and graduated the same year. McIlhenny had been talented enough to go into pro football, playing halfback for the NFL's Detroit Lions in the fall of 1956. Now he was back in Dallas to take graduate business classes at SMU in his off-season.

McIlhenny picked up the phone in his apartment. "Hey! How are you, Lamar?" he exclaimed.

"I'm fine, Don," Lamar replied. "Say, how about you and me and the wives going on a picnic this weekend? How does that sound?"

McIlhenny had always admired Lamar's unostentatious nature; he had more money than anyone but didn't flout it. In fact, he almost seemed embarrassed by it.

They arranged their picnic for a hillside overlooking White Rock

Lake. When McIlhenny and his wife arrived, they found that Lamar's brother Bunker was also present with his wife. The couples sat on blankets, ate sandwiches, and relaxed in the warm glory of a Texas spring afternoon, conversing on a variety of subjects. Then Lamar suddenly zeroed in on McIlhenny's experience with the Lions.

"What was it like in the pros?" he asked.

McIlhenny responded that he had a hell of a time; the Lions were a championship-caliber team quarterbacked by Bobby Layne, a Dallas native and former Texas Longhorns star renowned for drinking hard on Saturday nights and playing hard on Sunday afternoons.

Lamar fired more questions, getting down to specifics about the NFL. What was the salary range? How long were the practices? How good was the coaching? Did teams travel in style or cut corners? How were the fans? Which cities were enjoyable to play in and which were dead ends? McIlhenny believed that his wealthy friend, like many football fans, simply wanted the inside scoop.

But a couple of years later, when he read in the newspaper about Lamar wanting to start a new pro football league, McIlhenny turned to his wife and said, "Honey, remember when we went on that picnic and Lamar asked me all those questions about pro ball?"

His wife said she did remember. McIlhenny smiled and shook his head.

"I thought at the time he was just curious," he said, "but you know what? I think he was on to something."

Even after conceiving the idea of a new pro league in February 1959, Lamar still sought to bring the NFL to Dallas. He was just so proud of his hometown. On his travels around the country, he often found himself extolling its abundant virtues with childlike enthusiasm, boasting that Dr Pepper, the popular soft drink, was bottled there, that Neiman Marcus, the quintessential chic clothier, was headquartered there, and that the sprawling State Fair of Texas, held every October at Fair Park, east of downtown, was truly a spectacle. You could not top the Mexican food at Spanish Village, he would say, or the charbroiled hamburgers at Goff's on Lovers Lane. The towering downtown skyline had to be seen to be believed, he would exclaim, and there was always college football on the radio, with broadcasting legend Kern Tips at the microphone — nirvana for a sports fan. An NFL franchise would just add more excitement to the scene, he felt.

But there was a fundamental problem with his quest, an obstacle he simply couldn't get around. The NFL had put a team in Dallas before, with disastrous results. In 1952 a group of Dallas businessmen led by Giles Miller, a sports-loving young millionaire, had purchased the league's downtrodden New York Yanks and brought them to Dallas as a team called the Texans. The city rejected the franchise so resoundingly that it didn't even complete a full season in Dallas before pulling up stakes. Understandably, the memory of that experience persisted in NFL circles, cooling the league on Lamar's hometown.

Giles Miller had really believed that North Texas was ready to support a pro team; tens of thousands of fans packed high school stadiums on Friday nights and cheered for college teams on Saturdays, so why wouldn't they fill the Cotton Bowl on Sundays? The NFL had been similarly optimistic; with its teams concentrated in the Northeast, Midwest, and West, it embraced the idea of expanding to a new part of the country, especially a region so passionate about football . . . and so wealthy. The *New York Times* wrote that the NFL would benefit from having a team "where they grow money."

But Miller and his group did not actually have that much to invest. They also didn't know how to run an organization. They brought in a former Notre Dame quarterback, Jimmy Phelan, to coach the team, but Phelan knew next to nothing about the job. One of his ideas was to have players bat a football back and forth over the goalpost crossbar during practice.

The team's roster included Gino Marchetti and Art Donovan, two future Pro Football Hall of Fame inductees, but overall the Texans were shy on talent. At their first home game, just 17,000 fans were sprinkled around the Cotton Bowl, which could seat 75,000. The crowds quickly grew even smaller, partly because the Texans were a losing team, and also partly because they had several African American players. The Southwest Conference still hadn't integrated, and neither had the Cotton Bowl, where black fans sat in a "colored" end zone section.

By November the Texans had a record of zero wins and nine losses and were playing before a few thousand home fans. With Miller's group hemorrhaging money, the league yanked them out of Dallas before the season ended and ran them as a homeless squad based in Hershey, Pennsylvania. Improbably, they defeated Halas's Bears on Thanksgiving in Akron, Ohio, before a few thousand fans (after 33,000 had packed the stadium for a high school game that morning), but ended the season with only one win. They began anew the next year as the Baltimore Colts.

After that fiasco, the NFL had wanted no part of Dallas. When conversations about possible expansion or relocation occurred, several cities were mentioned — but never Dallas. As far as the league was concerned, Dallas had blown its opportunity. There was no sense putting a pro team in such a narrow-minded college football hotbed.

But Lamar Hunt was undeterred. In March 1959 he called Bert Bell again — after his fateful American Airlines flight — and asked if there was a chance the league might expand. The idea had gained some momentum lately. With the NFL and Major League Baseball both seemingly determined not to add teams, the frozen-out cities had raised enough of a ruckus to gain the attention of a congressional subcommittee on antitrust and monopoly issues, chaired by Estes Kefauver, a Tennessee senator. With Congress sniffing around, the leagues had started taking expansion more seriously, at least publicly. Baseball had announced parameters for new franchises. The NFL had convened an expansion committee chaired by Halas.

Bell told Lamar to call Halas. The cantankerous sixty-four-year-old "Papa Bear," as he was known, had been in the Canton, Ohio, auto showroom on the day the NFL was formed shortly after World War I, and he had been present for every important decision in its history. He was not only the league's conscience but also its wisest owl and fiercest warrior. He loved his Bears, but above all he loved the NFL. Although he was almost irrationally competitive, he was also a team player. The NFL's twelve teams might be rivals on the field, he said, but they were partners in the football business, sharing the goal of seeing their league succeed.

When the Bears' storied archrivals, the Packers, stumbled in the early fifties, Halas went on the stump to help them win a local election to obtain funding for a new stadium and then suggested they hire Vince Lombardi, a bright new coach. Suddenly, the Packers were back on their feet — bad news for the Bears but good news for the league.

The coterie of stubborn sportsmen who had banded together and shepherded the NFL through decades of hard times to its current increasing prominence included Bell, Pittsburgh's Art Rooney, New York's Tim Mara, and Washington's George Preston Marshall. But no one had a clearer vision of the league's past, present, and future than Halas. When he spoke, it was, in effect, the league speaking.

When Lamar phoned Halas at the Biltmore Hotel in Arizona, where Papa Bear spent the winter, and offered to come and discuss expansion, Halas discouraged him, saying the trip would be a waste of time. The NFL had no plans to expand, Halas said, and he reiterated that it wouldn't until the Wolfners decided what they were doing with the Cardinals.

Hanging up, Lamar decided it was time to move ahead with putting together a new league. The NFL expansion committee had never actually met, it turned out. Halas basically *was* the expansion committee, and he obviously wasn't bullish on the idea. Dallas might never get a pro football team if it waited for the NFL to act, Lamar thought.

He contacted Bud Adams and flew to Houston for a meeting. They had never met, and the two sons of oil millionaires noted their differences as they ate dinner at the Charcoal Inn, a steakhouse Adams owned. Adams was outgoing and brash, Lamar's opposite in many respects. As Lamar made small talk through the meal, never broaching the subject that had brought him to town, Adams found him shy and somewhat curious.

Finally, on the drive to the airport, Lamar brought up football. "I know you tried to buy the Cardinals. I did too," Lamar said. "Would you be interested in starting up a new league?"

Adams, at the wheel, quickly replied, "Yeah, I would."

Lamar nodded, got out of the car at the airport curb, and as he closed the door said, "Okay, I'll be back in touch with you."

Encouraged, Lamar began seeking owners in other cities who wanted to come aboard. Max Winter, a former part owner and general manager of the National Basketball Association's Minneapolis Lakers, had been denied an NFL team for the Twin Cities. He agreed to take an AFL team. Bob Howsam, a minor league baseball owner in Denver, also came aboard.

Dallas, Houston, Denver, and Minnesota were classic "outsider" markets in search of a place somewhere in pro football. But Lamar also believed the league needed teams in major cities to succeed, which meant encroaching on the NFL's turf in New York and Los Angeles.

He found a surprising partner in California: Barron Hilton, the thirty-two-year-old son of hotel magnate Conrad Hilton. His mother's second husband had been a football coach at College of Mines in El Paso, Texas, and Barron had enjoyed sitting on the bench during games. He jumped in enthusiastically when Lamar asked if he wanted to own a team in Los Angeles, even as Dan Reeves, a friend of his family's and the majority owner of the NFL's Rams, called and told him not to get involved.

On the other coast, Lamar recruited Harry Wismer, a well-known broadcaster, to own a New York franchise. A fast-talking Michigan native with an entrepreneurial mind and enormous ego, Wismer had broadcast the games of the NFL's Lions and Redskins, married into the Ford family, and gained a minority interest in the Redskins at one point while trying, without success, to get the television networks to broadcast NFL games in prime time — thought to be a crazy idea at the time. Lamar believed that Wismer could help the new league attract attention.

In Dallas, Lamar applied to the State Fair of Texas for a permit to play at the Cotton Bowl on Sunday afternoons. (The stadium was located in the middle of Fair Park.) But he continued to move cautiously, leaving his options open. In early June, he flew to Philadelphia to meet with Bert Bell and ask him, yet again, if the NFL might expand.

Bell, a rumpled fifty-six-year-old who had owned and coached the Philadelphia Eagles before becoming commissioner, liked the young Texan but had begun to find him somewhat annoying. Bell stated firmly that the league had no plans to expand.

Lamar flew back to Dallas and finalized his initial plans for what he would call the American Football League. He had six teams tentatively established and needed two more, having decided that eight, not six, was the optimal size. But before going public with his plans, he sent an emissary back to Philadelphia to warn Bell about what was coming.

The emissary was Davey O'Brien, a legendary former star quarterback who had played at Texas Christian University in the thirties and later for Bell's Eagles. O'Brien told Bell what Lamar was planning, but didn't offer many details. Bell, seemingly unconcerned, wished Lamar well.

Shortly after O'Brien's visit, Bell was scheduled to appear before Estes Kefauver's Senate subcommittee, which was investigating whether the NFL had a monopoly on pro football. Believing the start of a new league would help keep Congress off his back, Bell announced at the hearing on July 28, 1959, that a new entity called the AFL was planning to kick off in 1960.

Tipped off, Lamar flew to Washington and was in the subcommittee room as Bell spoke. Thinking through the odd circumstances, he didn't mind that Bell had revealed his big secret. The NFL's blessing could give his venture credibility, he decided.

That night, Lamar visited Bell at the commissioner's summer home in New Jersey. Bell gave him advice on how to proceed, which Lamar welcomed. He wasn't trying to start a war. He didn't see his new league as a potential threat to the NFL. Most of his franchises would be in new pro football cities. There was room for two leagues and they could coexist peaceably, he thought, perhaps even with Bell as commissioner.

Later, Lamar would characterize that vision as "perhaps the most naive idea in the history of sports."

After Bell told the Senate subcommittee about Lamar Hunt's new league and the plan to kick it off with a pair of teams in Texas, Dallas was no longer a forbidden city in the NFL's eyes. The established league suddenly was interested again in Lamar's hometown — very interested.

Halas sensed a real and dangerous threat. As young as Lamar was, he had more money than anyone in the NFL. So did Bud Adams and Barron Hilton. Dallas had failed as a pro football town before, but it looked more promising now as part of a new league with these men and their money behind it.

Within a week of Bell's remarks to Congress, Halas summoned Lamar and Adams to a secret meeting at his Chicago sporting goods store. Lamar was flattered to get the call, noting a change in Papa Bear's tone. The old man was a lot friendlier now, a lot more interested.

Lamar and Adams flew up to Chicago on Adams's private plane, picking up Bob Howsam in Denver along the way. On a sweltering August afternoon, the three men from the AFL sat down with Halas.

Papa Bear wore a short-sleeve white shirt and Coke-bottle glasses. He growled when he spoke, but he cracked sly smiles.

If Lamar had learned anything about the NFL in a year of knocking on doors, it was that Halas got what Halas wanted. His favorite referees tended to work the Bears' biggest games. When his opinion settled disputes at league meetings, the Bears tended to benefit.

And what Halas wanted now was to swat away this damn AFL like a fly hovering over a glass of sweet iced tea at a picnic.

After downplaying the likelihood of expansion for years, Papa Bear abruptly reversed course. In a backroom at his store, he offered Hunt a Dallas franchise that could kick off in 1961 and tendered the same offer to Adams for a Houston team. The league didn't want a team in Denver, he said, but he offered to help Howsam buy into an existing team.

"You've always wanted to get into the NFL. The time is right," Halas said with a satisfied smile to the men across the table from him.

Stunned, Lamar, Adams, and Howsam retreated to the Sherman Hotel in downtown Chicago and discussed Papa Bear's offer. Just like that, they could be part of the NFL, what they had wanted all along. But the longer they talked, the guiltier they felt. They had already committed to starting the AFL. They would be bailing on Hilton, Wismer, and their other new partners. They couldn't do that.

In the end, they called Halas and told him no.

Less than two weeks later, on August 14, 1959, the men who had committed to starting the AFL gathered for the first league meeting in Chicago. There was no commissioner, no president, no publicist; Lamar ran the meeting because the league had been his idea. He used the occasion to obtain $25,000 from each team for a league treasury.

Sportswriters from around the country were in Chicago to cover the annual exhibition game between the NFL champions and a squad of top rookies just entering the league — a popular event on the nation's sports calendar. Hours before the game, at a packed news conference across town from the all-star game, Lamar announced that the AFL would kick off in 1960 with teams in Dallas, Houston, Denver, Los Angeles, New York, Minneapolis, and two cities to be determined.

That evening Johnny Unitas and the Colts rolled to a 29–0 lead over the college all-stars at Soldier Field as 70,000 fans watched along with a national television audience of millions. Then a violent thunderstorm struck, stopping the game in the third quarter. But before the rains came, Halas had spent the evening circulating among the NFL executives in attendance, offering cautionary advice.

"We've got to stop Lamar Hunt," he said.

# 2

★

# "Those Texas Millionaires"

AMERICA HAD NEVER seen rich people like the Texas oilmen who seemingly came out of nowhere after World War II, living with an over-the-top extravagance unseen since the ornate craziness of the Gilded Age.

The country was used to ogling Vanderbilts, Rockefellers, and Gettys, eastern elites who attended prep schools and lived in mansions on New York's Fifth Avenue. But H. L. Hunt, "Big Clint" Murchison, Houston's Roy Cullen, Fort Worth's Sid Richardson, and Texas's other big-shouldered oilmen were not Harvard men who bartered equities and lorded over boardrooms. They were chicken-fried gamblers who had played a desperate zero-sum game, borrowing money they could not pay back to back speculative drilling operations, and when their wells spurted thick crude, they suddenly had fortunes matching those of Europe's grandest royal families.

And did they ever spend it.

They built sprawling mansions resembling Greek temples, with dining halls that could seat a hundred people. They dug Olympic-sized swimming pools in their backyards, traveled the globe in private planes and yachts, dreamed on a scale that titillated onlookers. Houston's

Glenn McCarthy poured his profits into an opulent eighteen-story hotel, the Shamrock, which opened in 1949 with a million-dollar gala featuring movie stars Ginger Rogers and Errol Flynn. John Mecom, another Houston wildcatter, bought a yacht as long as a football field. Richardson and Dallas's Algur Meadows assembled world-class art collections.

There was nothing, they believed, that their wealth didn't enable them to do. Dick Andrade, a Dallas bon vivant, threw weeklong parties at his mansion, and in a famous incident, he brought a live horse to his Louisville hotel suite during a party on the eve of the Kentucky Derby. Only a Texas oilman would do that.

Amazingly, they had amassed their fortunes out of the public's view, without a single headline being written until the late forties. Staunch political conservatives for the most part, they shunned the mainstream media, viewing it as a liberal cabal controlled by snotty Yankees.

But reporters eventually sniffed out the scent of money being piled as high as Dallas's skyscrapers. In 1948 a pair of popular magazines, *Life* and *Fortune*, published stories about a Texas oil boom and its brazen gamblers. Hunt, an unknown until then, was pictured walking down a Dallas street, with a caption reading, "Is this the richest man in America?" Lamar was as shocked as anyone when a ninth-grade classmate at the Hill School showed him the magazine.

Until the articles ran in *Life* and *Fortune*, people had viewed Texas and its citizens mostly through the lens of the Hollywood myth — cowboys and Indians, guns and horses. But a new Texas character quickly developed: the larger-than-life oil millionaire, impossibly rich, wearing a suit and a ten-gallon cowboy hat. Within a few years, the image was firmly stamped in America's consciousness, as evidenced by a poem written by a Los Angeles sports columnist when the NFL's Texans came to Dallas in 1952:

> *Oh, give me a home where the millionaires roam*
> *And three hundred grand is just hay.*
> *Where seldom's allowed*
> *A discouraging crowd*
> *And the Cotton Bowl's jammed every day.*

Edna Ferber, a Pulitzer Prize–winning novelist from New York, used Texas, the country's new fantasyland, as the setting for *Giant,* a sweeping 1952 novel about an oil family's rising and falling fortunes. When the book was made into a 1956 movie starring Elizabeth Taylor, Rock Hudson, and James Dean and earned a "Best Picture" Academy Award, the new Texas and its flamboyant oilmen were officially the stuff of American mythology.

In some respects, H.L. was the most outrageous of them all. At seventy years old in 1959, he had the financial clout to make or break kings, but preferred funding right-wing pamphlets and radio broadcasts from a perch on the fringe. And his personal life was downright bizarre. When Lamar was in elementary school, his family was devastated to learn that their father supported a secret second family, four children and another woman whom he may have married. When Lamar's mother died in 1955, the old man married a Hunt Oil secretary and started a third family.

But H.L. was old-fashioned in his belief that his children should make something of themselves, not just live off their inherited advantages. He tolerated Lamar's fascination with sports until he read in the Dallas papers that his son was seriously considering starting a league. Having been raised near St. Louis, a baseball hotbed, he didn't understand pro football and doubted it would flourish, remembering when it was a money loser in the thirties and forties.

He contacted two friends who were in pro football — Tim Mara, owner of the New York Giants (and a renowned high-stakes gambler himself), and James Breuil, owner of the Frontier Oil Company, who had owned the Buffalo franchise in the ill-fated All-America Football Conference in the forties. H.L. asked them to talk to Lamar, hoping they would dissuade him. H.L. knew Breuil had lost more than a half-million dollars in Buffalo.

Lamar received a phone call from H.L.'s secretary, who said, "Your dad wants to talk to you about football." Lamar went to his father's office, where Mara and Breuil were on a speaker phone. H.L. told them Lamar was thinking about getting into pro football and then asked what they thought of the idea. To H.L.'s surprise, they didn't give negative replies.

"Pro football is a good investment. It's something your son will really enjoy," Breuil said.

That wasn't what H.L. wanted to hear. He sighed at Lamar.

"Well," he said, "if you want to do it, son, I guess it's yours to do."

In the spring of 1954, when the editors of *Time* magazine were looking for the right Texan to feature in a cover story about the oil boom, they knew they had their man when they came across Clint Murchison Sr. A short, pie-faced fifty-nine-year-old with big ears, "Big Clint" was hardly an imposing figure at first glance. But in fact, he was a shrewd wheeler-dealer who set the standard for how to live large.

His Dallas residence was a palace of some 34,000 square feet. He traveled in a private plane, gave his second wife a sixteen-carat diamond engagement ring, and spent his weekends at Matagorda Island, a thirty-eight-mile strip on the Texas Gulf coast that he had purchased and developed into a private retreat where he brought friends for getaways replete with booze, cards, and women.

A native of Athens, in East Texas, Murchison had made his fortune in the thirties by drilling successful wells and by stealthily selling "hot oil," more than the federal government allowed per day from individual wells. He also was aggressively agile, like many of the other oil boomers. When his wells in West Texas brought up natural gas instead of oil, he piped the gas into nearby towns for people to use to heat their homes.

Unlike H.L., he had taken his fortune and reinvested it, buying a steam-operated railway line, a publishing house, a magazine, and much more. "Money is like manure, you have to spread it around for things to grow," Murchison said. As a venture capitalist and natural horse trader, he entertained a steady line of bankers and speculators who came to his Dallas office with business proposals in hand. He made the cover of *Time* on May 26, 1954, wearing a cowboy hat and round tortoiseshell glasses, under a banner that read, THOSE TEXAS MILLIONAIRES.

An early widower, he had raised his two sons, John and Clint Jr., sending them to elite prep schools and colleges. They returned to Dallas and initially worked alongside their father, but soon they were on their own, working at Murchison Brothers, the partnership their father had set up for them.

John, who had attended Yale, was quiet and deliberate and shunned the spotlight, while Clint Jr., more like his father, was a whip-smart risk-taker who, though shy, relished the excessive life of a Texas oil millionaire. Thirty-six years old in 1959, he was short, trim, and appeared bookish, with a brush-cut flattop and black-frame glasses. Unlike Lamar Hunt and his brothers, who had the same money but lived in normal-sized homes on quiet streets, young Clint had broken ground on what would become the largest home in Dallas, a 43,000-square-foot stone mansion with a movie room, bars, and curtains managed by push-button electronics. Married with four children, he traveled in a private plane and, like Big Clint, had bought his own island, a Spanish cay in the Bahamas, where he fished and staged lavish parties.

There was no doubting his mind. He had graduated Phi Beta Kappa from Duke with an electrical engineering degree and earned a master's degree in math from the Massachusetts Institute of Technology. By the mid-fifties, he and John had built an international empire of construction and real estate companies, taking on such complex and expensive projects as the removal of shale deposits at the Panama Canal, the building of a harbor tunnel in Havana, Cuba, and the building of massive subdivisions outside major American cities. The joke about the Murchison boys was that one couldn't say yes (John), and the other couldn't say no (Clint), but their effectiveness was indisputable.

Clint Jr. had tried to suit up and play football years earlier at Lawrenceville Prep in New Jersey, but a broken arm had convinced him to settle for enjoying the game from the stands. Now that he was a family man, he closely followed the SMU Mustangs, took his sons to Austin to see the Longhorns play, and excitedly took on the task of coaching their youth teams at the Town North YMCA in Dallas.

Few of his friends cared about pro football, but Clint Jr. enjoyed it as much as the college game, perhaps because he had spent time in the East, where it was more popular. He had purchased twenty season tickets to watch the pitiful Texans at the Cotton Bowl in 1952 and briefly considered buying out the team from Giles Miller before wisely passing. But that experience kindled an idea. He began looking to get into the NFL.

Big Clint, like H.L., was firmly opposed, believing that pro football would never be a moneymaker. But Clint Jr. thought a well-run team could turn a yearly profit, especially as the fast-growing sport gained popularity. And in any case, at a cost of around a half-million dollars, a franchise was a minuscule investment for him — actually for him and John, as they went fifty-fifty on every deal.

Mostly, young Murchison, like Lamar, just wanted Dallas to have a team. In 1953 he almost bought the San Francisco 49ers and moved them to Dallas, but Bert Bell blocked the deal, not wanting the league to abandon the Bay Area. Five years later, Clint Jr. almost bought the Washington Redskins from George Preston Marshall, their irrepressible longtime owner, who had brought marching bands and gala halftime shows to the NFL but was struggling financially. Murchison agreed to buy the team for $600,000 and let Marshall run it for five years in Dallas, and he even drew up a cashier's check to complete the purchase. But when Marshall demanded to be in charge for ten years, not five, Murchison called off the deal.

Undeterred, Murchison and his friend Bedford Wynne, a Dallas attorney who shared his passion for football, continued to explore getting into the NFL, staying in touch with Halas. When they contacted Papa Bear about expansion early in 1959, they received a far less negative response than Lamar. Halas viewed Murchison as an established businessman who could be trusted, unlike the young, hard-to-read Hunt.

In August 1959, when Halas learned about Hunt's new league starting up with a team in Dallas, he zeroed in on Murchison.

A few weeks later, Murchison and Wynne met Papa Bear in Houston, where Bud Adams had brought in the Chicago Bears and Pittsburgh Steelers for an exhibition game. Originally designed as a chance to draw a crowd and show Houston's interest in the NFL, the game was still on even though Adams had hooked up with the AFL.

Murchison knew he had the upper hand. The NFL had turned him away before, but oh, it wanted him now. He demanded that Halas publicly commit to Dallas. Papa Bear was reluctant, but he buckled when Murchison pointed out that Lamar Hunt already had the advantage, having arranged to play games at the Cotton Bowl. Murchison would need the NFL's immediate support if he was going to catch up.

Meeting with reporters in the press box before the exhibition game in Houston, Halas dropped the bombshell that the NFL now planned to expand, with two new teams kicking off in 1961 pending approval by the other team owners at their annual meeting after the 1959 season. Asked to name the cities most likely to get new franchises, Halas said Houston and Dallas were at the top of the list. Murchison was identified as the likely owner in Dallas.

Back in Dallas that afternoon, Lamar was clipping bushes in his front yard when an Associated Press reporter called.

"Could I get your reaction?" the reporter asked.

"My reaction to what?" Lamar responded.

The reporter explained that Halas had just said the NFL would be expanding, with Dallas and Houston likely to receive teams. Stunned, Lamar asked for a phone number and said he would call back. He needed time to gather his thoughts. Neither Halas nor Bell had ever hinted to him that such a move was in the offing. Lamar might never have gone to the trouble of starting the AFL if he had known this was the NFL's timetable all along.

Returning the reporter's call, he opened fire. "The American Football League has attempted, from its inception, to operate its relationship with the National Football League on the highest plane and with an amicable attitude on all matters," Lamar said. "It is now apparent that Mr. Halas and the rest of the National Football League are not interested in this type of relationship but are interested in continuing the stalling and sabotaging efforts that have kept pro football out of Denver, Seattle, Minneapolis, Louisville, Buffalo, Dallas, Houston, and Miami, despite repeated efforts from those cities to expand the National Football League.

"Everybody has been knocking on their door for years, and they've turned everybody down. It is obvious what they are trying to do, and it can get them in trouble. They're trying to knock out our Dallas and Houston teams. But this doesn't change our plans at all. We're moving ahead. The American Football League stands as a group, not wanted by anyone except the American public, ready to play in 1960, and interested only in furthering the game of pro football."

After hanging up, Lamar called Bert Bell to complain. Bell shrugged that it was out of his control; if the owners wanted to expand, they could. Bell continued to downplay the prospect of trouble, saying he believed there was enough interest in the pro game to support two leagues. But Lamar wasn't buying that anymore. If the AFL got off the ground and the NFL put a team in Dallas, his modest-sized hometown, lukewarm about pro football to begin with, suddenly would have two teams.

After reading Lamar's remarks in the Dallas papers and hearing from mutual friends how angry the young man was, Murchison invited Lamar to his offices the next day. They had met before at the dinner party given by Lamar's uncle three years earlier.

"If you want to own a team this badly, why don't you go ahead and take the NFL team?" Murchison asked.

Lamar declined.

"Well, then, at least come in fifty-fifty with me," Murchison said.

Lamar was tempted, saying years later that he might have accepted if Murchison's offer had come just two weeks earlier, before the Chicago meeting at which the AFL owners had gotten together for the first time. But that meeting had taken place, establishing the AFL. Money had changed hands.

Lamar turned Murchison down, repeating what he had told Halas a month earlier, that after working so hard to obtain commitments from these other men to get the AFL started, he couldn't bail on them now — not even with a brutal fight in the offing if the NFL really came to Dallas.

They hadn't planned it, but suddenly, Lamar and Clint Jr. were lined up opposite each other, representing different oil dynasties and different leagues, but sharing a goal — ownership of Dallas's pro football future. If both succeeded in bringing teams to the city, it would be like a Hollywood western in which two gunslingers reach a standoff and point their pistols at each other, ready to fire. The town wasn't big enough for both of them.

On the September 1959 afternoon when Lamar sat in Murchison's office and they charted the contentious course of Dallas's football future, their hometown was a place where the stirrings of the wildest imagination had a hard time topping reality. Neighboring Fort Worth, thirty miles away, was known as "Cow Town," but Dallas was "Big D," a sophisticated nexus of ideas and money—America's westernmost eastern city, it was said.

It was a place where bankers and stockbrokers took their wives to the symphony and art museum, where women from neighboring states came to shop at the city's high-end fashion stores; a place with an array of art deco movie houses, a pair of hard-charging newspapers, and a debutante scene to rival any; a place where Broadway road shows sold out and planes left every day for New York, Los Angeles, and Europe.

But while its East Coast urbanity dazzled, Dallas was unmistakably part of the Lone Star State. That millionaire walking down the sidewalk might be wearing a ten-gallon hat and a pistol at his waist along with his tailored suit and smile. That young blonde driving a shiny convertible and winking at strangers might be some big daddy's girl, possibly worth the trouble, but probably not.

Underwritten by the breathtaking flash of oil money, the city was governed by stolid businessman-politicians such as R. L. Thornton, an avuncular mayor known as "Uncle Bob," whose slogan was "keep the dirt flying"—build, build, build. The forward-thinking atmosphere was manna for the creative minds of young entrepreneurs such as Ross Perot, a high-flying computer salesman who would soon start his own company; Stanley Marcus, a retail visionary whose Neiman Marcus store embodied upscale fashion; and Trammel Crow, a developer whose fashion market would become as influential as any outside of New York.

Houston had just as many outlandish oil millionaires, but Dallas had a twinkling essence that stirred poetry. Every night at the Imperial Theater on Broadway in New York, in the second act of a popular musical called *The Most Happy Fella*, a foot-stomping song about Dallas, "where every home is a palace," brought sold-out crowds to their feet.

Thirty years earlier, Dallas had been a relatively quiet post-frontier town that ran on the buying and selling of the cotton found in the black-clay fields outside the city. One hundred thousand people lived there, but other than the fact that the Trinity River ran by it, no one knew why a wandering Kentucky woodsman named John Neely Bryan had stopped there, put a shovel in the ground, and founded the place in the 1840s.

All along, however, there were signs that big dreamers lay within its boundaries. By the 1920s, downtown Dallas was dominated by buildings so tall they seemed to stretch to the clouds. The magnificent twenty-nine-story Magnolia Petroleum Company Building was one of America's tallest edifices west of the Mississippi River. The twenty-two-story Medical Arts Building, Republic National Bank Building, Dallas Cotton Exchange, and Dallas Hilton Hotel also soared grandly, boggling minds.

After massive oil wells gushed in nearby East Texas in 1930, Dallas bankers agreed to accept reserves — crude *expected* to come out of the ground — as collateral on loans to wildcatters wanting to drill more. The bankers in other cities couldn't bring themselves to assume the risk, and Dallas boomed when its wells came in. Leaving cotton behind, it emerged as an oil industry center. Between 1930 and 1932, it experienced a tenfold increase in start-up oil-related businesses specializing in banking, drilling, exploring, and manufacturing.

When the American Petroleum Institute held its annual meeting in Dallas in 1934, Magnolia Petroleum consecrated the moment by erecting a symbol of the city's newfound importance on the roof of its skyscraper. It put up a fifty-foot tower resembling an oil derrick and topped it with a statue of a giant flying red horse. Forty feet long, thirty feet tall, and illuminated by neon, this stunning rendering of Pegasus, the winged horse of Greek mythology, instantly became a landmark, visible from seventy-five miles away as it rotated electrically — a fitting symbol for the high-flying city over which it loomed.

By 1941 the city's population had doubled in twenty years, and one in five residents depended on oil for their income. Having survived the Depression in better shape than most cities, Dallas was an attractive place to do business. Chance Vought Aircraft, a major defense contractor, moved down from Connecticut with thirteen hundred employees. Dresser Industries, a giant manufacturer, came from Cleveland. A spate of local businesses also bloomed, including the Southland Corporation, which operated convenience stores, and Texas Instruments, which had developed the integrated circuit, the engine for a contraption called a computer.

As the sixties approached, the Dallas city limits had expanded six-fold in the past fifteen years, and its population was close to 700,000. The flying red Pegasus no longer ruled downtown, having been topped by the Southland Center, a forty-two-story office tower.

Dallas was a city with broad shoulders, yet while it was major league in almost every respect, it had never experienced major pro sports other than that single disastrous season in the NFL. For decades, it had supported an array of minor league baseball teams, often somewhat tepidly, and like much of the rest of the country, it followed Major League Baseball and the NFL from a distance, often somewhat uninterestedly. The city's sports fans were satisfied supporting college and high school football, which were more interesting to them than pro sports anyway.

Their forefathers had fallen for those brands of football long ago, as Texas transitioned out of the Wild West of the nineteenth century into a modern place to live and work. Fielding winning high school teams had replaced herding cattle and shooting bad guys as the way for one town's boys to prove they were tougher and more self-reliant than the next town's boys. The first state high school football champion was crowned in 1913, and within a few years fierce rivalries from Amarillo to Brownsville were unfolding like battles between Greek city-states in the Age of Pericles.

Dallas's first great sports teams were the Oak Cliff High School and Forest Avenue High School varsities, both of which played for the state title in the twenties. Sunset High School, Woodrow Wilson High School, and Highland Park High School also became powerhouses as Dallas churned out young legends. Davey O'Brien went from Woodrow Wilson to TCU, where he won the Heisman Trophy in 1935, and then on to a long career in the pros. Bobby Layne played at Highland Park and Texas and led the Lions to two NFL titles, boozing and gambling as the football equivalent of an oilman. Doak Walker, a darting back from Highland Park, stayed home to play for SMU and became Dallas's first sports superstar.

SMU had gained football prominence in the thirties as the oil economy boomed and wealthy alumni backed the program. When the Mustangs met TCU and O'Brien in Fort Worth on November 29, 1935, with both teams undefeated and a Rose Bowl berth on the line, New York's finest sportswriters took trains in to cover the event and put Texas college football on the map. Syndicated columnist Grantland Rice wrote that SMU's 20–14 victory was "one of the greatest games ever played in the sixty-year history of the nation's finest college sport."

A month later, as SMU took on Stanford in the Rose Bowl on New Year's Day in Pasadena, California, a Dallas oilman named J. Curtis Sanford looked at the massive crowd and wondered why his city couldn't replicate such an event. He led a campaign to change the name of six-year-old Fair Park Stadium to the Cotton Bowl and bankrolled a game between TCU and Marquette on January 1, 1937. When only 17,000 fans attended, including four-year-old Lamar Hunt, Sanford lost money.

But Sanford was determined to make the event go, even after a smaller crowd watched Clemson play Boston College four years later. Sportswriters derided the annual bowl game as "Sanford's folly," but the oilman persevered and finally struck a crucial deal with the Southwest Conference to put its champion in the game every year opposite a top team from another region. That elevated the game's importance, playing to the pride Texans felt about their college teams. The New Year's Day game became a college football staple.

Meanwhile, SMU played on the school's University Park campus, at 26,000-seat Ownby Stadium, until Doak Walker's arrival in 1947. Breaking long runs and punt returns as a sophomore, Walker won the Maxwell Award as the nation's top player and led the Mustangs to a conference title. When they played Texas late in the season, with both teams unbeaten, the demand for tickets was so great that the game was moved to the Cotton Bowl, which then seated 45,000. The Mustangs won, and after they played Penn State to a tie on New Year's Day, they moved permanently to the Cotton Bowl the next year.

Walker became the first junior to win the Heisman Trophy in 1948 as the Mustangs, playing before sellout crowds, won another conference title and defeated Oregon State on New Year's Day. Walker's shrieking hordes of fans convinced the city to expand the Cotton Bowl — an upper deck with 30,000 seats was added.

Fans expected more magic during Walker's senior season in 1949, but he battled injuries and the Mustangs fell short of expectations. Their final game was against Notre Dame's undefeated, top-ranked Fighting Irish on December 3. With Walker unable to play, the Irish were favored by four touchdowns, but 75,000 fans still packed the Cotton Bowl as a national radio audience tuned in.

Notre Dame jumped ahead and held a 20–7 lead entering the fourth quarter, but the Mustangs rallied behind Kyle Rote, a junior back from San Antonio who could catch and throw the ball as well as run with it. Helped by a tiny end named Johnny Champion, Rote led SMU on two touchdown drives. Suddenly, the game was tied, 20–20. The great crowd could feel the upset brewing.

But Notre Dame took back the lead, and a gallant final drive by the Mustangs fell short. Notre Dame had scored a 27–20 win in what everyone immediately agreed was the best football game ever played in Dallas.

When the NFL's Texans came and left a few years later, it only reinforced Dallas fans' belief that pro ball was a humdrum affair by comparison.

But now, just seven years later, in 1959, the circumstances were different. Americans in the cold, snowy Midwest and Northeast were moving to where the climate was better and, they believed, so was the living — California, Texas, Atlanta, New Orleans, and elsewhere. Their pockets were full as the postwar economy boomed, and since fans could now sit at home and watch Major League Baseball and NFL football on television, they could see just how inferior their precious minor league teams were. Indeed, a whole generation of Dallas fans had grown up watching NFL games on Sunday afternoons and liking what they saw.

For decades, the major leagues and the NFL had amounted to a country club with severe membership restrictions, playing in just a few cities in the Northeast (New York, Boston, Philadelphia, and Washington) and Midwest (Pittsburgh, Cleveland, Detroit, Chicago, Cincinnati, and St. Louis) while relegating the rest of the country to the minors. But with the country's population shifting, major pro sports were changing. The small, restricted country club had started opening its doors to the cities where Americans now lived.

Pro football had jumped first when Dan Reeves moved his football Rams from Cleveland to Los Angeles after winning the NFL title in 1945. Reeves lost money in his first years in California but eventually drew massive crowds to the Los Angeles Coliseum. The All-America

Football Conference also put teams in new markets such as San Francisco, Miami, Baltimore, and Buffalo. Major League Baseball followed football's lead within the decade and also had teams in California, the Dodgers and Giants having moved west from New York.

As the sixties neared, the race was on among the major leagues and the NFL — and now, also, the AFL — to get into new markets that, like California, had the potential to benefit their leagues. Texas was near the top of the list. Dallas and Houston hadn't earned their bona fides as pro sports towns, but their state just had so ... much ... money. George Halas had long resisted expansion, but knowing its time was approaching, he had to concede Texas's potential. Papa Bear fretted when he heard about the AFL: Texas looked like the next pro sports frontier, and the NFL couldn't let some upstart steal it away, he screeched.

Halas had privately pledged that if he — er, the NFL — ever went into Texas again, he would find a more secure tap into the state's oil riches; he still couldn't believe the NFL's first attempt to put a team there had ended with, of all things, the owners running out of cash. In *Texas*? But that would never happen with Clint Murchison Jr., Halas felt, and there was reason to believe the city would respond more favorably to pro ball now that SMU had run out of steam, falling to a midlevel program in the Southwest Conference.

Was Dallas, the oil boomtown with a flying red Pegasus overhead, really ready to extend its football embrace to the pros? Papa Bear thought so. Or hoped so.

# 3

✦

# "You're going to break us all"

I N AUGUST 1959, when a *Morning News* reporter surveyed people on the street about Lamar Hunt bringing a pro football team to Dallas, he received mostly positive responses. "We didn't support pro football last time, but perhaps it would go differently this time around," a policeman said. Another resident said, "I sure would like to see the pros come back."

But many people still had doubts. Pro teams had black players, undeniably a turnoff for some. Die-hard college fans did not want the landscape to change. One well-known iconoclast wrote crusty letters to the city's two papers, the *Morning News* and *Times Herald*, saying he doubted Lamar's team would succeed and feared it might hurt the college game.

The letters were signed by H. L. Hunt.

It was fair to wonder. Lamar was the youngest person in this developing situation, working alongside and against formidable older men who had accomplished more. His AFL investors were mostly at least a decade older. The league's first commissioner, a World War II flying ace, was two decades older. Halas and some of the NFL's other lions were three decades older.

Ralph Wilson, a wealthy Michigan entrepreneur, was forty-one — fifteen years older than Lamar — when he called Lamar about obtaining an AFL franchise in the fall of 1959. He had taken over his father's insurance business after the war, invested in mines and factories, and moved into manufacturing, construction, and radio. No one told him what to do.

A football fan, Wilson owned a small piece of the NFL's Detroit Lions, but he wanted his own team and contacted Lamar after reading about the new league. He owned a winter home in Miami and thought it would be fun to put a team there. Like Dallas, Miami had experienced a brief fling with pro ball, one losing season by an AAFC team called the Seahawks in 1946. But college football was popular in Florida, and the city was growing.

Speaking with an authority that surprised Wilson, Lamar said, "Well, Ralph, you better get over here to Dallas right away and come see me. We've got about three people who want a team in Miami."

Wilson obediently got on a plane, went to Texas, and sold himself to Lamar, eventually obtaining the rights to the Miami franchise. When stadium issues prevented it from getting off the ground, Lamar persisted, offering Wilson a team in one of five northeastern cities. Wilson wound up sending Lamar a telegram stating, "Count me in with Buffalo."

People quickly forgot how young he was; he was just an insatiable optimist with a radical idea, boundless drive . . . and a lot of money.

But by the fall of 1959, he had more on his plate than any one person could handle.

His AFL investors, knowing that only Lamar understood what needed to transpire to get the thing up and running, had elected him president of the league. In that role, he was leading the search for a commissioner while also seeking to identify the league's eighth and final franchise to join Dallas, Houston, New York, Los Angeles, Denver, Minnesota, and Buffalo. Meanwhile, he needed to hire a general manager and coach for his Dallas franchise, decide on a name for the team, and — little detail — start signing players. It was an imposing to-do list.

Overall, Lamar was encouraged. Investors from around the country wanted to put money into the AFL even if they didn't own a team. Two oilmen from Midland, Texas, and a New York textiles manufacturer had bought a piece of the New York franchise. The Boston group seeking a franchise was fronted by Bill Sullivan, the president of a coal and oil company, and included Dom DiMaggio, the Major League Baseball star. A real estate developer in Oakland, California, wanted a team.

The AFL owners rushed to hire a commissioner. They interviewed the athletic director at the University of Michigan, but he was a college sports expert. Several other candidates expressed interest. In the end, they settled on a surprise selection, Joe Foss, a former Marine pilot who had served two terms as the governor of South Dakota. He had no football experience, but his political connections and inner toughness would come in handy as they battled the NFL.

Foss's hiring knocked one item off Lamar's to-do list. He knocked off another when he picked a name for his new team: it would be the Dallas Texans, same as the woeful 1952 NFL team.

"It's hardly original, but it just seems to fit," Lamar said. "Some people may have bitter memories about that team, but I feel the public associates the name with pro football."

He was pleased that so many fans in Dallas seemed to be on his side in his budding battle with the NFL. Upset that he had announced he was starting a team, the NFL had come barging in months later.

In a letter to the *Morning News,* a fan wrote, "I think the attitude the NFL is taking toward Lamar Hunt and the AFL is the most unsportsmanlike attitude we have witnessed in many a moon. The NFL for years ignored pleas for expansion from Dallas and Houston. Their sudden interest is obviously made for the purpose of 'nipping in the bud' the creation of Hunt's AFL, on which he has devoted his time, talents, and considerable money. I, for one, would like to see all Dallas and Houston sportsmen backing Lamar Hunt and the AFL to the hilt."

Curtis Sanford, founder of the New Year's Cotton Bowl game, avidly took Lamar's side. "The public is with Hunt. I've heard nothing but favorable comments about him," Sanford told the *Times Herald.* "He has some fine men coming with him (as AFL partners) and is going about it with the right approach. I see nothing but success ahead for him."

Sanford revealed to the paper that he also had approached Bert Bell in the past year about an NFL expansion team for Dallas, offering to put $1 million in the bank and guarantee 25,000 season tickets — quite a package. Bell had discouraged him, he said, claiming the NFL was lukewarm about Dallas and wasn't planning to expand.

The league obviously had changed its mind, Sanford said, "just to keep Hunt from operating." There were plenty of people who didn't appreciate the NFL's tactics, Sanford added, pledging to support Lamar wholeheartedly if and when the city divided into two football camps.

With league affairs keeping him busy, Lamar barely had time to get the Texans going. To help, he hired a general manager, Don Rossi, a former college player (at Michigan State) and NFL referee who had worked for Spalding, the sporting goods company. Rossi's job was to oversee the Texans' front office and help lure players. Lamar also hired a scout, Will Walls, who had caught passes from Sammy Baugh at TCU in the thirties and played for the New York Giants before becoming a coach.

As he patched together a front office, Lamar fielded several phone calls from Halas, who was doing everything he could to keep the new league from becoming a reality. Having convinced Murchison to let Lamar take a minority stake in a Dallas NFL franchise, Papa Bear left a message at the Hunt Oil Company headquarters, where Lamar had an office.

Before returning the call, Lamar walked across the hall and invited Mack Rankin, a young Hunt Oil lieutenant, to come listen to the conversation on a speaker phone.

"Mr. Halas, sir, this is Lamar Hunt calling from Dallas. How are you?" Lamar said.

Halas responded that he was fine but immediately got down to business. Murchison was willing to let Lamar take 45 percent of the new NFL team. How did that sound?

"I'm sorry, sir," Lamar said. "I appreciate you calling, and I've discussed this with Clint before. But I've been talking to you about a Dallas team for several years and you never would acknowledge it. Now we've started this league, and as you know, I've given my word to these other men. Besides, I don't want 45 percent. I want to run a team. I don't want to be a minority owner."

Rankin's eyes grew wide as he listened to Halas's furious response.

"Goddamn you, son, you're going to break us all with this new league," Papa Bear roared. "We're going to be competing for players and the salaries are going to go through the roof."

He repeated: "It's going to break us all. You're going to be sorry you did this."

Papa Bear went on the prowl after that, pressing to finalize a round of NFL expansion that might kill off the AFL. He kept up the heat while coaching the Bears during the 1959 season. After Bert Bell died in October, felled by a heart attack while watching his beloved Eagles play in Philadelphia, Halas respectfully but determinedly used the occasion of Bell's funeral to canvas his fellow owners on the subject of expansion.

Halas wanted to know if they would vote to let teams in Dallas and Houston start playing in 1960, instead of a year later, so they could compete with the AFL teams in those cities. A majority of the owners said yes, but there were exceptions. George Preston Marshall was firmly opposed; his Redskins, the NFL's southernmost team, benefited from having their games telecast throughout the South, and he wanted to protect that market. The Cardinals also were opposed, mainly because Violet Wolfner detested Halas and everything he wanted. Several other owners wondered if it was wise to return to Dallas.

Needing unanimous approval from the other owners to get a new team into the league, Halas had work to do. But he moved ahead. Ten days after Bell's death, he announced that, pending approval by the owners at their annual meeting in January, the NFL would indeed be expanding: a Murchison-owned Dallas team would kick off the next fall, in September 1960, along with another team — in Houston, Halas hoped — probably starting in 1961.

Murchison had pressed Papa Bear to make the announcement, wanting to get on with the business of putting together a team that could compete with Hunt's. The rush meant the Dallas team, tentatively called the Rangers, wouldn't be able to participate in the NFL's annual draft of college players, set for early December 1959. A team that didn't exist couldn't draft players, right? The Rangers would be stocked later, with fringe veterans from the other teams, in an "expansion draft."

Within a week, Halas's plan was dealt a blow when Rice University in Houston refused to rent its stadium to the proposed NFL team, saying it preferred that its stadium be used strictly for college games. Halas couldn't get Rice to budge. And Bud Adams had already locked up the city's only other suitable stadium, a high school facility, for his AFL team. Out of options, Halas would need to find a city other than Houston for his second expansion team. Dallas was now his only hope of establishing the NFL in Texas.

After trying yet again to negotiate a deal to get Lamar and Adams into the NFL — both refused — Halas finally just attacked.

Shortly after announcing in early November that Boston would get the AFL's eighth and final franchise, Lamar scheduled the league's inaugural college draft for later that month in Minneapolis, where the AFL ownership group, led by Max Winter, had become an early league cornerstone. But Winter, like many prospective pro football owners around the country, also had previously sought an NFL team for the Twin Cities, only to be turned away. So Halas called him.

"Forget Hunt and that damn AFL," Papa Bear said. "You can have that NFL team you wanted. We're expanding. Houston is out. You want in?"

Stunned, Winter and his group went with the NFL.

The news broke on the eve of the AFL draft in Minneapolis, where the league's nascent front offices had gathered. Winter at first tried to downplay the possibility that he was switching leagues, but finally confessed. The news cast a pall over the draft, which was a shambling affair: several teams still hadn't hired general managers and were forced to pick players based on newspaper and magazine articles.

The NFL's expansion plans had been finalized. Dallas and Minnesota would get teams, pending approval by the other owners. Halas sat back and smiled. He had staggered the new league, outfoxed H. L. Hunt's kid. Papa Bear could play this game.

But while Lamar was frustrated as he returned to Dallas from Minnesota, he was less discouraged than Halas imagined. He didn't start shouting or slamming phones. That wasn't how he operated. Yes, Max Winter had dealt his league a blow, but if anyone understood how tempting it was to join the NFL, Lamar did. He had been tempted himself numerous times. If Winter was gone, so be it. Lamar had plenty of prospective owners clamoring for franchises, people who would never turn on him.

Even though the other NFL owners had not voted his franchise into existence yet, Murchison felt confident that it would happen. He couldn't be absolutely certain, since there were enough owners who opposed the move, but with Halas supporting him so doggedly, he felt he would eventually prevail.

It was time to start putting together an organization. Murchison wanted someone to run it for him. That was his standard operating model, the way he ran his businesses — hire the best person and then get out of the way and let that person do the job. That was certainly what he needed to do with a football team. Although he was an avid fan and did not lack for knowledge — his playbooks for his son's YMCA teams, which he coached, were fairly complex — industry professionals obviously knew far more about how to construct and run an organization.

He put in a call to Halas, asking for recommendations. Halas gave him a name — a TV executive named Texas Earnest "Tex" Schramm.

Murchison initially wondered if Papa Bear was joking. A guy named Texas to run a team in Dallas? Good one, George.

But once Halas explained who Schramm was, Murchison understood that the old man was serious.

Although Schramm was living in New York and working for CBS Television as its assistant sports director, he was a football man . . . a very good one, Halas said.

Halas then went as far as to call Schramm, suggesting he consider getting back into the game with the proposed expansion team coming to Dallas. Schramm's eyebrows arched. Since joining CBS in 1957, he had turned down offers to run the Detroit Lions, the Canadian Football League's Montreal Alouettes, and the National Basketball Association's Detroit Pistons. The fact that his phone steadily rang was a testament to his reputation as a first-rate sports executive. But he was holding out for the right opportunity, one that truly stirred him. This might be it.

A dapper thirty-nine-year-old, Schramm had a bald head and twinkling blue eyes. A big presence in any room, he was a born raconteur who liked a glass or two of Scotch at the end of the day.

His father, a stockbroker, and his mother were Texas natives who had lived in Los Angeles for many years, but loved their home state so much they named their son after it and packed him off to study journalism at the University of Texas. Schramm wrote sports for the *Austin American* newspaper after graduating in the forties, but soon veered into football. His father knew Dan Reeves, owner of the Rams, and that helped him get a job as the team's publicity director. Schramm wrote newspaper articles about the Rams to attract attention. But he was destined for bigger things. Shrewd and feisty, he quickly outgrew that job and became the team's general manager in the late forties.

With Reeves's blessing, Schramm operated the NFL's most forward-thinking franchise out of Southern California. They put all of their games on local television — not just the road games but also the home games at the Los Angeles Coliseum; others in the league felt this controversial tactic might undermine attendance, but Schramm saw it as free advertising. To enhance those broadcasts and sharpen the team's identity in the marketplace, Schramm asked halfback Fred Gehrke — an industrial design artist in the off-season — to design a yellow ram's-horn logo to adorn the sides of the players' helmets. No NFL team had ever marketed itself in such a way, but within a dozen years every team in the league except one had followed the Rams' lead and designed a helmet logo.

Under Schramm, the Rams were the first team with a full-time scouting director; they spent far more time and money on the draft than their rivals, and their attention to detail repeatedly paid off. They also favored a high-scoring passing attack, with quarterbacks Bob Waterfield and Norm Van Brocklin throwing to star receivers such as Elroy "Crazy Legs" Hirsch and Tom Fears.

Their exciting brand of football and Schramm's progressive leadership caused a sensation as the Rams set offensive records, contended for titles, and drew massive crowds to the Coliseum in the late forties and early fifties. They played in three straight NFL championship games, winning in 1951.

But although Reeves was known as a forward thinker, he experienced money problems in the early fifties, brought in partners, and eventually lost his majority stake. As the other owners battled for control, the team faded in the standings. Growing weary of the infighting, Schramm left in 1957 for CBS Television in New York.

He enjoyed his new line of work. Television was growing crazily as a popular medium, with millions of Americans buying their first sets every year. It was exciting to make decisions that had an impact on such vast audiences. In the fall of 1959, Schramm was busy planning CBS's coverage of the upcoming Winter Olympics in Squaw Valley, California.

But his heart was in football. He remained closely connected to the NFL because CBS broadcast the games of many teams. (Each team had a separate TV contract with a network in the years before the first communal league TV deal.) A keen competitor, he missed the immense satisfaction he felt when his team won on Sundays. The television business was a fascinating challenge, but it could never replicate that feeling.

His experience with the Rams had taught him a lesson. He would get back into football only if he found what he called "the perfect situation" — a team where ownership was neither so volatile nor so involved. He wanted the freedom to run a team as he wanted, without interference.

After Halas played matchmaker, Murchison invited Schramm to Texas for an interview. They were not an ideal match in some respects — Murchison was understated, with a dry sense of humor, and Schramm was blustery. But they also were the same age, equally bullish on Texas, and fond of a good time. They got along well. Schramm loved hearing Murchison say he would leave the football operation to the experts.

There was a second meeting two weeks later in New York. Murchison could see that Schramm was smart and experienced, an ideal manager, and Schramm could see that this was potentially just what he wanted, a chance to take a new team and shape it without "advice" from ownership.

Before agreeing to take the job, Schramm wanted to make sure Murchison understood he would lose money in the beginning — quite a bit of money. That was the supreme test of any owner's commitment. Schramm asked Murchison to estimate the franchise's likely first-year losses. Murchison guessed $250,000. Schramm slowly shook his head from side to side. The Rangers would lose three times that much, if not more, in both their first *and* second years, Schramm declared. Murchison doubted those figures but smiled, saying he was prepared to lose that much as the Rangers slowly grew.

That was what Schramm wanted to hear. On the day before Thanksgiving in 1959, the Rangers announced that their new general manager — fittingly — was a man named Texas.

For the final time, college football ruled Dallas without competition from the pros in the fall of 1959.

In September, SMU drew 48,000 fans to the Cotton Bowl for its home opener against Navy. Led by Don Meredith, a handsome All-American quarterback, the Mustangs won. The Texas Longhorns came to town in early October and knocked off Oklahoma before a sellout crowd, then returned at the end of the month to derail Meredith and SMU, 21–0. The Longhorns would finish the regular season with a 9–1 record, earn a share of the Southwest Conference title, and play Syracuse in the Cotton Bowl on New Year's Day.

As SMU's season wound down, the Rangers and Texans both had their eyes on Meredith, whose potential value to a Dallas pro team seemed limitless. He was tall and rangy, possessed an accurate arm, and also was articulate and lighthearted, a fun young man who could charm a crowd and sell tickets. His sparkling blue eyes and bright smile lit his long, angular face as he spoke to reporters.

Growing up in Mount Vernon, one hundred miles east of Dallas, Meredith had sung in the church choir, belonged to the Future Farmers of America, and starred in basketball and football while his father ran a dry-goods store. As a high school junior in 1954, he had come to Dallas and carried his tiny school's varsity basketball team to the title game of the prestigious Dr Pepper Holiday Classic tournament, scoring fifty-two points in one game.

But football was his sport. He had picked SMU over numerous other suitors and gone on to pass for more than three thousand yards and twenty-five touchdowns in three seasons, setting a major college record as a junior by completing 61 percent of his throws.

Lamar felt great about his chances of signing Meredith. Both had gone to SMU. They shared many friends and experiences. Lamar could easily envision the young star joining the Texans and continuing to dominate the Dallas football scene.

To start the recruiting process, Lamar invited Meredith over for dinner early that fall, before the Mustangs' season began. Meredith brought along his older brother, who had played at TCU. Lamar planned to grill burgers, but he forgot to buy starter fluid, so he asked the Meredith boys to scour the backyard for mimosa leaves to use as kindling.

When they got around to the subject of football, Lamar talked up the AFL. Meredith said he had an open mind but wasn't ready to commit.

The Texans took Meredith with their first selection in the AFL draft in November. That caused consternation in the Rangers' offices just as Schramm came aboard. The Rangers also wanted Meredith, but since they weren't allowed to participate in the NFL's draft, they had no way of obtaining his rights. What could they do?

Schramm, thrilled about returning to football, devised a sly solution. Although the Rangers couldn't draft Meredith, there was nothing stopping Murchison from signing him to a personal services contract, securing his commitment. Schramm floated the idea by Murchison and Halas, both of whom approved. Papa Bear promised to find a way to get Meredith to the Rangers if they signed him.

Schramm contacted Meredith, and negotiations ensued during the final weeks of SMU's season. Lamar, showing his inexperience, had planned to wait until after the Mustangs' final game, at TCU, to get back in touch. Schramm jumped ahead as that game neared.

Two days before that final game, Meredith called Lamar and asked to meet. Lamar knew he was in trouble when Meredith arrived with an attorney aligned with Murchison. Scrambling, Lamar offered to exceed the Rangers' offer by $5,000 a year. Meredith said he would think about it.

On Saturday afternoon in Fort Worth, Meredith had one of his worst games as a horde of pro scouts watched. TCU's defense, led by a tackle named Bob Lilly, hounded him with a strong rush and limited him to 107 passing yards. The Horned Frogs won, 19–0.

Meredith was disappointed, but he perked up when he heard from Schramm upon returning to the SMU campus that evening. The Rangers offered him a five-year contract worth $150,000, payable even if the NFL never approved the Dallas franchise. Smiling broadly, Meredith signed. Then he called Lamar himself to deliver the news.

It was Lamar who broke the story in the media that night, telling the *Morning News* and *Times Herald* he had lost out. "We would like to have had him. But it's just one of the turns. We'll probably lose a few more," he said.

At the NFL draft a week later, Halas took the matter into his hands. The Rams wanted to take Meredith in the first round, but Halas talked everyone into not taking him, and then picked him with the Bears' third-round selection. Papa Bear pledged to trade Meredith to Dallas for a third-round pick in 1960 as soon as the Dallas franchise was approved.

If they didn't know before, Lamar and the Texans knew now that they were in for a keen fight. Schramm was a canny, competitive opponent, and the entire NFL had conspired to make sure Dallas got its player.

Frustrated, Lamar and his staff concocted a sarcastic new nickname for their rivals. They weren't the Dallas Rangers; they were the Halas Strangers.

With his quarterback locked up, Schramm plunged into the task of putting together an organization. Murchison gave him carte blanche, the oil millionaire bowing to the football expert.

Schramm's primary goal was to hire a head coach, but he also was concerned about getting players into the fold. The expansion draft in March 1960 would bring a slew of veterans, but with the league not allowing the Rangers to participate in the draft, they wouldn't have any rookies — at least not any deemed talented enough to have been drafted.

Austin Gunsel, the NFL's treasurer and interim commissioner since

Bell's death, refused to give Schramm blank standard contracts with which to sign free agents (players who had not been drafted). "Really sorry," Gunsel said, "but remember, you're still not in the league."

Schramm rolled his eyes but, as in the Meredith case, figured out a solution. He found a blank contract in a file, took it to a copier, and had a stack printed. Then he paid his former team, the Rams, for a look at their extensive scouting files, which included written reports on hundreds of players. Finally, he contacted Gil Brandt, an energetic twenty-six-year-old from Milwaukee, Wisconsin, who had done part-time scouting work for the Rams and 49ers.

"Go get us some players," Schramm barked.

Brandt had an unusual background for someone in football. He was not a former player or coach. He had just taken an interest in scouting as a student at the University of Wisconsin, going so far as to pose as a high school coach to obtain films of players from college coaches. Then he wrote reports — not for pay, but just because he enjoyed doing it.

Eventually, he caught on with the Rams, the only NFL team with a national network of part-time scouts. Brandt scouted his region for them, and later for the 49ers. Meanwhile, to support himself, he ran a baby photography business: he paid hospital nurses to take pictures of newborns at hospitals and then sold the pictures to parents.

Armed with counterfeit contracts and representing a team that didn't yet exist, Brandt figured he would struggle to sign players. It wasn't even clear whether the NFL would honor the contracts if and when it found out about them. But Brandt was a charmer, always smiling, talking a good game, never forgetting a name. He persevered.

His first stop was Hanover, New Hampshire, in search of John Crouthamel, a speedy Dartmouth College halfback. Although no NFL team had drafted him, Crouthamel was thought to have potential. The AFL was already on him; he had heard from Frank Leahy, the respected former Notre Dame coach who was now the Los Angeles Chargers' general manager. Brandt convinced Crouthamel to sign one of his counterfeit contracts, making him the first player to sign with the Dallas NFL franchise.

Thrilled to have outdueled Leahy, Brandt called Schramm.

"What are we paying him?" Schramm asked.

"Seventy-five hundred dollars if he makes the team," Brandt replied.

"We can't afford that!" Schramm shouted. "Gosh, we'll go broke if you keep signing guys for that much!"

Brandt feared he might get fired, but Schramm told him to stay on the road and keep hunting. They were putting a football team together. They needed players.

They also needed a coach.

It wasn't unusual for the owners of NFL teams to want to pick their coaches, so Schramm didn't take it for granted when Murchison told him to handle the job. Murchison didn't really have a choice after ceding control of the football operation, but Schramm appreciated the freedom.

He did not cast a wide fishing net. Schramm spoke first to Sid Gillman, the Los Angeles Rams coach, whom he had hired before when he plucked Gillman from the University of Cincinnati in 1955. Gillman had led the Rams to an NFL title-game appearance in his first pro season and was widely respected for his offensive mind, but his tenure in Los Angeles was winding down with a losing season in 1959, and he was about to be fired. (Gillman would catch on with the AFL's Los Angeles Chargers, taking a job with Barron Hilton in 1960.)

Meanwhile, having lived and worked in New York since 1957, Schramm kept hearing about Tom Landry, a brilliant, young assistant coach with the NFL's Giants. From the outset, Schramm thought this was probably his guy.

A former defensive back for the Giants, Landry was thirty-five, just four years removed from his playing days. But his coaching credentials were impressive. While with the Giants, he had pioneered the four-three defensive alignment and four-man "umbrella" secondary that most pro teams now used. He also was a Texan's Texan, having grown up in the Rio Grande Valley, played at the University of Texas, and married a Highland Park girl. He lived in Dallas in the off-season.

When Schramm contacted Landry in early December 1959, Landry was enthusiastic about the opportunity. The Giants had told him to expect to succeed their current head coach, Jim Lee Howell, when Howell retired, but Howell was just forty-four and Landry did not want to wait around.

There was no doubt he was going to be a head coach soon. Speaking bluntly, Landry said he had hoped to hear from the fledgling Dallas franchise. That was his hometown. While he had private doubts about how well pro football would go over there, he was willing to explore the possibility.

Lamar had contacted him earlier that fall about possibly coaching the new AFL team in Dallas; the Texans still didn't have a coach, and hiring Landry certainly made sense. They met one evening in New York. Wanting to shield the process from sportswriters, Lamar asked to borrow the apartment of a close friend, Tom Richey, a former Hill School football teammate, who lived on Manhattan's East Side.

Excited to help, Richey stocked the fridge with sodas, met Landry in the lobby, and escorted the coach up to his apartment, where Lamar was waiting. Richey then went back to the lobby and sat down to wait, thinking the interview would last hours. But Landry was down in less than an hour, having delivered the sobering news that he was an NFL man.

Years later, Landry revealed that he was less than impressed with Richey's dank apartment and that if this was the best the AFL could provide as a setting for hiring its coaches, the league probably was not going to last long.

In early December, with the Giants vying for the Eastern Division title, Landry heard from another AFL owner. One weekend when the Giants were on the road, Bud Adams booked a suite at their hotel and arranged a meeting, intent on hiring Landry to coach his Houston AFL team, called the Oilers. Adams also planned to interview players who might be interested in jumping leagues.

Landry arrived first and was speaking with Adams when there was a knock on the door. One of the prospective players had arrived early. Landry panicked. He did not want a player seeing him interviewing for a job in the AFL. Adams pointed to the bathroom door, and Landry ducked behind it. After Adams went to the front door and told the player to come back later, Landry emerged from the bathroom, relieved.

Adams offered him a huge contract. When Landry hesitated, Adams sweetened the offer, pledging to take his insurance business to Landry's father-in-law. Landry said he was flattered and wanted time to think. He was honest about the new NFL franchise also approaching him.

On December 27, 1959, the Giants lost to the Colts, 31–17, in the

NFL championship game. Adams hoped to hear from Landry but feared the worst when the coach did not call. Sure enough, the next morning a limousine whisked Landry, his wife, and their two young children to the airport, where they boarded one of Murchison's private planes, bound for Dallas.

In the end, Landry was an NFL man in the right place at the right time to coach Murchison's team. Although he continued to wonder whether Dallas would support pro football, he took the job, negotiating a five-year contract.

Two days later, the Rangers introduced Landry as their head coach. Standing beside each other at a news conference, smiling confidently, and taking questions, Landry and Schramm made quite an impression. Both had Texas roots and starry backgrounds, Landry in coaching, Schramm in management. They were pros, steeped in the football business, and accustomed to success. Murchison's Rangers were off to quite a start.

With a sporting goods rep as their general manager, Lamar's Texans looked amateurish by comparison.

# 4

———————— ☆ ————————

## "Son, that league isn't going to make it"

WHEN ABNER HAYNES heard rustling on the patio outside his bedroom window in Denton, Texas, early one morning in early December 1959, he initially thought it was a stray dog. When the noise persisted, Haynes climbed out of bed and peeked outside.

He saw a man sitting in a chair. A *white man*.

Opening a door to the patio, Haynes, an African American football star at North Texas State College, eyed the stranger cautiously.

"Can I help you?" he asked.

Like many small Texas towns in the late fifties, Denton could be a tough place for a young black male. But Haynes was well known and liked, having led North Texas to glory as the school's first black athletic star.

"Abner? Is that you?" the stranger asked, rising to shake hands.

"Yes, sir," Haynes replied. "Who are you?"

It turned out the man was Ed Kiely, a front office assistant with the Pittsburgh Steelers, who had selected Haynes in the fifth round of the NFL draft several days earlier.

Haynes, relieved, exhaled and asked, "How'd you find me?"

Kiely smiled. With the battle to sign college players suddenly on between NFL and AFL teams, front offices on both sides were under pressure to work fast and get names on contracts.

Kiely handed Haynes one. The Steelers would give him $1,500 to sign and a $10,000 salary in 1960.

"This looks great! Let me take it to Dallas and show it to my dad and my brother," Haynes said brightly.

Kiely smiled and said, "Okay. You can do that. But if you want to sign it now, we can go show it to them together."

Haynes didn't want to sign without first discussing it with his family. His father, R.L., was a Pentecostal church bishop, highly respected in Dallas's segregated black community, and his older brother, Sam, had been a star quarterback nicknamed "Jitterbug" a decade earlier at Prairie View, an all-black college near Houston.

After Kiely left, Haynes drove to Dallas, thirty miles away. His family lived just south of downtown, not far from the Cotton Bowl, on South Boulevard, a wide street of graceful homes built at the turn of the century by Dallas's first Jewish families, many of whom had since moved north to the city's growing white suburbs.

As he pulled into the neighborhood, Haynes felt at home. He was a hero here. Playing football at Lincoln, a black high school located down the street from the Cotton Bowl, he had piled up yards and touchdowns as a darting running back. Though small at five-ten and 160 pounds, he had a natural gift for eluding tacklers and could change directions in a blink. After he went wild against a team from Houston as a senior, scoring on three runs, a kickoff return, and a punt return, he was named "Back of the Week" by the *Times Herald*, a rare honor for a black player.

To his great disappointment, the teams in the all-white Southwest Conference had no interest in recruiting him. Colorado was the only school to offer him a scholarship, and although it sounded like the other side of the moon, he went. But he left after only two days, having had what he later termed a "misunderstanding" with the coach. On his trip back to Dallas, he stopped at North Texas, which was going to accept black students for the first time. Eagles coach Odus Mitchell was unimpressed by a youngster he would recall as "so skinny his pants just hung on him." Mitchell did not offer a scholarship.

Haynes contemplated heading to Prairie View, where his brother had starred, but his father stepped in. R. L. Haynes had some power in Denton, having served as the minister of a church there. He spoke to the president of North Texas State about letting Abner and Leon King, another former Lincoln High standout, try out for the Eagles as nonscholarship walk-ons. When the president said yes and the coach relented, the bishop spoke to Abner.

"It's fine if you want to go to an all-black school like everyone else," he said, "but if you go to North Texas and play there, and you know you can, you can show people that blacks and whites can get along. You can open some doors. You can help some other kids who come along."

Abner agreed to go. He and King were the only blacks on campus when they reported for preseason workouts. That fall they broke college football's color line in Texas as members of the school's freshman team. Initially, Haynes was cautious around his white teammates, and they were unsure about him. But they came together during a road game in Kilgore when rival fans taunted the two blacks with racial slurs. His teammates backed him up.

Life in Denton had not always been easy. The North Texas dorms and dining halls remained segregated. Haynes had to live off campus and occasionally hitchhike to and from practice even as he blossomed into a star. But he made friends and opened closed minds.

North Texas belonged to the Missouri Valley Conference, a second-tier college league. Abner dominated it. After starring on the freshman team in 1956, he piled up almost a mile and a half of rushing, receiving, and kick return yardage during the next two seasons, leading the Eagles to a conference title as a junior. His senior season was no less successful: the Eagles won nine games and had been invited to play in the Sun Bowl, with Abner finishing fifth in the nation in scoring and seventh in rushing.

By now he was so popular in lily-white Denton that he couldn't go to a movie without being swarmed by autograph hunters. When he took the field for home games, fans shrieked his name.

He had leapfrogged many better-known players from bigger schools in the NFL draft, becoming the 55th overall selection out of 240. His pro prospects seemed promising. But when his father and brother saw Pittsburgh's contract, they said he shouldn't sign. Sam had doubts about the NFL. Teams never seemed to have more than three or four black players at any time. Some didn't have any. There seemed to be an unspoken quota, which could curtail Abner's career.

Abner's father and brother wanted to hear what this new league had to offer. Minnesota had taken Abner in the AFL draft, but that franchise had dissolved to go with the NFL, leaving his status uncertain.

Lamar stepped in at that point. Having lost Don Meredith to the Rangers, he wanted to grab as many other local players as possible. They would help sell tickets, he thought. Haynes, who grew up a mile from the Cotton Bowl, was as local as could be.

Lamar didn't care that he was black. There wouldn't be a racial quota in the AFL. The new league was going to need every decent player it could get, regardless of color.

Having learned from the Meredith situation that he needed to be more aggressive, Lamar obtained Abner's rights in a trade, called the bishop, arranged a meeting, and came to South Boulevard one afternoon. Lamar, the bishop, Sam, and Abner sat on the porch and talked about football, money, and opportunity.

When the bishop revealed what the Steelers had offered, Lamar pledged to top it. Knowing that Lamar's father was one of the richest men in America, the bishop was not surprised.

When Lamar explained that Abner could benefit from playing at home, in front of fans who knew him, the bishop agreed wholeheartedly. After Lamar left, the bishop told Abner, "You should go with the Texans. You can do more good here. People know you."

College players weren't supposed to sign with the pros until after their final games, so with North Texas playing in the Sun Bowl on New Year's Eve, Abner couldn't immediately sign. But he announced in early December that he planned to sign with the Texans after the bowl game.

The Steelers didn't give up. One night at 2:00 AM, the great Bobby Layne banged on the bishop's door after a night of bar-hopping; the famed quarterback, a Dallas resident in the off-season, had been traded to the Steelers after winning titles in Detroit.

"Abner should sign with us," Layne slurred. "Us Texans need to stick together."

The bishop preferred Lamar's sales pitch. Haynes signed with the Texans after the Sun Bowl.

The NFL's worst fears about the new league were realized quickly, long before the AFL ever played a game. In late 1959, the scramble to sign college talent disintegrated into a wild scene across the country, sending the price of football flesh skyrocketing. Some players signed before their seasons ended, rendering them ineligible, but continued playing anyway. Some signed with teams in both leagues, leaving it to the courts to decide which contract took priority.

The nation's top college player, Louisiana State University running back Billy Cannon, agreed to three one-year contracts with the Los Angeles Rams, whose general manager, Pete Rozelle, coerced him into an agreement in late November by suggesting that the AFL might never get off the ground. But Cannon never signed the contracts or the check for his signing bonus, fearing he might not be able to play against Ole Miss in the Sugar Bowl. Then he signed with the AFL's Houston franchise in mid-December after Bud Adams offered him a three-year deal worth $110,000, a lot more than the Rams were paying.

The dispute landed in a federal court and ended, after six months of arguments and deliberations, with Cannon going to Houston, a major victory for the AFL. Calling the player "a provincial lad untutored and unwise in the ways of the business world," the judge rebuked Rozelle for maintaining a "shroud of secrecy" over his handling of the situation.

The anything-goes landscape fascinated Lamar's father; as he amassed his fortune, H.L. had often honored rules and laws only when they helped his cause. Pro football had never interested H.L. more than when his son's league started battling the NFL for players.

On the other hand, Lamar, with his limited business experience, was somewhat unprepared for the lawless battle royale. His general manager, Don Rossi, was more of a fast-talking salesman. But as always, Lamar had a plan. Abner Haynes was just one of the players he wanted. The others included Johnny Robinson, Cannon's backfield mate at LSU; Jack Spikes, a fullback from TCU; and Chris Burford, a receiver from Stanford.

The Texans had Robinson's AFL rights. Though smaller than Cannon, he had great speed and was impressive enough to have gone to the Detroit Lions as the third overall pick in the NFL draft. Then, like Cannon, he was goaded into signing with the NFL when a Lions executive came to Baton Rouge in early December and told him the AFL might never play a game. But Lamar jumped in aggressively, offering to pay Robinson more than the Lions. Robinson signed with the Texans after the Sugar Bowl, and as in Cannon's case, the dispute landed in federal court because the player had signed with both leagues. Eventually, the judge ruled that Robinson belonged to the Texans.

In early December, Lamar sought to land Burford, a precise route-runner in the mold of the Baltimore Colts' Raymond Berry, Lamar's friend and former SMU teammate. Burford had been taken by Cleveland in the ninth round of the NFL draft. The Texans had his AFL rights.

The Browns' Paul Brown had offered him a $500 signing bonus and $8,500 salary for 1960, but when Burford said he wanted to hear the Texans' offer, Brown imperiously pulled his offer off the table. That was supposed to intimidate Burford, but he was a straight-A student headed for law school, not a naive country boy. Brown merely irritated him.

Lamar and Rossi flew out from Dallas to pursue Burford. Cutting costs, they borrowed a car from a friend of Lamar's instead of paying for a rental and drove to Palo Alto, where Burford lived with his wife and their young child in a small house near the Stanford campus.

When Lamar showed up driving a battered, twenty-year-old Chevrolet, Burford wondered if he had blown his chance to make any money in pro football by feuding with Brown. But Lamar and Rossi made a strong pitch. Rossi, a gregarious salesman, did most of the talking.

"We don't want to leave without signing you. What's it going to take?" Rossi asked.

A friend had told Burford he was in a good position with two teams fighting over him and shouldn't sign for less than $12,000.

"I want twelve thousand," he said.

Rossi and Lamar nodded. No problem.

"And I want two thousand of that in advance," he said, showing his inexperience by asking for an advance instead of an actual bonus.

"We can do that," Lamar said.

Burford put his name on a contract, becoming the first player to actually sign with the Texans. He figured he would be getting his advance check that day, but Lamar had forgotten to bring a checkbook.

"I'll have to put it in the mail once I get home if that's okay," Lamar said sheepishly.

The check arrived a few days later.

Lamar and Rossi then set their sights on Spikes, who had led the Southwest Conference in rushing as a senior. The Steelers had picked him in the first round of the NFL draft, and Steelers owner Art Rooney had called Spikes personally to welcome him.

The Denver franchise had obtained Spikes's AFL rights, but Lamar called him to say that would be changing. "We're going to figure out a way to get your rights," Lamar said. "We want you to come play for us in Dallas."

That interested Spikes. A native of Big Springs in West Texas, he had gone to TCU four years earlier partly because his father could follow his exploits in the local paper. The same would certainly be true if Spikes played professionally in Dallas instead of Pittsburgh.

"Whatever you do, don't sign any contracts," Lamar warned.

Spikes said he wouldn't. And then Lamar, as promised, quietly obtained his AFL rights from Denver.

When TCU traveled to Houston to play in the Bluebonnet Bowl before Christmas, the Steelers made their play. Buddy Parker and Bobby Layne flew in from Dallas and went to Spikes's room at the Shamrock Hotel. Parker knew of the Texans' interest and told reporters, "You never know which direction these AFL guys are attacking from. But I've got my checkbook, and I'm going to sign Spikes."

Parker offered him $200 to sign and a $9,000 salary for 1960. Spikes said he wanted to hold off until he spoke to Lamar.

Lamar, also in Houston for the game, offered more — $2,500 to sign and a $12,000 salary. Spikes and his schoolteacher wife were living on $240 a month; to them, the higher offer was crucial. Spikes went back to Parker, detailed the Texans' offer, and said he was leaning toward them.

"Son," Parker said, "that league isn't going to make it. We're not going to make a counteroffer. You just come and talk to us when Hunt folds his tent."

Having lost Haynes and Spikes, Parker, a Texan himself (from Kemp, near Dallas), lamented drafting any players from the Lone Star State.

"I figured those oil men from Dallas and Houston would outbid me for guys from SMU and Rice, but they're getting the guys from other schools too," Parker told the *Morning News*. "Tell those guys to have a heart. Tell them I'm from Texas too."

Parker's warning about the AFL rattled Spikes. He signed with Lamar but kept thinking about what the NFL coach had said. Finally, he went to Lamar. "The Steelers tell me you're going to have a hard time making this thing work. Would you mind personally guaranteeing this contract for three years if the league doesn't make it?" Spikes asked.

Lamar didn't hesitate. "Sure," he said. "You've got yourself $36,000 if the league doesn't make it. But I'm telling you, it's going to make it."

A month or so later, the phone rang at Spikes's house. Someone from the new NFL team in Dallas, the Rangers, was on the line.

"We want you to come play for us," the person said. "It's NFL football, not some new league."

Spikes said he appreciated the interest but explained that he had already signed with Lamar and the Texans.

"Oh, don't worry about that," the person said. "A lot of guys are signing with both leagues. It can be worked out."

Again, Spikes said he appreciated the call but wasn't interested. "I've already cashed my signing bonus," he said. "I'm going with the Texans."

He never heard from the Rangers again.

Lamar was encouraged. In Haynes, Burford, Spikes, and Robinson, he could see the outline of an exciting young team forming. But he needed someone to coach them.

The other AFL teams were hiring established coaches, names that were familiar to fans. New York's Sammy Baugh had been a legendary quarterback for the Washington Redskins. Buffalo's Buster Ramsey was a former NFL player and longtime assistant coach with the Lions. The Chargers' Sid Gillman had coached the Rams for five years. Denver's Frank Filchock had been an NFL player and head coach in Canada. Boston's Lou Saban had been a head coach at Northwestern and Western Illinois. Bud Adams had a solid alternative to Landry ready — Lou Rymkus, who had been in the NFL as a player and coach since 1943.

Lamar had also intended to hire someone well known to coach the Texans, but he had been repeatedly turned down — not only by Landry but also by the University of Oklahoma's Bud Wilkinson, who had led the Sooners to three national titles, and by Michigan State's Duffy Daugherty. He could not get anyone to coach his team.

Throughout his search, he kept a lesser-known candidate in mind: an assistant at the University of Miami who was the antithesis of the AFL's developing stereotype for coaches. He had never coached in the pros or been a college head coach, and he wasn't a hulking former pro player who marshaled his forces with a military general's bearing. He was short, glib, and unknown to most fans, yet he was one of those individuals who made an indelible impression. Once you met Henry Louis "Hank" Stram, you did not forget him.

Stram's Polish-born father, Henry Wilczek, was a custom tailor in Chicago who worked part-time as a wrestler in a traveling circus (the circus bosses had changed his last name to Stram), and the son had inherited his father's dapper effervescence and flair for showmanship. Stram wore expensive suits and shiny shoes and chatted up reporters and fans with an easygoing nonchalance, always effectively selling his point of view.

He had been an assistant at Notre Dame, SMU, and his alma mater, Purdue, before spending the 1959 season at Miami. A decade earlier, while at Purdue, he had recruited a star quarterback from Ohio named Len Dawson. Dawson was sweet-talked by countless coaches, but only one wore trendy slacks with no back pockets. "Where does he put his comb?" Dawson wondered, mesmerized. The youngster eventually bought Stram's relentless sales pitch, bypassed Ohio State — where everyone had expected he would go — and signed with Purdue.

Stram specialized in the wide-open offense. Most teams used a standard set with three backs and one split receiver, but Stram changed alignments from play to play, flanked multiple receivers, and even used different line formations. He had developed star quarterbacks such as Dawson, Notre Dame's George Izo, and Miami's Fran Curci.

He had been an assistant at SMU when Lamar suited up for the Mustangs, and Lamar liked his style. Stram was smart and optimistic, yet also believed in discipline and had a knack for explaining strategy. Miami had gone from two wins in 1958 to six in 1959 after bringing in Stram to build a better offense around the 150-pound Curci.

Lamar had first contacted Stram about a possible job in the spring of 1959, before the AFL had even formed. Stram barely remembered Lamar, but the two agreed to meet after a spring football practice on Miami's campus. During the practice, Stram gazed at the crowd of onlookers, looking for a young man with fancy clothes and jewelry, the trappings of wealth. There was no way the owlish guy with horn-rimmed glasses and a rumpled raincoat could be Lamar, Stram thought, but indeed, that was the guy who sought him out after practice.

After the two talked for a while, with Lamar explaining his plans for the AFL, they went to dinner. When the check came, Lamar reached for his wallet but realized he had no cash. Embarrassed, he asked Stram if he could pay the bill, which Lamar would reimburse. Stram came away from the evening somewhat perplexed by the rich young man who couldn't pay for dinner.

As the 1959 season unfolded, Stram became a hotter coaching commodity. He had turned down a chance to be an assistant with the NFL's Philadelphia Eagles several years earlier. Now he was among the finalists for the University of Florida's head coaching job. Wichita State also wanted him.

In December, Stram was giving a speech at his former high school in Gary, Indiana, when he was told there was a call for him on the kitchen phone. Lamar was on the line, wanting him to come to Dallas and talk about coaching the Texans. Lamar had made a decision. Stram was not a "name" hire, but he was a born salesman and a clever coach — an undiscovered jewel, Lamar believed.

Stram flew to Dallas and interviewed with Lamar. Stram thought it went well, but Lamar didn't make an offer. After their conversation, Lamar said he would drive Stram to Love Field and asked Stram to fetch his car from a nearby garage. Stram expected to find a fancy car there, but it was a beat-up Oldsmobile that sputtered and died as Stram drove it back to Lamar's office. Stram got a push to a gas station and finally made it to the office, where Lamar apologized profusely.

Back in Miami, Stram waited for a call from Lamar for a week. He didn't get the Florida job, but Wichita State stepped up its pursuit. Stram held out. The idea of coaching in the pros intrigued him, and his wife, pregnant with their fourth child, approved of the idea. They still owned a home on Northaven Road in Dallas, which they had used when Stram coached at SMU.

Finally, Lamar called and offered him a three-year contract with a salary of $15,000 per season. Stram asked for $20,000. Lamar hung up and called back in an hour, agreeing to the higher figure.

When Lamar announced Stram's name at an introductory press conference in Dallas the next week — in late December 1959 — Lamar's brother, Bunker, loudly exclaimed, "Who?" The sportswriters had a good laugh about that. Not even Lamar's brother had heard of the guy being hired to coach the Texans.

But Stram impressed the writers. Dressed in a dark suit, he flashed a broad smile, promised an exciting brand of football, and showed knowledge of the Texans' young personnel. The son of a circus performer was in the center ring himself at last, intent on putting on a show. Lamar liked that about him.

Sure, Lamar was rolling the dice. Wilkinson or Daugherty would have brought more credibility. Landry's knowledge of defensive football was unmatched. Baugh, a Texas legend, would have sold more tickets. Stram was an untested leader. But this whole business of starting up a new league was a risk, Lamar figured. Why go conservative now?

# 5

★

# "Is Big D big enough ... for two teams?"

WHEN THE NFL OWNERS' meetings dragged on at the luxurious Kenilworth Hotel in Miami, Florida, in January 1960 without any resolution on expansion, Clint Murchison Jr. and Tex Schramm picked different ways to release their nervous energy. The prospective owner sat by the pool with his cronies running up a ferocious bar tab and sharing some laughs. The intense GM-in-waiting just paced back and forth in his suite.

They had flown in together from Dallas on Murchison's plane, expecting to receive good news within several days and head back to Dallas, franchise in hand. Halas had assured them the Rangers would be approved to begin play in the fall of 1960.

But their prospects took a wrong turn as soon as the meetings began. The owners couldn't agree on a successor to Bert Bell as commissioner. Austin Gunsel, Bell's interim replacement, had the support of the old guard, but the new guard supported Marshall Leahy, an attorney from San Francisco. A stalemate ensued, the dispute grew bitter, and it suddenly seemed that nothing positive would get accomplished at the meeting.

The Dallas delegation waited more than a week, growing increasingly nervous. If the Rangers had to wait another year before kicking off, they might as well cede Dallas to Lamar and not even start up. Holed up in his suite, Schramm alternately muttered to himself and complained on the phone to his friends in the league.

But on the twelfth day of the impasse, after twenty-three ballots had failed to produce a commissioner, the sides finally agreed on a surprising compromise choice: Pete Rozelle, the Rams' boyish-looking thirty-three-year-old general manager, whom Schramm had hired a decade earlier as the team's public relations director.

With that issue finally settled, the owners turned to expansion. Halas had sat quietly through the commissioner debacle, slyly abstaining from voting because there were expansion supporters on both sides and he didn't want to risk alienating them. But he took center stage now. The NFL's elder statesman believed that putting new teams in the right markets was just as important to the league as a new commissioner.

Halas's first move was to shepherd through an amendment to the league's bylaws. Until now, a unanimous vote by the owners had been needed to approve new franchises, but Halas pointed out that a perfect consensus on *any* matter would be difficult to obtain, and the other owners agreed. Halas suggested that approval from ten owners become the new requirement, and the idea sailed through.

Papa Bear had some breathing room. But he still had to make the case for letting the Rangers start in 1960. He took a day to present his side. Murchison had deep pockets, he said, and obviously knew what he was doing, having hired Schramm and Landry. Gil Brandt, the team's young personnel whiz, had already signed twenty-eight free agents. The city of Dallas was growing fast and, unlike in 1952, was ready now for the NFL. And the team really needed to kick off in 1960.

Halas felt he had a strong case, but George Preston Marshall and Walter Wolfner wanted to put off expansion for at least a year, and the Giants' owners were lukewarm.

That evening Murchison sought to sway Marshall. The two hadn't spoken since Murchison tried to — and almost did — buy the Redskins in 1958. Marshall was still furious about a prank Murchison had pulled after that failed deal. Marshall had fired his longtime band director, who had penned "Hail to the Redskins," the team's fight song, and owned the rights. The angry bandleader knew an associate of Murchison's, a mischievous Washington attorney named Bob Thompson; seeking revenge, he sold Thompson the rights to Marshall's song for $2,500. Marshall was apoplectic when he learned that he didn't own his beloved fight song.

Now, when Murchison went to Marshall's suite to discuss expansion, Marshall opened the door and yelped, "You took my fight song!" Murchison smiled, talked his way into the room, charmed the older man, and agreed to give back the song in exchange for a yes vote on expansion.

The next day, when Marshall announced that he now supported expansion, the issue was settled.

On January 28, 1960, fifteen days after the meetings had begun, Halas entered a motion to vote Dallas into the league. The motion was seconded by Jiggs Donoghue, the Philadelphia Eagles' executive vice president. Eleven owners, including Marshall, voted in favor. Wolfner abstained.

At 6:10 PM, Rozelle strode into the press room and announced that the Dallas Rangers would kick off in 1960. He also announced that Max Winter's Minnesota team, approved without opposition, would kick off in 1961.

Standing among the reporters listening to Rozelle, Murchison's friend Bedford Wynne smiled and said, "Thank God." Schramm literally sagged with relief. Jack Mara, president of the Giants, approached Charles Burton, the Dallas *Morning News* reporter on the scene, and exclaimed, "Welcome to the National Football League!"

Murchison, showing his typical dry humor but little emotion, said that he was excited to be admitted but would now have to pay his whopping bar bill from the past two weeks.

Back in Dallas, the reaction was decidedly mixed. Some fans were excited by the prospect of supporting an NFL team and watching legendary opponents such as the Bears, Giants, Browns, and Colts come to town. Others thought the city didn't need another team with Hunt's Texans already up and running; they were annoyed with the bullying NFL.

Charles Burton posed the central question, and then answered it, in a *Morning News* article the next day: "Is Big D big enough to support two teams? The answer lies with you, the people."

While the NFL owners met in Florida, the AFL owners met in Dallas at the downtown Statler Hilton, where, no doubt, Barron's father offered a break on the group rate. Commissioner Joe Foss had pledged to stay in session until the league decided on its eighth franchise, which had been up for grabs since Minnesota switched leagues. Seattle had come close to locking it up, but now Oakland had emerged as the favorite.

Foss reacted angrily to the news that the NFL was officially coming to Dallas.

"This is an act of war, an out-and-out attempt to put the AFL team in Dallas out of business," he thundered. "The NFL is out to continue its monopoly on professional football. We will go to court or Congress to prevent them from killing off the Dallas team. You have antitrust laws to take care of such situations."

Rozelle replied, "It is a shame to hear the commissioner of the AFL resort to issuing threats when all we are trying to do is establish a harmonious relationship with the new league. Besides, they have moved into our territory in New York and in Los Angeles and in San Francisco. Why shouldn't we be allowed to move into Dallas?"

Lamar responded to that question, pointing out that New York, Los Angeles, and the Bay Area were large sports markets with millions of residents, potentially capable of supporting two teams, while Dallas was clearly a one-team market.

"It's not the same situation at all," Lamar said.

Schramm, in a statement given to reporters, sought to position the Rangers as cool heads, above the fray: "We don't feel Dallas is either a one-team city or a minor league city. We have always felt it is a major league city, and we're gratified that Dallas has been granted a franchise in a major league. In the final analysis, this is a matter for decision by the people of Dallas."

Having finally been granted life, the Rangers moved into offices on the second floor of the Triple A Building, located north of downtown on Central Expressway. Schramm worked his final assignment for CBS, the Winter Olympics in Squaw Valley, and came to Dallas permanently in early March.

His first piece of business was to change the team's name. Dallas's minor league baseball team was also called the Rangers. Murchison had taken the name only after the baseball team's owners said they were disbanding, but they had reversed course and planned to bring their team back for another season, leaving Dallas with two Rangers teams. Murchison had volunteered to be the one to change.

Knowing how important this decision was, Murchison and Schramm deliberated for weeks, talking to friends and soliciting opinions. Wynne, a big University of Texas supporter, wanted to call the team the Steers, but Schramm thought it was a mistake to take a name so closely associated with another team. When he asked people around the country what they envisioned when they thought of Texas, many said, "Cowboys." They settled on that name. In a testament to Texas's gun-toting heritage, the team would be the Dallas Cowboys.

The *Morning News* gave the name a thumbs-up in an editorial, saying that one of the teams needed to change to avoid "endless confusion."

The Cowboys' next task was to fill out their roster. Of the $600,000 Murchison had paid for the franchise, $50,000 went to the league and the rest went to the other teams in exchange for the thirty-six players — three from each team — the Cowboys would select in the expansion draft at the league's spring meeting in Los Angeles in March.

Not surprisingly, the mechanics of the draft, the first of its kind in the NFL, stirred an argument. The debate was over how many players each team would be able to "protect" from the Cowboys. Halas thought twenty-two was a fair number, since it would enable teams to protect their offensive and defensive starters, but Marshall yelped that the Cowboys would be getting "too many damn fine ball players." He thought teams should be able to protect twenty-eight, leaving the true dregs for Dallas.

In the end, it was agreed that teams could protect twenty-five, a number the prickly Marshall still didn't like and pledged not to honor.

The Cowboys knew the draft wouldn't provide them with much regardless of how many players were protected. But they tried to make the most of it. Landry and Brandt visited the other eleven teams, studying game films and seeking to discover more about players who might be available. Landry eventually dismissed the process as a waste of time.

In another negotiated decision, the teams were allowed to keep their protected lists from the Cowboys until just a few days before the draft. Finally, over several mid-March days in Los Angeles, while the owners dealt with other issues such as approving the Cardinals' long-awaited move — the Wolfners were taking them to St. Louis — the Cowboys selected their players.

A few were relatively big names whose best days were behind them, such as Duane Putnam, an offensive guard for the Rams who had been to four Pro Bowls; Jim Doran, a tight end who had played on three title-winning teams and compiled almost three thousand receiving yards in nine seasons with the Lions; and Don Heinrich, a quarterback who had logged important minutes in important games for the Giants.

Then there were some solid veterans with Texas ties, such as Don McIlhenny, the former SMU running back (and Lamar's friend and college frat brother) who had played for the Lions and Packers; L. G. Dupre, a former Baylor runner who had played five seasons with the Colts; and Jerry Tubbs, a 49ers middle linebacker from Breckenridge, Texas.

But the majority of the selections were unknowns on the NFL fringe, such as Bill Striegel, Buzz Guy, Tom Franckhauser, Joe Nicely, Gene Cronin, and Dave Sherer. Frank Clarke, a speedy young receiver from the Browns, was one of the few with genuine promise; Paul Brown was letting him go because he didn't block hard enough, Brown felt.

Landry tried to sound optimistic, saying the team had grabbed a number of capable players, but privately he shook his head. He was supposed to mold *these* guys into a competitive team? There wasn't a bona fide star in the bunch. His job became even harder when capable selections such as Ed Modzelewski, a Browns fullback, and Charlie Ane, a Lions center, retired rather than go to a new team.

To anyone who knew football, it was instantly clear that the Cowboys wouldn't win many games; they would be over their heads as an expansion team taking on established winners such as the Colts, Giants, and others. They were going to get whipped.

Lamar's Texans, starting from scratch along with everyone else in the AFL, almost surely would have more success on the field.

When Murchison expressed dismay, Schramm stressed that the battle for the fans' allegiance would be a marathon race, not a sprint. The Texans might fare better on the field in the beginning, he said, but the Cowboys would take a patient, long-range approach and eventually win too.

From his days with the Rams, Schramm knew that intelligent scouting and drafting could provide a team with winning material. The Cowboys would duplicate that model, he said, and focus on bringing in a core of talented young players. Gil Brandt, who had signed so many free agents since December, was being hired as a full-time director of scouting, a position that few other NFL teams saw fit to fill. He would be given a budget to build a national network of area scouts who could file reports on players and tip him off to unknown talent. That investment would eventually pay big dividends, Schramm said.

Besides, Schramm said, the Cowboys had the advantage of playing in an established league, the benefits of which became apparent as soon as the NFL approved them. As Dallas's fans divided into two camps, with some supporting the Texans and others picking the Cowboys, the city's sports establishment clearly backed the Cowboys. Field Scovell, promoter of the Cotton Bowl game, said he looked forward to seeing famous NFL teams playing in Dallas. The Salesmanship Club, an influential businessmen's group that had sponsored a series of successful NFL exhibition games at the Cotton Bowl, drawing as many as 50,000 fans, said it would continue to sponsor a game every August with the Cowboys, not the Texans.

In a white-collar city run by businessmen, it was inevitable that the establishment would favor the established NFL over the start-up league that might or might not survive, even with Hunt money backing it. The Cowboys banked on that as they dug their cornerstone in Dallas, seeking to identify and cultivate a support base. They had the backing of institutions and organizations, groups whose success stories were already written. They would need that support as they lurched unsteadily into existence.

· · ·

The last thing Lamar Hunt was, in either background or tempera-
ment, was an extremist who picked fights. But he was in a fight now,
an increasingly hostile fight, and despite his wealth and last name,
he was clearly the underdog. He knew he couldn't proceed in the me-
thodical manner he preferred. He had to be aggressive, throw first
punches, scratch for advantages. Unlike the Cowboys, he couldn't
sit back and wait for a winning team to grow. He had to get out and
compete.

When Jim Stewart, executive director of the State Fair of Texas,
contacted him about reserving dates for the Texans' home games at
the Cotton Bowl that fall, Lamar didn't try to play fair. He asked for
four straight Sundays early in the season, from mid-September to mid-
October. Stewart had promised him that he would get the dates he
wanted because he had signed before Murchison. He needed to make
the most of that promise.

His plan was to maximize the effect of the Cowboys' likely early
struggles and try to score an immediate knockout by winning games
right away, getting as many fans as possible to the Texans' games,
playing exciting football, and stealing the city's heart before the Cowboys got going. If he bombarded the city with a blizzard of marketing
and promotional stunts that introduced the new team *that was winning*, maybe fans would check out the Texans, like what they saw, and
sign on.

Stewart sighed when he saw Lamar's request for four straight Sunday afternoons. He knew the Cowboys wouldn't be pleased. Stewart
hadn't expected to encounter problems when Hunt first came to him
about pro games in 1959; no one else wanted the Cotton Bowl on Sundays. When Murchison called later, also wanting to reserve some Sundays for *his* new team, Stewart explained that Hunt had first choice
and said he hoped the teams could work out any difficulties. Murchison promised they would. But it had just been a theoretical issue then.
Now it was real.

When Schramm heard about Hunt wanting to lock up the stadium for a month, he phoned Stewart and, voice rising, said Hunt was
deviously trying to keep the Cowboys away from their fans. Stewart
shrugged. What could he do? Plenty, Schramm barked. Never lacking

for an angle to exploit, he said the Cowboys would find a way to play at home early in the season, regardless of what Hunt wanted.

Both Schramm and Stewart knew what that meant. The Cowboys could shift games to Saturdays, which the Cotton Bowl definitely didn't want. It had a long-standing relationship with the Southwest Conference and the area's college teams, all of which feared the pros coming in. They wanted Saturday to remain their day for football.

When the Dallas papers reported that the Cowboys were thinking about playing on Saturdays, the colleges immediately complained. TCU athletic director Dutch Meyer said the Southwest Conference would boycott the Cotton Bowl game on New Year's Day if the stadium scheduled Saturday pro games. "I hope we don't have to, but we will if that's how they want to play ball. They'll live to regret it," Meyer said. Ed Olle, athletic director at the University of Texas, wrote to Stewart that "to allow use of the Cotton Bowl for pro games on any day other than Sunday would not be treating college football right and would do our institutions irreparable harm."

Having orchestrated the uproar, Schramm then played the innocent in public, seeking to portray the Texans as the bad guys. "We seem to be catching the brunt of the criticism, when in actuality, the only reason the Saturday night dates have ever come up is because the Cotton Bowl is tied up on four consecutive Sundays by another team," Schramm said dryly.

Stewart was a veteran administrator who had witnessed his share of disagreements over the years, but this one was ornery. So he abdicated, passing the issue on to his athletic committee. Seeking to calm down the colleges, the State Fair released a statement saying this would be the only season in which games "might" have to be played on Saturdays. Pete Rozelle chimed in, saying the NFL had "no intention of harming the colleges. We want to cooperate with them in every way possible."

Both teams needed to settle on home dates so their league offices could finalize schedules for the upcoming season. Everyone was angry. Finally, in early April, a settlement was reached. Lamar agreed to take the Cotton Bowl on three straight early-season Sundays as opposed to four, and the Cowboys agreed to play just one game on a Saturday night — their home opener against the Pittsburgh Steelers on September 24.

"We can assure you next year [in 1961] every pro game will be played on a Sunday," Stewart said.

With the schedule finally determined, Lamar focused on generating publicity and selling tickets. Sitting with Rossi in the Texans' offices, he hatched plans to get the team in the news and people behind it.

His approach, quite simply, was anything goes.

To combat the Salesmanship Club's influence, he started a season-ticket sales group for the Texans called the Spur Club. At a kickoff barbecue at Memorial Auditorium, the city's downtown arena, Lamar said that anyone who signed up and sold one hundred season tickets would get choice seats at games, premium parking spots, and the chance to travel with the team to away games. When he called for volunteers, the first person in line was Curtis Sanford, who purchased one hundred season tickets with a check for $3,200.

Lamar's next idea was among his most outrageous. Since Texans loved football and pretty women (not always in that order), why not merge the two? He hired thirty schoolteachers as summer employees and rented thirty sports cars once the school year was out. The teachers were given neighborhoods and businesses to canvas, selling tickets door to door. Soon the red cars were seen all over town. Lamar had told the teachers that the one who sold the most tickets would get to keep her car.

At a Spur Club dinner in April, he handed out bright red sports jackets with Texans breast patches to those who had already sold one hundred season tickets. A month later, he announced the formation of the Huddle Club, a group for kids. Youngsters could get into games for a dollar and also were given a T-shirt, a contract with their name on it, and the chance to attend clinics with Texans players. Hundreds of kids attended several sign-up sessions held at Dallas parks.

Watching from a distance, the Cowboys shook their heads. They had a season-ticket drive of their own going, helped by the Salesmanship Club. They were focusing on football more than business, hiring assistant coaches, signing veteran players to contracts. They smirked at

Lamar's red jackets and youth groups. Winning games was the best way to sell tickets, they figured.

Lamar wasn't about to sit back. In early June, as both teams were gearing up for their inaugural training camps, he fired his biggest shot. The AFL filed a $10 million antitrust lawsuit against the NFL in a federal court in Washington, DC, claiming the older league was "conspiring to monopolize pro football." The suit claimed that (1) the NFL had threatened players and coaches with being blackballed if they joined the AFL; (2) players who had signed with the AFL were being encouraged to break their contracts; and (3) the NFL had expanded to Dallas and Minnesota to knock out the AFL in those markets.

Lamar hadn't started the AFL intending to go to war, but the NFL clearly felt challenged and had come after him . . . hard. Since August, when Halas announced that the NFL was thinking about expanding to Dallas and Houston, Lamar had considered a lawsuit and felt it probably was inevitable. His lawyers told him he had a terrific case.

Joe Foss had taken a keen interest in the matter. A former politician, Foss had friends in high places. In January, before the NFL granted Dallas a franchise, he met with Estes Kefauver, the chairman of the Senate's Antitrust and Monopoly Subcommittee. Kefauver pledged to follow the situation after Foss explained that Dallas had been denied an NFL team until Lamar started the AFL. But the senator reversed course after Dallas's NFL franchise was approved, saying disputes over cities were for rival leagues, not Washington, to work out.

Foss then tried Emanuel Celler, a Democratic congressman from New York who chaired the House Judiciary Committee. Foss convinced Celler to put his committee's investigators on the case. They took affidavits from Foss, Hunt, Bud Adams, and the AFL's other major players. After weighing the evidence, the committee recommended that the Justice Department investigate the NFL and also asked the U.S. attorney general to issue an injunction that would keep the Cowboys from taking the field. "The injunction could last three to five years," Lamar told the *Morning News*.

But no injunction had been filed, and the Justice Department was just beginning its investigation in early June 1960, so Lamar and Foss went on and filed their antitrust suit. "Our lawyers feel things have happened which definitely are applicable to antitrust laws," Lamar said. "I'm glad to see the case out of the talking stage. Personally, I believe a suit is long overdue."

Pete Rozelle said he was sorry to see the AFL "resort to such tactics." The Cowboys weren't pleased about Lamar trying to knock them out in court. But Murchison and Schramm honestly weren't concerned. Halas was on record five years earlier saying the NFL would consider expansion. The chances of an injunction successfully knocking the Cowboys off the field were almost nil, they thought.

"We are confident there is nothing to it," Schramm said. "In the final analysis, the decision as to what Dallas wants in pro football will rest solely in the hands of the people. Apparently Lamar Hunt and his league aren't willing to risk a decision on this basis. We don't think they will find sympathy either in court or with the people of Dallas."

Officially, and inevitably, the battle had become nasty.

# PART II

# 6

★

# "I trained on biscuits and gravy"

W HEN THE COWBOYS' coaches and front office staff met at
Love Field in early July for their trip to training camp in Forest Grove, Oregon, Tom Landry was noticeably grim. Charles
Burton of the *Morning News* wrote that the coach "appeared about as
excited as if he were preparing to drive to Grand Prairie for a civic club
luncheon."

In the coming years, Landry's sober public persona would become
familiar. He was serious about football, viewing it as more an academic
exercise than a blood-and-guts sport. He didn't consider "rah-rah" pregame speeches or fiery criticism of players to be part of his job; pros
should motivate themselves. Having studied engineering in college, he
had mastered the geometry of play design and defensive strategy, the
physics of movable forces, the science of chance and predictability.

Some players found him remote and difficult to engage on the sideline, but he wasn't snubbing them; he was just concentrating, his mind
whirring ahead.

Bald and lanky, he was taller than people imagined, with deep-set
blue eyes and a long forehead. He had earned a reputation for being
smart and steady as a player, but there was little doubt his true calling
was coaching. After the Giants won the NFL title in 1956 with the "um-

brella" secondary he had designed — two cornerbacks guarding split receivers, backed by two safeties — other teams quickly poached the idea. They didn't realize Landry also was analyzing their tendencies — what plays they ran in various down-and-distance situations — and giving his players "keys" that tipped off what likely was coming.

He didn't follow pro football's developmental curve; he set it. His boss with the Giants, Jim Lee Howell, called Landry "the greatest coach in the game today." And he was just an assistant then.

Growing up during the Depression in Mission, a small town in the Rio Grande Valley, he had seldom worn shoes until he reached junior high school, but now, after a decade of playing and coaching on the East Coast, he wore tailored suits and a fedora on the sidelines. The fancy clothes conveyed an important message. He was from a burgeoning new breed of coaches, smart and snappy, demanding from his players their full attention and a lucid grasp of complex strategies.

The NFL had been a rough-and-rowdy place in the fifties with its heavy population of crusty war-era veterans who lived hard and didn't always take the game that seriously. But recess was over as coaches like Landry and his former Giants colleague Vince Lombardi took command.

The idea of coming home to coach thrilled him. He loved the Texas myth. Sharing an attic bedroom as a boy with an older brother and younger sister, he had caddied at the local golf course, thrown a paper route, and dreamed of becoming a cowboy, not a Cowboy. He loved books and movies set in the Old West, and a decade on the East Coast had not changed him. When he left on road trips, his wife, Alicia, made sure he packed a frontier novel written by Louis L'Amour, his favorite author.

He had initially played center on the Mission High varsity because the coach trusted him to know when to snap the ball, but he soon moved to quarterback because he had a strong arm and a knack for eluding tacklers. As a senior, he led the Eagles to a regional championship (they didn't compete for the state title) before packed stands of adoring fans. The team scored 322 points and allowed just one touchdown.

Recruited by the University of Texas as a quarterback, he was on campus for just one semester before entering the Army Air Corps in

1942, at the height of World War II. Stationed in Europe, he partic- ipated in thirty B-17 bomber missions as a copilot and gunner, was discharged as a first lieutenant in 1945, and returned to college and football in his early twenties. Taking one look at a recruit named Bobby Layne, he switched to defense and cocaptained teams that won the Sugar Bowl and Orange Bowl in his final two seasons.

Giving the pros a shot, he spent 1949 in the All-America Football Conference with the New York Yankees. The Giants grabbed him when that league folded. Although he was slow afoot, he became a mainstay in their secondary by analyzing and anticipating what quarterbacks would do. He earned All-Pro honors in 1954, intercepting three passes in one game, and was voted to the Pro Bowl in 1955.

All along, he considered quitting the game to sell insurance or work as an engineer. Both professions paid better, and he was a family man now, with others to consider. But when he finally stopped playing after the 1955 season, he turned to coaching, becoming a full-time assistant.

The Giants began 1956 with Landry running the defense and Lom- bardi, then another impressive assistant, directing the offense. Al- though they were opposites in many respects — Lombardi a volatile and emotional New Yorker, Landry a stoic and analytical Texan — they were a devastating tandem. Howell joked that his top assistants were so good that "all I have to do around here is pump up the balls."

In training camp that season, Sam Huff, an undersized rookie defen- sive lineman from West Virginia, became discouraged about his pros- pects and tried to walk away. Lombardi talked him into coming back, and Landry, observing Huff's mobility, put him behind the defensive line instead of on it. Huff blossomed into a ferocious linebacker, and the Giants rolled to the NFL championship behind Landry's swarming defense.

Lombardi, eight years older, had become the head coach in Green Bay in 1959 and immediately turned around the moribund Packers, earning the NFL's "Coach of the Year" award. Now, a year later, Landry was getting his chance. But as he boarded the plane that day at Love Field, bound for Oregon and his inaugural training camp, he doubted he would find success as quickly as Lombardi.

Oh, some experts had suggested the Cowboys might surprise the football world in their first year, strictly because of Landry. Giants halfback Frank Gifford, a budding broadcaster, had told Dallas reporters, "I bet that you win more than you lose. I wouldn't say that if anyone other than Tom were coaching. He is going to surprise you." Former Giants quarterback Don Heinrich, whom Landry had selected in the expansion draft, predicted the team would be "comparable to the Redskins and Cardinals, maybe even the Packers and Rams."

Landry knew they were just trying to help build enthusiasm, but the predictions were absurd. He didn't have much of a team. The Cowboys were going to have a rough season, lose a lot of games. The NFL's refusal to let them participate in the 1960 draft meant their younger players were almost all free agents, not worthy of having been drafted. And the most accomplished of the veterans from the expansion draft, such as Duane Putnam and Jim Doran, were nearing the end of their careers, while the rest were journeymen who could play a supporting role on a winning team but could not carry a major load.

Landry had originally hoped the expansion draft would provide the cornerstone of a competitive team, but once the other teams agreed to protect twenty-five players, enabling them to keep all of their starters, the Cowboys were doomed to field a team of leftovers. Their roster was so alarmingly incomplete that they had to give up future draft picks — precious commodities to a team that had never participated in the draft — to help field a reasonably competitive team in 1960.

Shortly before they left for Oregon, they reluctantly sent their first-round pick in 1961 to the Redskins for Eddie LeBaron, a veteran starting quarterback. They had no choice, they felt. Heinrich was a career backup whom Landry wanted around mostly to mentor Don Meredith, and the rookie hotshot from SMU was not remotely ready to play.

That spring, Landry had brought Heinrich, Meredith, and a few others to Dallas for a quarterback camp, a classroom-style introduction to his offense. When tested on how he would respond to certain defensive alignments, Meredith had sputtered, stammered, smiled thinly, and finally admitted he had no idea. SMU, he explained, had run a simple offense.

Landry had fully expected that Meredith would need time to develop, but found his lighthearted lack of understanding mildly irritating.

Lacking a viable full-time signal-caller, the Cowboys jumped at the chance to obtain LeBaron, who had started for the Redskins since the early fifties, earning three Pro Bowl selections along the way. At five-foot-seven, he appeared too short for the job, but he was a deft ball-handler, an accurate passer, and smart as hell. He had worked his way through law school while playing, graduating at the top of his class.

After taking a beating that included broken ribs during the 1959 season, LeBaron had told the Redskins he was retiring to practice law in Midland, Texas. When Schramm and Landry heard he was nearby, they talked him into coming back with the Cowboys. (A prospective job with Bedford Wynne's law firm helped.) When George Preston Marshall reacted furiously, the Cowboys had to give up two picks, including their precious first, for LeBaron's rights.

They kept dealing, out of necessity, as training camp neared. Their fifth-round pick in 1961 was sent to the 49ers for the rights to Gene Babb, a fullback and former Golden Gloves boxing champion who had spent the past year coaching football and running the art department at a junior college. They sent a tenth-round pick to the Packers for Fred Cone, an old-pro kicker who had booted more than fifty field goals.

They stole Babb from the Houston Oilers, who had convinced him to come out of retirement, leave his art classes behind, and play more football. Babb was preparing to go to camp with Houston when the Cowboys obtained his rights and convinced him to sign with them. He gave his bonus money back to the Oilers and headed for Oregon to practice with the Cowboys.

They hated giving up draft picks, but for now the Cowboys weren't concerned about the future. They had to field a team that could survive the 1960 season in one piece, win or lose. In Landry's opinion, they had about a fifty-fifty shot.

The plane carrying Landry, Schramm, and Brandt to Oregon made fuel stops in West Texas, Colorado, Utah, and Idaho before finally reaching Portland, where the three men got off and drove thirty miles to Pacific University in Forest Grove, a suburban logging town. They were a long way from home, but Schramm and Landry hadn't wanted to hold camp in the brutally hot Texas summer.

Forest Grove was ideal, cool at night and just warm enough in the afternoon, with Mount Hood's majestic snowcapped peak visible in the distance and salmon running in nearby rivers. The quiet campus of Pacific, a private school known for its music and optometry schools, was lush with evergreens and white birch. The local residents were so excited to have an NFL team around that they fought to loan their cars to the players for use on the team's days off.

Practices rotated between the college stadium and a field located behind a fish cannery. On the first day, the players had to run a mile. Landry had sent out letters explaining this would be his first order of business. He wanted players to complete the run in six minutes. (Linemen were given thirty more seconds.) The rookies reported first, several days ahead of the veterans, and their version of the "Landry Mile" unfolded disastrously — none of them beat the six-minute mark. Landry complained to reporters that he had warned them about having to do this. To himself, he thought, *If this doesn't reinforce how bad we are, nothing does.*

One of the team's few heralded rookies, Don Perkins, a running back from the University of New Mexico, had been told by Landry he would play fullback, so he had put on twenty pounds. ("I trained on biscuits and gravy all spring," he admitted.) Carrying the extra weight, he simply wasn't up to running a mile. He trudged through the first three laps, lagging far behind the others, and then spent the final lap staggering, falling, rising, and taking a few steps before staggering and falling again as Landry and his four assistants watched in silence, beyond stunned.

The Cowboys had gone to lengths to obtain Perkins. Clint Murchison had invited his friend Clinton Anderson, a U.S. senator from New Mexico, to sit on the team's board of directors, and Anderson, a football fan, had accepted and offered some scouting advice: "Get this running back at New Mexico."

Perkins had rushed for more than two thousand yards in three seasons at UNM. The Baltimore Colts owned his NFL rights, but the NFL allowed the Cowboys to sign him to a personal services contract, as they had with Meredith. He signed in the senator's office.

Landry had hoped Perkins could contribute as a rookie, but Perkins was so humiliated after the mile run that he wanted to quit football. "I think I'm going to go home and do something else," he told Landry.

Landry explained to the young man that the coaches understood why he had failed — the extra weight — and suggested he take time to reflect before making such a decision. Perkins, Meredith, and two other rookies were scheduled to leave camp soon and spend three weeks in Chicago with the College All-Stars, the select team that would play the NFL champion Colts in mid-August. It was an honor to have been selected; Perkins was no slouch. He calmed down before leaving for Chicago and promised Landry he would return in better shape.

The Texans were looking for a few good men — or even some who weren't so good. Two weeks before their training camp opened in mid-July 1960 at the New Mexico Military Institute in Roswell, New Mexico, they were hunting for "camp bodies" — players to take hits for a couple of weeks and then likely be on their way.

Well-known rookies such as Johnny Robinson, Abner Haynes, Chris Burford, and Jack Spikes would be in camp, as would several dozen older guys who had been out of the NFL, but the Texans needed more bodies for drills and scrimmages — football fodder.

Ever mindful of opportunities to generate publicity, Lamar devised the idea of an all-comers tryout. *You want to play pro football? Here's your chance.* The Texans promoted it with newspaper ads, asking anyone who wanted a shot to come to Jesuit High School in North Dallas on July 1.

That morning, as a withering sun rose, more than one hundred young men gathered on the school's football field, which had been baked hard by the summer heat. No one would have supposed these were candidates for jobs in pro football. It was a motley crew. Some were tall, some were short, some were fat, and some were trim. Some wore cleats, shorts, and T-shirts, and some came in tennis shoes and sweatpants, which they regretted as the temperature soared toward one hundred degrees.

As he waited for the tryout to begin, Stewart "Smokey" Stover glanced at the other players. Who *were* these guys? Most were dreamers with no hope, but the Texans had invited a few legitimate players, guys who didn't warrant free agent contracts, yet had qualities that made them interesting prospects. Stover was one. A six-foot, two-hundred-pound fullback-linebacker from tiny Northeast Louisiana State College, he had played with an edge, delivering enough hard hits to attract attention even though his team had won just two games in 1959. He had received feelers from the NFL's Giants and a team in Canada, and then Will Walls, the Texans' scout, called and suggested he try out.

Stover had not planned to play beyond college. He was going to earn a master's degree in geology and get to work in the oil business; he had a wife and young child and needed to support them as best he could. But since the pros had shown interest, however minimal, he wanted to give it a shot before he gave up. He agreed to try out for the Texans. Dallas was closer to his Louisiana home than New York or Canada, and maybe the fledgling AFL was the right place to try to make it.

The first order of business at the tryout was a physical. The medical tests quickly ended the dreams of several dozen candidates. Those with high blood pressure or heart murmurs were sent home, as were those obviously too fond of hamburgers and milk shakes.

The survivors returned to the field, where Hank Stram, dressed crisply in red shorts and a white shirt, blew his whistle and led the players through jumping jacks, sit-ups, and other calisthenics. Stover was in shape, having figured he wouldn't last long otherwise, and was relieved he had put in the work when an assistant coach replaced Stram after fifteen minutes and led another fifteen minutes of exercises before handing off to yet another assistant.

The players, soaked in sweat, grew weary and pale, and several dropped out, walking off the field with their heads down.

After the calisthenics finally ended, the players were told to sprint across the field once, twice, four times, eight times. More dropped out. Stover kept pace, again relieved he had prepared. As the sun burned down, the coaches didn't allow anyone to sip water, thinking that was a sign of weakness.

By the end of the one-mile run that concluded the day's work, half of the original candidates were gone. The survivors were given a small per diem and sent to a cheap motel down the road, with orders to return the next morning. They walked down a scalding-hot sidewalk to the motel, crammed into double rooms, and flopped on their beds, exhausted.

The second day unfolded similarly, with the coaches putting the players through several hours of calisthenics, sprints, and agility drills.

The shrinking pool of survivors returned for a third, fourth, and fifth day, their routine unvarying. Stover walked from the motel to Jesuit in the morning and trudged home in the afternoon to a room without air conditioning. He ate dinner, slept hard, and did it all over again the next day.

After a second week of drills, only twenty-five players remained. Stram congratulated them for getting that far, but explained the Texans would take only seventeen to Roswell. He posted the survivors' names on a board and left.

Stover held his breath before he checked; if his name wasn't on the list, his playing days were probably over. He stood up, walked to the board, and looked at the list. His name was there. He couldn't suppress a smile. The pride of Northeast Louisiana State wasn't done with football just yet.

There were more than eighty players in the Cowboys' camp when the veterans reported to Forest Grove. They also had been warned by letter about having to run a mile, and while many didn't quite beat the six-minute mark, they came close. Frank Clarke, the young receiver whom the Browns had let go, won the race, beating the six-minute mark by ten seconds.

Landry initiated a regimen of two-a-day practices with classroom meetings in the evenings. He was never without the clipboard he carried around listing his daily schedule and objectives. The emphasis was on teaching. As he installed his offense and defense — and make no mistake, he was in charge of both units, unlike some coaches who delegated — Landry patiently explained his thinking and answered all questions.

At times he almost seemed like a math professor, lecturing with a level voice as he etched out complex designs on a chalkboard. Some players embraced the environment. Jack Patera, a linebacker who had spent five years with the Colts and Cardinals, told reporters he was learning more than in his other NFL stops combined. Tom Braatz, a linebacker from the Redskins, was highly impressed with the young coach. Landry's blueprints certainly made sense.

Landry was determined that the players would do things his way, down to the littlest detail. He knew best, he believed. In his eyes, the worst transgression a player could commit was failing to follow his carefully crafted plan.

Don McIlhenny, the running back who had come from Green Bay in the expansion draft, knew Landry personally; both were married with young children and sold insurance in Dallas in the off-season. In fact, McIlhenny had seen Landry at a business meeting after the 1959 season and used the opportunity to say he would like to be plucked off the Packers' roster in the expansion draft.

Their association led McIlhenny to think he might earn an on-field wink or two from Landry. But after he improvised on a running play early in camp, hitting a different hole than Landry had diagrammed because he thought he could break a long run, he was met by an ice-cold stare.

"What were you thinking?" Landry asked.

"I thought I could break it," McIlhenny replied.

Landry grimaced and rolled his eyes disgustedly, as if to say, *Give me a break!*

During another practice, Landry blew his whistle and rebuked the backs for failing to run out plays — continuing to run for twenty yards after completing a play. When McIlhenny took a handoff on the next play, he burst through the hole and raced fifty yards, sprinting up the hill at the far end of the field before he finally stopped. As the other players snickered, Landry didn't spew venom at being shown up. He just gave McIlhenny his coldest possible stare.

Ed Husmann, a defensive lineman who had spent five years on the woebegone Cardinals with teammates who didn't always care, appreciated that Landry was demanding professionalism. Fred Dugan, a receiver who had been with the 49ers and hard-nosed coach Red Hickey, appreciated that Landry took time to explain his offense from a defensive point of view and pointed out how the opposition was likely to react to certain formations. *This guy can really coach*, Dugan thought.

But by the second week, some players were rolling their eyes. Just who was this young guy who thought he knew so much?

L. G. Dupre had come from the Colts, winners of the past two NFL championships. Although he was a native Texan who had played at

Baylor and was personally pleased to come home and run the ball for a Dallas team, he was dismayed about going from the league's number-one team to this new outfit coached by a young know-it-all. Dupre and some of the other veterans from hard-nosed old-school teams such as the Lions and Steelers could barely contain their contempt. They got together after practices to drink beer, complain about Landry, and talk about how much better things were done on their old teams.

Ray Mathews, a tough end-halfback who had rolled up almost five thousand yards of offense in nine years with the Steelers, was openly contemptuous. At thirty-one, he was old enough to have played against Landry and, in fact, had fared quite well against him.

"Tom, you couldn't cover me. I beat you like a stepchild," he said one day in front of some players.

Landry had little reaction, and McIlhenny pulled Mathews aside later and issued a warning.

"Ray, he's the coach. He's wearing long pants, not a uniform. He's your boss now. I don't know if I would taunt him," McIlhenny said.

Mathews dismissively waved his hand. He was a free spirit who had played with Bobby Layne, the league's ultimate good-time guy.

"But it's true, he couldn't cover me," Mathews said. "So why is he such an expert?"

Landry had regarded Mathews and Dugan as his likely starting receivers, but he told Schramm and Brandt to look for new blood. Mathews was irritating as well as over the hill. Schramm and Brandt located an excellent replacement: Billy Howton, a decorated veteran who had caught 342 passes in nine seasons with the Packers and Browns. He had retired to Houston, his home, where he planned to manage a shopping center, but was willing to come back and play if he could be so close to home.

The Cowboys sent the Browns a draft pick — *another draft pick* — and Howton joined the team. Mathews went from the top of Landry's depth chart to the bottom and would catch just three more passes before his career summarily ended.

On many days it was easy to understand why Landry was so grim. His camp resembled a home for the aged and infirm. Cone and Doran were thirty-three, Mathews thirty-one. LeBaron was thirty, as was sore-kneed Leo Sanford, who had last played in 1958 but was giving the game a final try because he lived in Dallas and the Cowboys needed a center. Sanford could barely walk some days, and he had company in that regard. Two weeks into camp, trainer Clint Huoy treated twenty-seven sore knees one morning, surely a record.

At times it almost seemed there were more characters and odd-balls than real players. Wahoo McDaniel, a rookie linebacker and full-blooded Choctaw-Chickasaw Indian, regaled reporters with wild stories from the reservation. Gene Babb, the fullback, painted western landscapes. Another fullback played piano. This was an NFL team?

Charlie Ane, the veteran center who had retired to his native Hawaii rather than play for the Cowboys, fielded a bevy of phone calls from Schramm and Landry. Please come back, they said. He declined. He could see what was going to happen and didn't want any part of it.

Ironically, Landry, the defensive expert, mostly feared that his first Cowboy defense would not stop anyone. There was such a talent short-age on that unit that Landry finally moved players over from the of-fense. Offensive linemen John Gonzaga and Don Healy became starters on defense. Pete Johnson, formerly a halfback, became a cornerback.

Cruising unobtrusively through this unsettled environment was Meredith, the team's future leader. Before leaving for the College All-Star camp in Chicago, the rookie went through drills and meetings with his eyes firmly fixed on LeBaron and Heinrich, the veterans men-toring him. Although he was raw, he threw a tight, accurate spiral.

"He might be one of the best quarterbacks to come into the league in the last four or five years," Landry admitted.

Bright and curious, Meredith asked numerous questions, pulling aside veterans such as McIlhenny, who had played with Bobby Layne. "How did Bobby play that hard on Saturday and still play so well on Sunday?" Meredith asked. McIlhenny just smiled. Meredith didn't party as hard as Layne — no one did — but his happy-go-lucky atti-tude reminded some veterans of the legendary signal-caller. Meredith walked around with a smile, whistling songs, snapping his fingers, and hailing teammates.

Privately, though, the young quarterback wasn't happy. The old, lame, and disgruntled Cowboys were not exactly an uplifting intro-duction to pro football. Landry was smart and all, but he was awfully serious about this game they played. The team itself was kind of depressing.

It was too late now, the carefree Meredith thought, but maybe he should have gone with Lamar Hunt and the Texans.

# 7

## "Someone is going to get hurt here"

UNLIKE THE COWBOYS, who had ventured to the crisp Pacific Northwest, the Texans had picked a training camp site no one would consider a tourist destination. Roswell was as miserable as Dallas in July, with temperatures reaching the high nineties on airless afternoons. The New Mexico Military Institute's austere campus of Gothic buildings seemed as forbidding as a horror-movie set. Alamogordo, the remote site of atomic bomb testing in the forties, was within earshot. That was enough to give anyone the creeps.

Somehow Don Rossi, the Texans' general manger, had identified this as an ideal location for camp. If an AFL players' union had existed, a complaint probably would have been filed. The players were assigned to dim double rooms in the barracks featuring squeaky cots, military-issue mattresses, and one small window without a screen. The thought of air conditioning was laughable. A fifteen-watt bulb dangled from the ceiling. Players were buzzed by mosquitoes when they opened the window in search of a breeze. At the dining hall on the first night, they watched dully as unidentifiable slop was doled onto their gray plastic trays. The cooks called it barbecue but later admitted the "meat" had been in the kitchen a while.

Stram was unfazed by the dismal surroundings. The same age as

Landry, he also had interrupted his college years to serve in the military during World War II. Born in Chicago and raised in Gary, Indiana, he had earned an athletic scholarship to Purdue before enlisting in the Army Reserves in 1943 and being summoned to active duty at age twenty. Like Landry, he returned to campus after the war and resumed his athletic career, playing football and baseball for the Boilermakers.

The similarities between Stram and Landry, however, ceased there. Stram was much shorter, at five-foot-seven, a bit rounder, and not nearly the same caliber of athlete; he went straight into coaching at his alma mater after graduation, working as a backfield assistant in football and the head baseball coach.

Stram also had a different personality than Landry. While, as the father of four, he certainly believed in old-school discipline, he was positively postmodern in his desire to understand and calibrate his players' emotions, which he deemed crucial to winning performances. Landry had little interest in that aspect of the coaching profession.

Stram had positive feelings as his players reported to NMMI. Unlike Landry, who was discouraged about his team's prospects for the upcoming season, the Texans' coach was optimistic. Every team in the AFL was starting from scratch, and the Texans seemed to have more talent than many of the others. One hundred and fourteen players were trying out, so many that Stram had to cut four before the first practice. He had brought too many guys, it turned out. The unlucky quartet donned the team's white pants and red jerseys and posed for a photograph on the first morning, then were handed plane tickets back to Dallas at lunch, having never put on their helmets.

Half of the prospects were straight from college, and the rest were grizzled older guys who either had never played in the NFL or had fallen out of the established league because of an injury, a military obligation, a lack of talent, low pay, poor prospects, or some combination of those factors. (The AFL was not pursuing players under contract to NFL teams, figuring such raids would cause legal headaches.) Desperate to find a few gems with pro experience, Lamar, Stram, Rossi, and Will Walls had reached out to anyone with a pulse who lived in Texas and played football.

Ray Collins, a thirty-three-year-old defensive tackle who had most recently played in Canada, looked positively ancient to the younger players. Paul Miller, a twenty-nine-year-old defensive end, had been out of pro ball since undergoing career-ending back surgery in 1957. Dick Frey, a thirty-year-old defensive end, had never played pro ball after leaving Texas A&M almost a decade earlier. Cotton Davidson, a former star quarterback for Baylor, had been coaching at his alma mater. Jerry Cornelison, an offensive tackle from SMU, had spent two years in the National Guard. Defensive backs Don Flynn and Jim Harris had been working in the oil business.

Many had been fine players at one point. Paul Miller had earned two Pro Bowl selections in the NFL. Ray Collins had earned one. Davidson had been a first-round NFL draft pick.

Harris had played quarterback at Oklahoma and defensive back for the NFL's Eagles and Rams, but had quit football for a job in the oil business in Dallas after the Rams (specifically Pete Rozelle, then their general manager) low-balled him when he said he wouldn't play for less than $10,000 in 1959. He was already established in his new career in 1960 when Lamar called, thinking Harris was just what the Texans needed — an NFL-caliber player seemingly unattached. When Lamar offered him $13,000 to play in 1960, Harris enthusiastically accepted.

But the biggest name among the "veterans" making comebacks with the Texans was Jim Swink, a celebrated former TCU halfback. A native of Rusk, a small town in East Texas, he had dazzled the college football world in the mid-fifties with his broken-field running, leading the Horned Frogs to a pair of Southwest Conference titles. As a junior in 1955, he had scored twenty touchdowns and put on a performance against Texas that ranked with the best the college game had ever seen — 235 yards rushing and four touchdowns on just fifteen carries.

Swink had been drafted high by the Chicago Bears in 1957, but in a stunning development, he turned down a pro football career to go to medical school. He didn't think he would make as much money as a halfback as he would as an orthopedic surgeon, and despite repeated phone calls from Halas, Swink had walked away from the game and enrolled at Southwestern Medical School in Dallas.

Lamar had watched Swink from the opposing bench when SMU played TCU in the mid-fifties, and he had enduring respect for the former star. He called Swink on a lark, and Swink confessed he missed football and wanted to play again. When Halas heard about that, he immediately phoned, encouraging Swink to sign with the Cowboys rather than the Texans. But Swink turned Papa Bear down again and signed with Lamar, figuring he would take his medical school classes at night.

Stram sought to separate the players from the pretenders as camp opened. He lined up the young guys and, one by one, had them take a handoff and run right at Bob Hudson, a crotchety offensive lineman who had played eight seasons in the NFL. With no blockers fending him off, the old pro leveled the youngsters, grinning unashamedly.

The goal was to see who could take punishment — who wanted to play and, more important, who didn't. As Chris Burford, the All-American receiver, waited in line, he watched Hudson flattening players who had come from small colleges and weren't prepared for such brutality.

*Someone is going to get hurt here,* Burford thought.

When his time came, Burford took a stance opposite Hudson, right hand in the dirt. A coach barked a signal and handed him the ball as he lurched forward. Hudson slammed into him, leading with a forearm. The crushing blow knocked Burford over, but he rose, dusted off his pants, and handed the ball to the coach. He might be from a fancy school, but he could play this game.

Stram's daily schedule consisted of long two-a-day practices in the mornings and afternoons, a grueling regimen in the brutal heat. As the afternoon session ended one day, several veterans eyed the water-filled irrigation ditches NMMI used to keep the field in shape. They shrugged and jumped in, drawing laughs as the muddy water cooled their soaring body temperatures. The next day dozens of players peeled off their shoulder pads after the final whistle and jumped into NMMI's luxurious "bath springs."

By the end of the first week, half of the players had been cut. They returned to the real world with tales about poundings from grinning old guys, wretched food, mosquito attacks, and afternoon workouts so miserable they reduced sane adults to thinking it was wise to plunge into an irrigation ditch.

Yet out of the limping mass of old guys and kids, the outline of a decent team began to form. Johnny Robinson and Burford could really play, as could Jim Harris, Don Flynn, and ancient Ray Collins. Perhaps most important, Cotton Davidson quickly separated himself from the other quarterbacks Stram had recruited.

A slender native of Gatesville, a small town in central Texas, Davidson had played so well at Baylor in the early fifties that the Baltimore Colts made him their first-round pick in 1954. A year later, he was in line to become the starter when a military call-up halted his career. He stayed in shape while in the service, quarterbacking Fort Bliss to the championship of a military league, but when he rejoined the Colts in 1957 another young signal-caller had taken his job — a guy named Unitas.

Davidson backed up Unitas and punted for a year, then left the Colts for a team in Canada in 1958, thinking he could still be a starting quarterback. When a shoulder injury cut short that experiment, Davidson went home to Texas and ruefully watched the Colts beat the Giants to win the NFL title; he knew he could have been on that team.

With his shoulder aching and spirits sagging, he took a job as an assistant coach at Baylor in 1959, figuring his playing days were over. Then he ran into Stram at a coaching clinic.

"Do you still want to play?" Stram asked.

"I think I still can," Davidson said.

"Well, let's talk about getting you on board," Stram said.

A week later, Stram and Lamar drove to Waco. Davidson had never seen a rich guy so modest, and he was impressed by Lamar's passion for the new league. He had heard people doubt the AFL's viability, but after a day with Lamar, he was convinced it would fly. He said he would give the Texans a shot. He could earn more money playing than coaching, and at twenty-eight, he might have a few years left.

He had arrived at NMMI to find himself competing for a job with Dick Jamieson, who had been with the Colts the year before; Hunter Enis, a rookie from TCU; and Fran Curci, another rookie, who had played well for Stram at Miami the year before. Davidson briefly wondered if he had run into a teacher's pet in Curci, but when scrimmages started, he stood out. "He looks good, makes all the throws impressively," Stram said.

It was also quickly apparent in scrimmages that Jim Swink had not lost much, if anything. The doctor-halfback ran hard and broke tackles, showing few signs of rust. Lamar was overjoyed. If Swink could play anywhere close to the level he had displayed at TCU, the Texans would have a backfield star who could really sell tickets.

Watching Swink's star rise, Abner Haynes was discouraged. He felt he also was performing well, breaking his share of runs, but he couldn't crack the first-team backfield. Swink and Johnny Robinson were the halfbacks, and they were bigger names from bigger college programs. TCU's Jack Spikes would be the fullback.

Haynes and his camp roommate, Clem Daniels, a halfback from all-black Prairie View A&M, spent their evenings swatting mosquitoes and fretting about their chances. They knew they could play as well as these white guys if given a shot, and they had hoped they would get that shot in the AFL. But only a handful of blacks had tried out in Roswell, and now only four were left, with several major cuts remaining.

Haynes wrote his wife a mournful letter one evening, expressing concern that he might not be around much longer.

"I'll be home in a week," he lamented. "They won't even let me run back kicks out here."

At times there was an amateurish feel to the Roswell camp. During practices, players would glance at an adjoining field and see Lamar punting and passing balls back and forth with his brother, Bunker, as if they were warming up to play. And only one sportswriter was on hand at first, Sam Blair from the *Morning News*. The *Times Herald* wasn't covering camp because Blackie Sherrod, the paper's respected sports editor, was unsure about the AFL lasting and feared blowing his travel budget on a team that might soon vanish from the scene. (Not that it was costing much: Blair had flown out for free on the charter and was eating for free in the mess hall.)

After reading Blair's stories for a while, Sherrod relented and sent twenty-five-year-old Gary Cartwright out to cover the team.

After almost a month at NMMI, the Texans prepared to break camp for a slate of six preseason games that would take them from one side of America to the other. Stram and his assistants had tough decisions to make as they pared their roster for the trip. They discussed each player, weighing his abilities, size, and potential. Some would clearly make the team, but Stram needed to see more of others.

A free-spirited linebacker named Sherrill Headrick was especially intriguing. He had been an all-conference performer as a junior at TCU in 1958, but had flunked out of school and spent the past year as an oil roughneck in New Mexico. Both the Cowboys and Texans had located him and sent him contracts. He started to go with the Cowboys because they reached him first and offered him $500 to sign, but he hesitated and called the Texans, whom he preferred because of Lamar's Southwest Conference roots. He went with the Texans when Lamar doubled his signing bonus to $1,000.

Headrick had to come to Roswell with a gleam in his eye. When old-pro Bob Hudson whacked him, he whacked Hudson back even harder. *There's a linebacker,* Stram thought. But then Headrick injured his back and was knocked out of scrimmages. All he had done was stay in shape. Stram was anxious to see what he could do in a game, so he survived the final camp cut.

Then there was Smokey Stover. Stram had originally put the obscure youngster from Northeast Louisiana State at fullback, but Spikes owned that position and Stover's knack for delivering hits was more suited to playing defense, so Stover joined the large pool of candidates trying to make the team at linebacker. He had some positive qualities, but he was so darn small, Stram thought. He had weighed two hundred pounds at the start of the tryout camp, but after two weeks in Dallas and a month in Roswell, he "looked like a bag of bones," Stram told an assistant, wondering if a guy that feathery could be a pro linebacker.

Aware that his low weight was an issue, Stover ate as much as possible in Roswell, but the food at NMMI was awful and a man could only eat so much Dairy Queen. Figuring he probably weighed 180 pounds, he resorted to a desperate trick. The coaches wanted to know what each player weighed as they broke camp, and before Stover stepped on the scale, he took a pair of ten-pound free weights and taped one under each armpit. Then he pulled on a shirt to cover his subterfuge.

Bill Walsh, the offensive line coach, was handling the weigh-ins. When Stover stepped on the scale, Walsh manipulated the measuring weights and eyeballed the results.

"Two hundred pounds, hmm," Walsh said.

Stover looked at him, hoping the coach didn't suspect he was being tricked.

"Next," Walsh said.

Stover stepped off the scale with a sly smile, believing he still had a shot to make the team.

The Cowboys could no longer delay the inevitable. It was time to play a game . . . and probably lose. After three weeks in Oregon, they traveled to Seattle, Washington, for their exhibition opener against the 49ers — their first-ever contest — on August 6, 1960.

It was hard to know what to expect, but Landry had a hunch. He thought his offense might fare decently with Eddie LeBaron and Don Heinrich under center, but feared his makeshift defense wouldn't stop anyone. Asked by the *Times Herald*'s Bud Shrake to predict how the team would perform, he replied, "Fair."

Seattle hosted an NFL exhibition every summer to indicate its continuing interest in obtaining a franchise. The game was part of Seafair, a citywide festival that included a salmon fishing derby, a jazz concert, and a Chinese carnival. On an eighty-degree Saturday afternoon, the Cowboys and 49ers drew an estimated 22,000 fans to the University of Washington's Husky Stadium, a scenic U-shaped facility overlooking Lake Washington and the Cascade Mountains.

As a steady breeze whipped the stadium's flags, the Cowboys kicked off just seven months after having been granted life — truly a rush job in cleats. The players wore their new home uniforms, which Schramm had designed, featuring royal blue jerseys with large white patches on the shoulders, white pants with blue piping, and white helmets with blue stars on either side.

The game was being broadcast on television and radio back in Dallas, but anticipation wasn't exactly running high. Charles Burton's "advance" story on the game in the *Morning News,* headlined "Cowboys Open NFL Wars," was played below the account of a high school all-star game from the night before.

The 49ers let twenty-four-year-old John Brodie start for old pro Y. A. Tittle, and Brodie drove the 49ers into scoring range late in the first quarter, but the Cowboys' defense held and a field goal attempt fell short. After Heinrich, starting largely because he resided in Seattle in the off-season, failed to produce a first down, a rookie center snapped the ball over Cowboy punter Dave Sherer's head and out of the back of the end zone. The gaffe gave the 49ers a safety, putting the Cowboys down by two points. Welcome to the NFL.

But Landry's defense held up surprisingly well, stopping the 49ers on several possessions while the Cowboy offense consistently generated first downs behind McIlhenny's productive running; he would gain over one hundred yards during the game. The offense never actually threatened to score, however, and late in the second quarter Brodie suddenly heated up, completing two long passes before hitting a rookie receiver on a thirty-four-yard scoring play. The 49ers led at halftime, 9–0.

Both teams changed quarterbacks after halftime, the Cowboys turning to LeBaron and the 49ers to Tittle. LeBaron drove the Cowboys into scoring range late in the third quarter. The drive stalled, but Fred Cone kicked a seventeen-yard field goal on the first play of the fourth quarter to give the Cowboys their first points. Tittle responded by passing the 49ers right back down the field for a touchdown, putting them up 16–3, with ten minutes to play.

Landry was pleased by his team's response to being down. On a first down at the Dallas 46, Frank Clarke, the receiver obtained from Cleveland, sprinted past a defensive back on a "streak route." LeBaron saw him and lobbed the ball downfield. Clarke ran under it, grabbed it, and raced across the goal line, completing a fifty-four-yard scoring play, the Cowboys' first-ever touchdown. The extra point made it 16–10.

The Cowboys' defense then stopped Tittle, returning the ball to LeBaron and the offense at their 37 with four minutes to play. Another touchdown might win the game! LeBaron threw to Clarke for twelve yards. McIlhenny ran around right end for eleven. Another run moved the ball to the San Francisco 28 with ninety seconds left. The fans stood, hoping for a dramatic ending. LeBaron dropped back, looked left, and threw for Clarke, but a defensive back read the route, stepped in front of Clarke, and intercepted, ending the rally and securing the win for the 49ers.

In a conversation with Dallas reporters the day before, 49ers coach Red Hickey had disparaged the Cowboys, predicting their roster of journeymen would have a miserable season, even with Landry as their coach. But the competitive game had changed his opinion.

"They surprised me. They aren't patsies. They're not going to finish last," Hickey said.

Landry said, "I'm encouraged. It was better than I expected. We really competed. I know the players are encouraged too. We think we can beat someone now."

The Cowboys returned to Forest Grove for another week of practice, broke camp, and traveled to San Antonio, Texas, for an exhibition game against the St. Louis Cardinals. Playing their first contest in the Lone Star State, they didn't quite pack a high school stadium, drawing 18,000 fans, 5,000 under capacity, on a balmy Saturday night. High school games routinely sold out the stadium in the fall.

Sluggish on offense, they trailed by six points at halftime and by two touchdowns entering the fourth quarter. Heinrich tossed a long touchdown pass to a rookie, but the rally ended when Clarke, trying to lateral after a reception, was hit hard and fumbled. The Cowboys had now played two games and lost both.

The referee blew his whistle and brought his right arm down, signaling for play to begin. The Texans' Jack Spikes advanced toward the teed-up football and booted it. As it spun through the cool air coming off San Francisco Bay, the Texans' kickoff coverage team ran downfield, white uniforms and red helmets glinting in the afternoon sun.

Watching from the top of the seating bowl at Kezar Stadium, Lamar beamed. At long last, his team was playing a football game.

He had spent the past eighteen months getting the AFL started, building a franchise, acquiring players, arguing with (and suing) NFL bigwigs, talking to reporters and lawyers, putting out fires, and selling the Texans to fans in Dallas — selling them hard. But his goal all along was to get the Texans onto the field along with the AFL's other seven teams. It had been a huge task, and as he watched the Oakland Raiders run back Spikes's kickoff, he couldn't help feeling satisfied.

The AFL's battle for survival was just beginning. Naysayers predicted the league might not last beyond one season. Lamar was pleased to see 18,000 fans at the Raiders' first exhibition game. That was a decent crowd. The Raiders were semi-vagabonds, playing in San Francisco all season because they couldn't find a suitable stadium in Oakland. That was hardly an ideal way to build a fan base. Lamar hoped those on hand today would be entertained and want to come back.

It was the first game ever for both teams, so no one knew what to expect. "We're going to have to kind of play this one by ear," Stram had chuckled. On the first possession, the Texans' defense gave up a couple of pass completions and held at midfield, forcing a punt. On the Texans' first offensive snap, Johnny Robinson took a handoff, swept right, and fumbled. The Raiders recovered and quickly scored a touchdown.

Lamar hoped things would improve. The game was being broadcast on radio back in Dallas, with Charlie Jones handling the play-by-play call. The Texans were working hard to attract fans — a lot harder than the Cowboys, Lamar believed. They had started the Spur Club and Huddle Club, held a beauty pageant to name a Miss Dallas Texan, and sent those thirty young schoolteachers in sports cars around town selling tickets. They had flown their entire team back from New Mexico during training camp for a public scrimmage at Dallas's P. C. Cobb Stadium, which 10,000 fans attended. They also flew to Wichita Falls to scrimmage. But Lamar knew all that work would be fruitless if the team fell flat on the field. It was imperative, he felt, that the Texans play interesting football and win some games. Nothing lured fans more than winning, and with the Cowboys likely to be looking at a losing season — maybe a few — the Texans really needed to win. Although exhibition games didn't count, positive results and positive headlines could only help.

Trailing 7–0, the Texans drove to midfield, but Abner Haynes fumbled. Haynes had not been himself since running into a goalpost during a practice in New Mexico a few days earlier. He would spend most of the game on the bench.

Cotton Davidson, playing in a game for the first time in two years, looked rusty early, missing several open receivers, but finally heated up midway through the second quarter. He lobbed swing passes to Robinson and Jim Swink coming out of the backfield, and both picked up first downs. Spikes barged up the middle for twelve yards. A square-out to Burford moved the ball to the Oakland 5. Finally, Davidson found Burford in the corner of the end zone for a touchdown.

Instead of kicking the extra point, the Texans experimented, going for a two-point conversion — a popular college play that was illegal in the NFL. Lamar loved the excitement it generated and had demanded that it be legal in the AFL. Lining up at the 3, Davison handed to Spikes, who ran up the middle and over the goal line. The Texans led, 8–7.

Burford led them to another touchdown early in the second half. Playing before his college friends from nearby Stanford, he ran precise patterns and gave head fakes; Davidson hit him for gains of twenty-one and nineteen yards. Spikes ran up the middle for twelve and scored from the 3. When the two-point try failed, the Texans led 14–6.

Oakland came back with a touchdown, but the Texans' defense delivered a major blow midway through the final quarter. Pressured by Paul Miller, the defensive end who had played in the NFL, Oakland quarterback Tom Flores threw a wild pass toward Mel Branch, a rookie defensive end from LSU. Branch grabbed the ball and ran to the Oakland 13 before being tackled. Spikes scored a few plays later.

Final score: Texans 20, Raiders 13.

Lamar came down from the stands with reporters Sam Blair and Gary Cartwright. Normally impeccable and calm, he looked disheveled as he entered the locker room, his tie loose, his hair matted. Like a parent watching his child perform onstage, he had experienced jangled nerves, but he was satisfied. The game had looked like an actual game with fans, refs, teams, and bands. The AFL was up and running. And Dallas had won.

"I'm tickled to death," Stram told him. "We were terrible starting out, but we got better."

Davidson had missed on a majority of his pass attempts ("I can do a lot better," he said), but the Texans had dominated with Spikes, Robinson, and Swink each rushing for over sixty yards. On defense, Miller and Ray Hudson had led the charge, with rookie linebacker Smokey Stover right behind. If this inaugural game was any indication, the Texans had the makings of a decent team.

# 8

☆

# "This is not a harassment situation"

F OR THEIR THIRD EXHIBITION game, the Cowboys came home to Dallas to play the Colts, the NFL's two-time defending champs, in the Salesmanship Club contest at the Cotton Bowl. The city's premier businessmen's group had promoted an annual preseason game for a decade, bringing in two teams to play before as many as 50,000 fans. Now that Dallas had a team, it was natural to include the Cowboys. Although many of the club's members knew Lamar's father, they never considered supporting his son's upstart league.

Tickets sold briskly. Fans were excited to see their new NFL team play in person for the first time — against Unitas and the Colts, no less. Landry felt pressure to put on a good show. This would be the Cowboys' only home appearance before the regular season began in September. It was no time for a pratfall. He worked the players hard at P. C. Cobb Stadium, the city's premier high school venue, with the gates locked to keep out curious fans . . . not that any showed up.

Don Meredith was back with the team after spending three weeks with the College All-Stars, whom the Colts had routed, 32–7. Meredith had played well in a losing cause, passing for 156 yards, and Landry said he hoped to get the rookie a few snaps against the Colts in front of the hometown crowd. A large photo of Meredith dominated the ads the Cowboys ran in both papers all week. (Don Perkins, the rookie running back, had returned from the all-star camp with a broken foot that ended his season. Disappointed, the Cowboys sent him home with instructions to stay in shape. Perkins took a job pumping gas in Albuquerque.)

On Friday, August 19, 1960, the Cowboys played in Dallas for the first time, kicking off at 8:00 PM as the sun set on a hot, cloudless day. Fair Park and its environs slowly came to life before the game started as fans parked by the railroad tracks, by the Hall of State, or on lawns in the nearby neighborhood and walked through the fairgrounds to the stadium, stopping to buy a game program for fifty cents or a hot dog from a vendor.

The Cotton Bowl was a vast, bare-bones expanse of peeling wooden bleachers set on concrete risers, with seat numbers stenciled into the wood. The crowd of 40,000 filled most of the lower bowl and spilled into the upper decks that rose steeply on either side of the field — the decks that had been built when Doak Walker was running wild for SMU.

The crowd was almost entirely white and generally amiable. Alcohol was not served, and tailgating before kickoff was not a common practice. The men wore short-sleeve cotton shirts and slacks, the women print dresses. A thick layer of cigarette smoke hung heavily, just above their heads. The concession booths that lined the concrete corridors under the bowl sold hot dogs, peanuts, candy, and soda. Vendors walked through the stands pouring Dr Pepper into plastic cups.

The Cowboys came out in their home jerseys, dark blue with white numerals, white pants, and stark white helmets with stars on the sides that glimmered under the stadium's lights. The Colts had donned the uniforms they wore in their classic overtime championship victory over the Giants in December 1958 — white jerseys, white pants, and white helmets with an upright horseshoe on either side.

After all the buildup about Meredith's debut, he never got off the bench. He just wasn't ready, Landry felt, and with the organization viewing this game as more than a meaningless exhibition, it was no time to experiment. Meredith shrugged. He wanted to get out there. He had played well against the Colts the week before. It was slightly annoying to pace the sideline with his helmet in his hand; he had played some great games in this stadium for the Mustangs. But Landry was in charge of his career now.

Playing with heightened intensity, as if this were a regular-season game, the Cowboys' defense stopped Unitas on several early possessions, eliciting cheers from the fans still adjusting to the idea that this was their team. But on the last play of the first quarter, the All-Pro quarterback struck. On a first down at the Dallas 46, Unitas surveyed the field and found halfback Lenny Moore running free on the right sideline. Moore grabbed the pass at the Dallas 20, dodged a tackler, and stepped into the end zone. Baltimore was ahead, 7–0.

The most motivated Cowboy was L. G. Dupre, the veteran halfback whom the Colts had let go in the expansion draft. He hadn't wanted to leave Baltimore, where he had played since 1955, and was determined to show Colts coach Weeb Ewbank that a mistake had been made. He smiled when his former teammates taunted him on the field early in the game, but their barbs stung, and he replied with sarcastic comments. He would later deny having cursed in Ewbank's face.

Early in the second quarter, Dupre took a pitchout at his 35, sailed around right end, and broke into the clear. As the crowd thundered, he sprinted down the sideline until two Colts knocked him down at the Baltimore 2. The drive stalled, however, when LeBaron was trapped for a loss on second down, and Cone kicked a field goal.

The score remained 7–3 through the third quarter as Landry's makeshift defense gave an inspired performance. John Gonzaga, who had come from the 49ers as an offensive lineman, pressured Unitas into hurried throws. Don Healy, a bulky tackle from the Bears, plugged up the middle. The linebackers, Jack Patera, Jerry Tubbs, and Tom Braatz, roamed the field making tackles. Landry had taken a collection of spare parts and seemingly patched together a solid unit.

The Cowboy offense struggled, but LeBaron kept trying to make a play, and he finally succeeded early in the fourth quarter. Fred Dugan broke free on a crossing pattern at midfield, and LeBaron's toss was on target. The veteran receiver stumbled and fell as he caught the pass, but he got up and weaved through the secondary until being tackled at the Baltimore 15. After another completion moved the ball to the 1, LeBaron sneaked over for a touchdown. Cone's conversion gave the Cowboys a 10–7 lead. The crowd cheered the hometown underdogs.

Unitas tried to lead one of his patented comebacks. The Cowboys' defense stopped him once, then stopped him again. As the clock ticked down, the franchise's first victory became a real possibility. But given one final chance in the final minutes, Unitas came through.

On a first down at his 32, he watched Moore circle out of the backfield and break open in the middle of Dallas's umbrella secondary. His pass hit Moore in the chest, and the fleet back turned and streaked toward the end zone, reaching the 6 before being tackled. Unitas went right back to him on the next play, hitting him in the left flat for a touchdown. The extra point gave Baltimore a 14–10 lead, and when a final Dallas drive fizzled, the Cowboys had lost their third straight game..

The fans smiled as they departed for their cars. The game had been so close! Schramm was encouraged. If the Cowboys could compete like that against top NFL competition once the regular season began, they would have little trouble winning over the city's fans.

But could they consistently compete like that? Landry still had doubts. These other teams weren't playing their hardest in August. Things would be different in the fall.

The Texans traveled to Tulsa, Oklahoma, to play the Houston Oilers. Seeking to introduce his team and league to fans across the Southwest, Lamar had scheduled exhibition games in Little Rock, Arkansas, and Abilene, Texas, as well as in Tulsa and Dallas (and Boston).

The Oilers, stepping onto a field for the first time, had a forgettable experience in Tulsa. A dozen of their blue jerseys were stolen from the locker room the night before the game, forcing them to play in red jerseys borrowed from the Texans, who wore their white road tops to go with their white pants and red helmets with the map of the state of Texas on the sides. Lamar hated seeing the AFL look so amateurish.

Abner Haynes barely got off the bench in the Texans' victory, and he was stewing by the time they played again, facing the Boston Patriots in Boston on August 14. He knew he could run as effectively as these other backs, if not better. But he had totaled only six carries for thirteen yards in the first three games.

The Patriots had reached into a local playground league for their quarterback, signing thirty-six-year-old Butch Songin, a former Boston College football and hockey star. To say he was an unknown quantity was an understatement, but he had played well in leading the Patriots to wins in their first two exhibition games, and he was the main reason 11,000 fans came to watch the Patriots' first-ever home game.

Songin was a pass-happy gunslinger with a permanent green light, an archetype the AFL would become known for. He moved his offense fairly well but tossed five interceptions in the first two quarters, and the Texans led, 14–0, at halftime. But Songin kept firing and finally threw to the right jerseys. The score was tied at the start of the fourth quarter, and Stram was irritated with his sputtering offense.

"Haynes! Get in there!" he shouted.

Haynes had been on the bench, glumly weighing his seemingly diminishing prospects, but he grabbed his red helmet and sprinted onto the field. Davidson called for him to carry around left end. Haynes took the pitchout and ran as if his career depended on it, which, perhaps, was the case. He brushed past one defender, spun past another, and sprinted down the sideline for eighteen yards before being pushed out of bounds.

Getting the call again, Haynes picked up seven yards off left tackle, and Davidson followed that with a twelve-yard completion to Burford. When the drive stalled, Spikes booted a field goal to put the Texans ahead, 17–14. Songin tried to rally the Patriots, but the Texans' Don Flynn grabbed an interception. Haynes rejoined the offense and heard his number called in the huddle — another run around right end. A block sprung him into the clear, and he sprinted downfield, then cut back sharply, dodging defenders and picking up twenty-four yards before being tackled.

Staying with the hot hand, Davidson flipped Haynes a short pass going the other way out of the backfield, and Haynes gained twelve yards. The offense finally was rolling. At the Boston 27, Davidson faked to Haynes and flipped a short pass to Robinson on the other side. Robinson picked up a pair of blockers and sprinted untouched to the end zone.

In the locker room after the 24–14 win, Robinson received a game ball from his teammates, but Stram praised Haynes as the difference-maker. Haynes sat in a corner, smiling broadly as he answered reporters' questions. He had proved his point, he believed. And indeed, he would never ride the bench again.

After losing to the Colts in Dallas, the Cowboys traveled to Delafield, Wisconsin, near Milwaukee, and set up a camp at St. John's Academy, a military institution. Gil Brandt, a native of the area, had suggested it as an ideal spot to train, and the players initially concurred as their bus rolled past lush playing fields up to a castlelike dorm right out of the movies.

But reality soon interceded. The rooms were depressing, with war-issue mattresses draped on squeaky springs, no electrical outlets, and dim bulbs providing little light. The dank locker room had lukewarm showers and no benches. The surrounding towns closed up before dark. After a couple of days, lineman Gerry DeLuca cracked jokes about rattling a cup against the bars of his cell, and some players discussed hanging Brandt in effigy. (DeLuca would not make the team.)

After a week of grumbling, the team commuted to Louisville, Kentucky, to play Landry's old team, the Giants, on a makeshift field in a minor league baseball park. Numerous key players from both teams were out with injuries, including marquee Giants such as quarterback Charlie Conerly and linebacker Sam Huff. On a hot, humid Saturday night, a sparse crowd of several thousand came out to watch a listless affair populated by rookies. The NFL was still not a hot ticket in many places across the country.

The Cowboys jumped ahead early when LeBaron and Clarke hooked up on a seventy-three-yard touchdown play. Landry put in Meredith after that, giving the rookie his first chance. It didn't go well. The Giants' defense harried and confused him, changing formations before the snap and blitzing from different places. Feeling the heat, Meredith threw at receivers who weren't open. By halftime, he had attempted twelve passes and completed one.

The Cowboys led at the half, 7–3, as their defense continued to exceed expectations, and after LeBaron accomplished little in a scoreless third quarter, Meredith returned to finish the game. He called a fullback dive in the huddle, trotted to the line, and barked out signals.

"Brown right, thirty-one!" he shouted.

The Giant defenders, familiar with Landry's numerical system, guessed what was coming and shifted positions to stop the play. Seeing them move, Meredith stopped and audibled.

"Um, red, thirty-four!" he shouted.

The Giants reacted again, shifting to cover the new play. Flustered, Meredith started to call a third play.

"Um . . . brown. No, red . . ." he stammered, and finally just threw up his hands: "Aw, shit! Time-out!"

Players on both sides cracked up.

Meredith wasn't the only Cowboy confused by Landry's sophisticated offense. Instead of letting the rookie call the plays, Landry handled that chore himself, sending in calls with substitutes, one of whom was Dick Bielski, the tight end from the Eagles. After Landry barked the play-call to him — "green, left-pitch twenty-nine, wing-t pull" — before a third-and-four play, the bulky tight end jogged toward the huddle trying to remember the complicated signals. When he got to the huddle, he paused, shrugged, and said, "Landry wants some kind of pitchout to the left."

Meredith, trying to follow orders, called such a play and led the team up to the line, but once he got there he realized he had the players in a formation that wouldn't allow a pitchout to the left. Trying to audible, he used too much time and was penalized five yards for delay of game.

Facing third-and-nine, he called his own play in the huddle, a pass, and Clarke, emerging as a genuine threat, broke open at midfield. Meredith hit the receiver in stride, the bullet pass a reminder of why the Cowboys had wanted him. Clarke sprinted to the end zone to finish another seventy-three-yard scoring play, his second of the game.

Although Meredith wound up completing just four of nineteen passes, his "accidental touchdown" gave the Cowboys a comfortable lead. When the final gun sounded a few minutes later, they had their first victory, a 14–3 decision over the Giants.

With three wins in three games, the Texans strutted into a "Meet the Texans" luncheon at a Ramada Inn near Love Field — another of Lamar's publicity stunts. One hundred fans paid two dollars to eat and hear from Stram, Lamar, and the players, whose spirits were high. A few days later, they made it four in a row with a 38–14 victory over the New York Titans in Abilene.

Titans coach Sammy Baugh, a Texas football legend, was from Sweetwater, near Abilene, and eight thousand fans packed a high school stadium to see him and cheer his team, even if it was from New York. But the Texans—led by Robinson, Spikes, Swink, and Haynes, whose names were becoming familiar—battered the Titans. A photo from the game in the *Times Herald* shows Swink dashing downfield on a forty-yard gain, looking very much like the player who had starred at TCU.

Since Abilene's little stadium consisted simply of wooden bleachers on either side of a field, the game's promoters had turned an adjacent outbuilding into a locker room and run plumbing to it so the players could shower. They wanted the pros to feel like pros. The Texans planned to shower after the game and take their bus back to Dallas before heading on to Little Rock, the next destination on their barnstorming tour.

But their bus rolled over an exposed pipe in the parking lot as the players returned to the locker room after the game. As water spewed, the players looked at each other grimly. No showers tonight. They piled onto the bus in their uniforms and laughed at the stench as their bus rolled through the warm night on the way to Dallas.

Welcome to the American Football League.

To close out their preseason, the Cowboys trained at St. John's Academy for two weeks while playing a pair of games. Looking like an outmanned expansion team for the first time, they lost to the Rams, 49–14, on a dusty field laid over a rodeo corral in Pendleton, Oregon. Then they lost to Vince Lombardi's Packers, 28–23, in Minneapolis, to finish their exhibition season with a 1-5 record.

Schramm and Brandt scoured the waiver wire, looking for players who had been cut loose by other teams but might be able to help the Cowboys. In a telling sign of what they thought of the talent on their team, they signed seven such castoffs on the brink of their regular-season opener, including three who immediately became starters—center Mike Connelly, fullback Walt Kowalczyk, and cornerback Don Bishop.

Kowalczyk had been cut by the Lions, who had obtained him from the Eagles before training camp. Having been on winning teams, he balked at coming to Dallas. He told the league he wouldn't report and holed up at his mother-in-law's house outside Philadelphia. Finally, Pete Rozelle himself called the house.

"I'm not a piece of meat. I don't want to go," Kowalczyk said.

"Well, you've got twenty-four hours to get there or I'm going to start docking you pay," Rozelle replied.

Kowalczyk caught a plane to Dallas. The Cowboys had a new, if reluctant, fullback.

The idea of the Texans practicing and playing an exhibition game in Little Rock hadn't been fully considered. Arriving in a city that had made national news in 1957 with its bitter opposition to school integration, the Texans were told their African American players couldn't stay at the team hotel, which was strictly segregated. The white players got on the team bus while Abner Haynes, Clem Daniels, and the other black players took a smaller bus to an all-black motel on the outskirts of town.

Having experienced his share of racism as a black college football star in Texas, Haynes believed he had to accept the situation even though it angered him. Chris Burford, raised in progressive Northern California, voiced his opposition. "How can we let this happen? Aren't we supposed to be a team?" he asked. Stram shook his head sadly, saying they couldn't do anything other than pledge not to return.

One evening after practice, Haynes and Daniels were sitting in their motel room when they heard music thumping in the distance. Having found little to do in the segregated neighborhood near their motel, they decided to investigate.

They walked behind the motel and along a footpath through a grove of trees, following the music, which slowly became louder. After passing some buildings, they found themselves in front of what appeared to be a nightclub. Walking in, they encountered a startling scene. Hundreds of black patrons were on a dance floor, twisting and spinning to a rhythm-and-blues band playing on a stage. The lead singer wore dark glasses as he played boogie-woogie on a piano.

"Holy shit! It's Ray Charles!" Haynes exclaimed.

The blind, southern-born singer was a superstar in black America, having reached the top of the sales charts the year before with a hit single, "What'd I Say?" His appearance in racially tense Little Rock had received little advance publicity. Haynes and Daniels had stumbled onto it. They soon made their way to the dance floor.

A long night ensued. Living apart from their teammates and coaches, the players had no curfew. They dragged themselves back to their motel shortly before dawn and were not at their best at practice the next day. But they regaled their teammates with stories from their epic night.

The presence of black players on both teams severely curtailed attendance for the game against the Denver Broncos on Saturday night at War Memorial Stadium, where all-white college and high school teams usually played. A sprinkling of fans, around five thousand, watched the Texans destroy their outmanned opponents, 48–0. The Broncos were struggling to field a competitive team. Lamar was worried their season might be a disaster. Stram tried to keep the score down by pulling his starters early, but the Texans' reserves kept piling up points.

A week later, the Texans played their final exhibition game against the Oilers on a Friday night at the Cotton Bowl. The date was September 3. Lamar had focused on the team's first home appearance for months, hoping his relentless sales and marketing efforts would result in a large crowd. He had hooked up with another charity after being spurned by the Salesmanship Club. Sam Blair and Gary Cartwright had churned out positive stories for weeks in the *Morning News* and *Times Herald*. Films of the Texans' games had been shown on channel 4 after the evening news. The five-game winning streak had helped, and with the Cowboys out of town, the Texans had Dallas all to themselves.

To Lamar's delight, 51,000 fans came out for the game, filling the Cotton Bowl's lower tier and spilling into the upper deck. Not many actually had paid to get in, as high school bandsmen, members of the Huddle Club, and thousands of others were admitted for free. But Lamar didn't care. He had sought to give Dallas a legitimate pro football entity that fans could get excited about, and if this crowd was any measure, he had succeeded. The Cowboys had drawn 11,000 *fewer* fans to their home exhibition game.

Backed by the shrieking crowd, the Texans delivered another winning performance, beating up on the Oilers again, 24–3, as their bright red jerseys and red helmets sparkled in the stadium lights. Ray Collins fell on a fumble in the first minute, setting up a touchdown pass from Davidson to Swink, and the Texans never looked back. Davidson, erratic at times in earlier games, was on target, hitting Robinson, Burford, and Haynes for gains. Houston's quarterback, George Blanda, a ten-year NFL veteran, was hounded. The Oilers couldn't compare to the Baltimore Colts, whom the Cowboys had played in Dallas in August, but the Texans looked sharp as they completed an undefeated exhibition campaign.

In the locker room after the game, Lamar couldn't help himself when asked if he felt his sales and marketing efforts had paid off. He took a shot at the Cowboys, whom, he believed, were not working nearly as hard to build their gate, relying instead on the simple fact that they played in the NFL.

"We'll always try to interest the people," Lamar said. "When you quit trying to promote your product, you're getting lazy."

Knowing his crowd had surpassed the Salesmanship Club gate, he continued: "Actually, I thought we might draw fifty-five or sixty thousand tonight. I think we would have if not for the rain before kickoff."

When asked if he felt the competition between the Texans and Cowboys was heating up, he nodded.

"A major thing that has helped us," he said, "is the spirit of our players and their desire to take part in this struggle. The players know what the situation is here. It has given them a focus, helped their morale. They want to prevail."

On this September night in 1960, it seemed they might.

Tex Schramm was at the Cowboys' training camp in Wisconsin when he heard about the big crowd for the Texans' game at the Cotton Bowl. The Cowboys had just returned from a miserable trip to Oregon, where the Rams had blistered them on a field laid over a rodeo corral. The Cowboys had played terribly, falling so far behind that the bored players had tossed handfuls of horseshit at each other late in the game.

"The last time I felt like crying for my coach was in high school, but I felt like crying for Landry tonight," Cowboys lineman Buzz Guy said.

Now Schramm felt like crying. He knew the eyes of the NFL were on him and his new team, and he knew the league would be unsettled by the fact that the Texans had drawn more fans to their home exhibition game. It was a stunner. Even though the Cowboys almost surely had attracted more paid customers, the Texans were building a following. Fans liked winners, and the Texans were winning. No one seemed to care that the Cowboys were playing tougher competition.

Schramm was becoming irritated with Hunt. Getting an NFL team up and running in a matter of months was difficult enough without having to battle a well-funded, energetic rival trying to steal your fans. Schramm wished Hunt would just go away.

Deep down, Schramm was convinced the NFL's experience and innate superiority would eventually win out. But for the moment, he was in a battle with a formidable opponent.

Yet the established league couldn't afford to appear worried, so when the *Times Herald*'s Bud Shrake asked Schramm about the Texans drawing so many fans, Schramm cleared his throat, gritted his teeth, and told a whopper.

"I think it's a great thing," he said. "It proves Dallas is a great sports town now. Maybe the city will lose its inferiority complex. People have been saying it can only support one pro football team, and deep down I think a lot of people thought it couldn't support any team at all. So the fact that there have been two exhibition games drawing ninety-two thousand people is very heartwarming. That inferiority about Dallas not being a major league city ought to be finished. The people have proved they're great fans. I think it's possible both teams will draw big crowds this season.

"Of course, I wish it had been fifty-one thousand at our game and forty-one at theirs. But I think the fact that we had such a competitive game against the Colts added another twenty thousand to the crowd for the Texans game. People are finding out that pro football is entertaining. I'm very happy with the way this thing is turning out."

Yeah, right. While there was some truth to his comment about the city proving it was a better pro football market than it had been in 1952, Schramm wasn't happy at all to see the Texans gaining a foothold. They were taking a real shot at the Cowboys, and Schramm felt strongly that the Cowboys should shoot back, subtly but resolutely.

He had targeted Jim Harris, the former Oklahoma quarterback now starting at cornerback for the Texans. Harris had played for the Eagles and Rams before going into the oil business. Lamar had lured him back into uniform, but Schramm believed that his return violated the contract he had signed with the Rams in 1958.

Like all NFL contracts, Harris's contained a clause stipulating that the Rams had the option to retain him for a year if he left football and later returned. Schramm obtained his NFL rights for a low draft pick, and when the Texans flew to Dallas from New Mexico in late July for a scrimmage, a Dallas police deputy greeted Harris and handed him a subpoena as he came off the plane. The Cowboys were taking him to court, seeking an injunction to keep him from playing for the Texans.

Schramm had dual motivations. The Cowboys desperately needed competent defensive backs, and Harris had played well for the Rams in 1958, intercepting four passes. But just as important, this was a chance to irritate Lamar.

At its core, the case was about basic contract law. The AFL's standard player contract had the same option-year clause as the NFL's, but the new league interpreted it differently, saying a retired player wasn't bound to his former team for life. The AFL had signed numerous former NFL players on that basis.

But beyond its legal ramifications, the case was mostly just about Schramm giving the Texans a hard time.

"This is not a harassment situation," Schramm insisted. "We have gone into this very thoroughly. We feel that Harris is a fine football player and a valuable piece of property, and that he belongs in the NFL, with the Cowboys."

In early August, a district court granted the injunction. Harris filed an appeal and continued to practice with the Texans, but an appeals court denied his attempt to overturn the injunction. Harris was forced to the sidelines. He could either join the Cowboys, surely for less money, or continue to fight in court and hope for a ruling allowing him to join the Texans.

Asked by a reporter if he wanted to play for the Cowboys, he said, "Not now. Not after this." He opted to pursue the case in court. But meanwhile, the Texans couldn't use him.

The thought brought a smile to Schramm's face. That so-and-so Hunt couldn't *always* get what he wanted.

After their final exhibition game, the Texans pared their roster to thirty-three. Several old pros survived the final cut, including ancient Ray Collins and Dick Frey, who had never played pro football. Davidson would start at quarterback, backed up by Hunter Enis, the rookie from TCU. (Stram had cut every other quarterback, including Fran Curci, his protégé from Miami.) The starting backfield would feature Robinson, Haynes, and Spikes, with Swink and Clem Daniels backing them up.

The coaches spent hours debating their linebackers. Ted Greene, a twenty-eight-year-old who had been out of football since the mid-fifties, had been the middle linebacker during the preseason, but he wasn't spectacular. Stram had hoped to get a look at Sherrill Headrick, the former TCU star, but the young man had barely played.

Finally, in the last preseason game at the Cotton Bowl, Headrick got his chance. The Oilers kept picking up yardage on "trap" plays, fooling Greene into charging into the backfield and then sending backs into his vacated territory. Hearing Stram vent frustration, Enis, the quarterback, encouraged him to try Headrick, a former TCU teammate.

"Sherrill can stop that trap play. He did it at TCU. Sherrill can stop anything," Enis said.

Stram relented, sending in Headrick with instructions to "stop that damn trap." The first time the Oilers ran it, Headrick stayed in his position and slammed the runner to the turf. Enis looked at Stram with a smile, and Stram nodded. As the game unfolded, Headrick made tackles all over the field, exhibiting lateral agility and a hard-edged nature. This was the player the Texans had expected.

In less than one game, Stram had seen enough. Headrick was his middle linebacker. And two rookie long shots, Smokey Stover and Walt Corey, would start alongside him as outside linebackers.

Corey, the youngest of sixteen children from a family of Pennsylvania mill workers, had played in college at Miami, where Stram liked his tenaciousness. After going unselected in the AFL and NFL drafts, he had lined up a job as an elementary school teacher, thinking he was done with football. But then the Texans called. He had impressed the coaches with his hard hitting and no-nonsense attitude throughout training camp and the exhibition season. He deserved a starting slot.

Stover, of course, had almost literally come out of nowhere, starting his drive to make the team at the humbling tryout camp in July. He had battled his way up the depth chart during the preseason, exhibiting an inner toughness you couldn't teach. If Stram had known how little he weighed, he probably wouldn't have made it. But Stram didn't know, or perhaps just didn't want to know.

"Not only have you made the team, you're starting Saturday night," Stram told him before the Texans' regular-season opener against the Los Angeles Chargers in California.

Stover tried to act nonchalant, but a smile slipped out. Two months after arriving at the tryout camp as an utter unknown, he would be playing at the Los Angeles Coliseum, one of America's great sports venues. He called his wife in Louisiana to tell her to pack their belongings and their young child, come to Dallas, and find an apartment. Stewart Stover was a pro.

# 9

⭐

# "It's going to take time for this thing to grow"

A s THE 1960 pro football season began, Mike Rhyner could barely contain his excitement. A ten-year-old living in Oak Cliff with his parents and younger sister, he had just discovered pro football the year before, watching the Chicago Bears on channel 4 on Sunday afternoons, reading about games and players in the newspapers, and, best of all, collecting trading cards with the players' pictures and statistics. It was all impossibly exciting, and now, almost magically, it was coming to Dallas. His hometown was going to have a team — actually two!

Mike was interested in the Cowboys because they played in the NFL, and he was interested in the Texans because they were exciting. But he would only be going to see the Texans at the Cotton Bowl. His father, an insurance salesman with a suppressed entrepreneurial spirit, had made it clear that only the Texans would get his money. Howard Rhyner admired what Lamar Hunt was doing — starting a new enterprise, taking a chance — and didn't appreciate the NFL ginning up a new Dallas team just to try to put Lamar out of business.

The Rhyners, father and son, had attended the Texans' exhibition game against the Oilers at the Cotton Bowl. The noise of the crowd, the shiny green grass, and the bright lights had dazzled young Mike. The fact that he didn't recognize many players disappointed him. He knew

George Blanda, who had played for the Bears, and had heard of Max Boydston, a Dallas receiver who had played for Oklahoma. Otherwise, he didn't have these players' trading cards. Who were they?

He knew he would recognize more players at a Cowboys game, but as both teams' regular-season home openers approached in late September, his father wasn't budging.

"Let's go see the Cowboys play," Mike said.

"No," Howard responded.

"Why not?" the boy asked.

"I support Lamar Hunt and the Texans," Howard replied.

It turned out that both teams were opening their home schedules at the Cotton Bowl on the same weekend. The Cowboys would play the Pittsburgh Steelers on Saturday, September 24, kicking off at 8:00 PM, and the Texans would play the Los Angeles Chargers the next day, starting at 2:00 PM.

Dallas had hosted busy football weekends before, usually consisting of SMU playing within hours of the Texas-Oklahoma game in October. But this was a different creature. Although the Cowboys and Texans wouldn't actually play each other, they were certainly competing to win fans and cause the bigger stir. They were fighting to own the town.

As the weekend approached, fans throughout North Texas faced a crucial decision. It was time to pick a team to support. Established league or upstart? Hunt or Murchison? Bright red or dark blue uniforms?

Buddy Macatee, the owner of a building supply company in Dallas, went with the Cowboys, purchasing a slate of season tickets. He and Landry had attended college together in the forties, even double-dating once; Macatee knew him less as a football star than as an engineering student with a slide rule in his pocket. They had remained in touch; within the past few years, Landry, working an off-season job, had tried to get Macatee to invest in an office building project put together by Curtis Sanford.

Macatee also felt more loyalty to the Murchison family and believed that H. L. Hunt was a bit of a lone wolf, somewhat mysterious, and not as wholly engaged in Dallas's business and social scene. Finally, as Macatee would recall years later, "the Cowboys, being from the NFL, just seemed like a more stable outfit with a better future."

Like much of the city's business elite, Macatee belonged to the Salesmanship Club, whose membership was almost unanimously supporting the Cowboys, citing reasoning similar to Macatee's.

Their snub made Lamar's task that much harder. He simply did not
have as much support in the business community. But he still culti-
vated his share, piecing together an "advisory board" that included his
childhood hero, Doak Walker, now in business in Dallas; Gordon Mc-
Clendon, a radio pioneer who owned KLIF, one of the city's largest AM
stations; Ryan Petroleum president Jerome Crossman; investment
banker D. Gordon Rupe; E. B. Germany, an industrialist and indepen-
dent oil producer; and Curtis Sanford, who had been on his side from
the outset.

But while corporate support was obviously crucial, fan support was
what the teams really craved. The size of their crowds would be a critical metric in their battle. A sports cartoon in the *Times Herald* on the
eve of the inaugural weekend depicted the situation. Two figures wearing cowboy hats, boots, and holsters face each other, one representing the Cowboys, the other the Texans, each poised to draw a pistol.
The Cowboy drawls, "This time I'm a-gonna show you who's the best-
est draw in these parts," as the Texan says, "I outdrew ya once and I
can outdraw ya again." The cartoon was headlined "Box Office Show-
down."

Across the region, fans picked one team over the other, citing a variety of reasons. Walt Garrison, a sixteen-year-old high school football
star in Denton, home of North Texas State, went with the Texans because he was a fan of Abner Haynes. (Garrison would later play for the
Cowboys.) Louis Tobian, an executive at the Dallas Cotton Exchange,
bought ten Cowboy season tickets because he liked established enter-
prises and the NFL was a known quantity. Billy Livingston, a twelve-
year-old in Oak Cliff, planned to support both teams, but he and his
father, who worked downtown in the oil well supply division of U.S.
Steel, would attend the Texans' game on Sunday; Billy thought the
Texans were flashier with their bright uniforms, and their undefeated
exhibition season had caught his attention. He had already signed up
for their youth group, the Huddle Club.

Nancy Nichols, a youngster living in North Dallas, had been directed to one side by her father, Jim, an avid football fan who ran a

printing company. After contacting Lamar when he read about the Texans starting up in 1959, Jim joined the Spur Club and wound up handling the team's printing business. Then he was elected Spur Club president. He was all in for the Texans, and his tomboy daughter had caught the fever. She had been to a luncheon, met some players, and picked out a favorite. She had a crush on Chris Burford, the handsome receiver from Stanford.

As the weekend approached, a startling letter to the editor of the *Times Herald* underscored the challenge both teams faced. The author wrote that he wouldn't support either team because he preferred the Southwest Conference's all-white squads.

"I've heard a lot of complaints," the letter stated. "A lot of people at the Texans-Oilers exhibition were shocked at the number of Negroes on the Dallas roster. It seems the teams would be more considerate of fans in this section of the country and hold the number of Negroes to a minimum if they have to field a winner. I'm sure the University of Texas doesn't need Negroes to field a winning team. The Supreme Court might force our children to sit in school with Negroes but they can't force us into the stadium to watch a football game played mostly by Negroes."

The letter prompted heated responses from fans encouraging the teams to use more black players. But clearly a portion of the football public had its mind made up. It would take time — and in many cases, an attitude change — before they got behind the pro game.

Lamar blanketed Dallas with ads and promotions in the final days before Sunday's game, relentlessly seeking to build the crowd. Discounted tickets were available at department stores and airline offices. If you filled up your car with a certain brand of gas, you received a free ticket. If you bought ten dollars of groceries at certain markets, you received a free ticket. Lamar stopped at nothing. Tickets were put in packages of Fritos and stuffed inside helium-filled balloons set loose over the city. People were waking up and finding Texans tickets in their backyards.

The game itself would feature the debut of a cheerleading squad named the Texanns, as well as performances from marching bands, trick ponies, and circus clowns. The Optimist Club was sponsoring a

"Friend of the Boy" promotion that would enable youngsters to sit in the end zone for free.

But the Cowboys weren't letting the Texans just dominate the scene. They also blitzed the city with ads, promotions, and discounts. Five kids could get into their game for free with an adult purchasing a $2.75 general admission ticket. Roy Rogers, the television crooner, was in town all week promoting the game with his wife, Dale Evans, and his horse, Trigger. He sang at a televised Cowboys "pep rally" in the parking lot outside channel 8's studios on Wednesday and was scheduled to sing before the game and at halftime on Saturday, accompanied by the Hardin-Simmons College band.

The Cowboys believed that having to debut on Saturday night put them at a disadvantage; they knew some fans would stay home to protest the pros encroaching on the college game's turf. But by reserving the Cotton Bowl for three straight Sundays, Lamar had boxed them in. Fortunately for them, on this Saturday SMU was playing at Ohio State and TCU was at Southern Cal, so no nearby college team had a home game. College fans could bring their radios and listen while they watched the pro game.

The weather was no help. Rain fell intermittently all day Saturday, and even though the skies had cleared by kickoff, some fans surely had been dissuaded. In the end, just 30,000 fans were in the Cotton Bowl to watch the Cowboys begin their NFL existence. Steelers owner Art Rooney would grumble about his paltry cut of the small gate.

On the game's third play, Eddie LeBaron zipped a pass over the middle to Jim Doran. A block by Don McIlhenny cleared the tight end's path, and he raced to the end zone untouched, completing a seventy-five-yard scoring play. The shocked fans loosed a loud cheer. What a start!

A few minutes later, LeBaron found Frank Clarke open on the right sideline for a fifty-eight-yard gain, setting up another score. The Cowboys had a 14–0 lead and the first quarter wasn't even over.

Many fans had come to see Bobby Layne, the Highland Park–reared legend, who now quarterbacked the Steelers. They had little doubt he would make a game of it, especially since Landry had cut the Cowboys' most experienced pass defenders, deciding they wouldn't help in the long run, and gone with three second-year players (cornerbacks Don Bishop and Tom Franckhauser and safety Bill Butler) and a rookie (safety Fred Doelling) in the secondary.

Predictably, Layne picked the youngsters apart, hitting receivers Buddy Dial, Jimmy Orr, and Preston Carpenter on passes that produced a pair of touchdowns in the second quarter. The Cowboys countered with another score and led, 21–14, at halftime.

Roy Rogers and Dale Evans sang several songs during the break, and then Roy climbed onto Trigger and slowly circled the stadium, waving. When they reached the north end zone, some teenagers hurled ice and cups at them, showering Roy and causing Trigger to rear. Roy grabbed the reins to calm his horse and shouted that the little buggers would be sorry. The police rounded up several dozen teenagers and took them to a nearby precinct station for a lecture. Roy's ice bath received extensive coverage in the papers, hardly the kind of publicity the Cowboys had sought.

When the game resumed, Layne handed the ball to halfback Tom Tracy on what appeared to be an end sweep, but Tracy stopped and threw a long pass to Dial, who was wide open behind the confused defense. The seventy-yard scoring play tied the score, 21–21.

But LeBaron continued to exploit the Steelers' weak defense. On a second down at his 46, he saw Doran open over the middle and hit him in stride. The tight end picked up a blocker, cut back twice, and chugged to the end zone, completing a fifty-four-yard scoring play. The Cowboys were back on top.

The fans stood and shouted; this game was proving to be more exciting than anyone had expected. But Layne had a habit of delivering in close games, and he was determined to prevail in his hometown, although he would hit the bars later regardless.

Late in the third quarter, Layne dropped back and watched Carpenter, his tight end, fake one way and zip past a rookie safety. He lofted a spiral well ahead of Carpenter, but the bulky receiver ran under the ball and grabbed it as he crossed the goal line, completing a forty-nine-yard touchdown play. The Cowboys' rookie safety, Fred Doelling, pulled a leg muscle on the play and was replaced by another rookie, Gary Wisener, a former receiver who had played defense for exactly one week.

With the score tied early in the fourth quarter, LeBaron drove his offense to the Pittsburgh 33 but was sacked for a loss and then tossed an interception. The Steelers went for it on a fourth-and-one at midfield a few minutes later. Layne eschewed Parker's play-call, sent in from the sideline, and called his own play, sending Tom Tracy on an end sweep. The Cowboys' Jerry Tubbs sniffed out the play, pursued Tracy, and slammed him down for a loss. Dallas ball!

But the Cowboy offense sputtered, and the Steelers took over at their 35 with three minutes to play. Layne dropped back, dodged a pair of onrushing linemen, reared back, and hurled the ball far downfield toward Tracy, who had circled out of the backfield, passed the rookie sub Wisener, and sprinted free down the right sideline. Tracy corralled the ball at the 20, sidestepped a tackler, and trotted to the end zone.

The crowd fell silent. When a final Cowboy drive fizzled, the visitors walked away with a 35–28 win.

Tubbs, the linebacker, sat motionless in the folding chair by his locker for twenty minutes after the game, his frustrations welling inside him. He had never lost a game while playing for Breckenridge High School and the University of Oklahoma, a pair of powerhouses, and he was still unaccustomed to the losing feeling, even though he now performed for an expansion team.

But despite his disappointment, Tubbs saw many positives in the Cowboys' performance. They had competed well in their first official game, exhibiting a big-play knack on offense as LeBaron passed for 349 yards and three touchdowns. Layne had prevailed in the end with his five touchdown passes, but Landry's patchwork defense had busted his chinstrap and made him sweat. That was encouraging.

Landry explained to reporters that the Cowboys had changed from a man-to-man pass defense to a zone in the second half, hoping to keep Layne's receivers from getting so open, and there had been a mix-up on the final scoring play, leaving Tracy free.

"We just got caught there, a shame," Landry said. "We'll get better. There were a lot of things to like tonight. We made some big plays."

Schramm declined to reveal how many fans actually had bought tickets, but Rooney said later that the check for his split of the gate reflected 13,000 paid admissions — no one's idea of a sizzling start.

• • •

The Cotton Bowl was more than half full for the Texans' game the next afternoon. It was again unclear how many fans had actually paid to get in, but Lamar was ecstatic to see a crowd of 42,000 in place as the Texans kicked off to the Chargers. They had outdrawn the Cowboys.

The Texans had already played a pair of regular-season games, the AFL having started two weeks earlier than the NFL because its teams were playing a fourteen-game schedule, as opposed to the NFL's twelve.

The Texans had opened against the Chargers in Los Angeles, thinking they might roll easily through the league after winning six consecutive preseason games. The first half of the game did little to change their thinking. Their offense produced a pair of early touchdowns, and their defense shut down the Chargers. They led at halftime, 20–7.

Lamar watched the first two quarters from the stands; with an announced crowd of 17,724 salted around the enormous Coliseum, he could sit practically anywhere. The lopsided first half so excited him that he came to the locker room at halftime.

"Do you think maybe we need to ease up?" he asked Stram, explaining that it was better for the league if the game was competitive.

Stram looked him incredulously. This game was far from decided, he said. Sid Gillman, a damn good coach, was over in the other locker room making adjustments.

Sure enough, the Chargers came out with a different defensive strategy that slowed Dallas's offense, and their quarterback, Jack Kemp, started finding open receivers in the seams of Stram's zone pass defense. After the Chargers rallied to win, 21–20, Lamar pledged never again to believe a game was decided at halftime.

As meager as the crowd was, only one of the AFL's other three opening-weekend games drew more, the contest between the Patriots and Broncos attracting 21,597 in Boston. Only 12,703 saw the Oilers beat the Raiders in San Francisco, and just 5,727 braved a steady rain to watch the Titans beat the Bills at the Polo Grounds in New York. It was a slow start at the gate, but when an Associated Press reporter called Lamar for a reaction, he preached patience.

"It's going to take time for this thing to grow. I don't think any of our owners are going to make any money this year. But they knew that," he said.

Rather than return to Dallas, the Texans remained in California to take on the Raiders in San Francisco a week later. It proved to be a more satisfying occasion. They won easily, 34–16, with Davidson throwing a pair of scoring passes but mostly just watching Spikes, Robinson, and Haynes run; the rookie backs totaled more than two hundred yards from scrimmage.

The fans at the Texans' first home game a week later hoped for a high-scoring rematch with the Chargers, but the defenses dominated. "It was like a taffy pull; nothing really happened," Stram said. The Texans finally broke a scoreless tie just before halftime, eliciting cheers from the crowd. The Chargers tried to rally in the second half, as they had in Los Angeles, but the Texans intercepted four passes to blunt the comeback. The Texans walked away with a 17–0 win.

Nancy Nichols, the young daughter of the Spur Club president, watched the game with a group of friends in the Cotton Bowl's south end zone, while her parents sat with other Spur Club members at midfield. The fact that the game was a low-scoring defensive affair didn't bother her in the least, and neither did the splinters she picked up from the peeling bleachers. She had never experienced anything more exhilarating. The kids in the end zone couldn't always see what was happening, but they stood and shrieked whenever the Texans did anything right, and sometimes even when they did something wrong.

Best of all, as the final seconds of the game ticked off, Nancy's father appeared in the tunnel leading from the field to the locker rooms, motioned to her, and helped her over the railing to the stadium floor. The players came walking by moments later, the fans shouting their names. *Abner! Abner! Jack! Jack!* Nancy waited for her favorite, Chris Burford, the receiver. When he walked up the tunnel, helmet in his hand, he looked at her and winked as she meekly waved.

"Hi, Nancy," he said.

Life could get no better.

Smokey Stover and Walt Corey jogged up the tunnel shortly after Burford, waving at the fans who called to them. They sat down heavily on metal folding chairs by their lockers and smiled at each other, exhausted but satisfied. Both had played superbly, stopping the run, pressuring Kemp, and dropping niftily into pass coverage. Corey had picked off two passes, Stover one. Add Sherrill Headrick's one and the Texans' linebackers had grabbed four interceptions in all. They were the talk of both locker rooms. Stram praised them for playing "just outstanding ball," and Gillman said Headrick, credited with thirteen tackles, was "one of the best I've ever seen."

Headrick's coaches and teammates just shook their heads at him. They were getting to know him, and well, he was quite a spectacle. The former oil patch roughneck vomited before games because of nerves, eschewed hip pads because he believed they limited his mobility, and was usually the first player out of the locker room after practices and games, making a beeline for the nearest bar. But he had also made it clear in these first games that he had canny instincts for football: he could predict what offenses would do and was inevitably waiting on ball-carriers and receivers to smack them as plays developed.

On this Sunday, he was gone from the locker room within minutes of the final whistle, passing through the shower at a virtual sprint, throwing on clothes, and hitting the door before Stover and Corey had their pads off. The departing fans, stuck in traffic outside the Cotton Bowl, would be surprised to know the Texans' middle linebacker was among them, anxious to punctuate the win and calm his jangled stomach with some beers.

# 10

★

# "They thought the Texans were a lot more fun"

TEX SCHRAMM WAS in a sour mood after Dallas's first head-to-head pro football weekend. Things were not going his way. The Texans had outdrawn the Cowboys at the Cotton Bowl, even though Schramm believed few of the Texans' fans actually had bought tickets. Now a second straight head-to-head weekend loomed, with the Cowboys again relegated to an "alternative" slot — Friday night this time — because the Texans were playing on Sunday again.

As if that weren't frustrating enough, a judge had ruled against the Cowboys in the Jimmy Harris case, lifting the restraining order the team had obtained during the summer to prevent the defensive back from playing for the Texans. Harris immediately suited up and practiced. "We're thrilled to have him and we're going to play him this weekend," Lamar said with a broad smile.

But it was Lamar's latest promotion that really galled Schramm. With the Cowboys up against high school football's sacred time slot — Schramm had decided on Friday night rather than play Saturday night two weekends in a row — Lamar was offering free admission on Sunday to anyone with a game ticket stub from an area high school game played that Friday night.

Schramm had no problem with most of the stunts Lamar cooked

up, believing the promotions were harmless and, for the most part, ineffectual. Lamar had also labeled this Sunday's contest "Barber Day." Anyone wearing a white barber's smock got in for free. Lamar thought that would get people talking about the Texans at barbershops. Schramm had to laugh at that one. Barber Day! What a joke!

But Schramm did find it annoying that freebies were enabling the Texans to outdraw the Cowboys and claim victory. "About the only thing left for them to do is just open the gates and forget about [selling] tickets," he groused. And his temples pulsed with anger when he heard about what Lamar was calling the high school game ticket stub gimmick — the "Teen Salute." This was dirty pool, Schramm thought. Lamar was blatantly attempting to discourage fans from coming to see the Cowboys. Why not just cut off the electricity in the Cowboys' executive offices while he was at it?

The Cowboys tried hard to sell the Friday night game, running wildly enthusiastic ads in both papers. "See the passing duel of the year! It's Eddie LeBaron vs. Norm Van Brocklin! See the color, excitement, and thrills of football as only the National Football League teams know how to play it!" But the public wasn't interested. Only 18,000 fans came to the Cotton Bowl Friday night. Half appeared to be youngsters getting in free with adults buying general admission tickets. Schramm would never admit it, but he was "papering" his house too.

The Cowboys were playing the Philadelphia Eagles, whose quarterback, the brilliant Van Brocklin, figured to have his way. But Landry's fledgling secondary was more cohesive after a week of practice, and Van Brocklin struggled at first. LeBaron also had problems adjusting to Philadelphia's unusual defense, consisting of three linemen and five linebackers. The two veteran passers would throw a combined nine interceptions during the game.

The Eagles led at halftime, 13-6, but Landry adjusted his offense to deal with the odd alignment, and LeBaron hooked up with Frank Clarke on a fifty-five-yard touchdown in the third quarter. The Eagles' Bobby Freeman rushed in from the right side to block the extra point, leaving Philadelphia ahead, 13-12. As the final quarter began, both offenses suddenly kicked into gear. Van Brocklin threw a touchdown pass. LeBaron ran for a score. Van Brocklin drove the Eagles back downfield, and a veteran back, Billy Ray Barnes, ran through a gaping hole for a touchdown.

Trailing by eight, the Cowboys produced another scoring drive as McIlhenny and Dupre broke long runs and LeBaron hit Gene Babb on a twenty-seven-yard score. But Bobby Freeman rushed in from the right side and blocked the extra point again, and the Eagles ran out the clock, securing a 27–25 win.

Both teams had scored three touchdowns and two field goals; the difference was the two missed extra points.

Landry tried to remain calm after the defeat. He took off his fedora and wiped his brow with a forearm as he began to take questions from reporters. But he was furious. His voice rose as he waved his arms with his palms up, indicating his incredulity. "That's the worst exhibition of extra-point kicking I have ever seen in my life," he stated pointedly. "It kills you when you can't kick an extra point. That's supposed to be an automatic. But we didn't block that guy on the end, and it left us in a hole all night."

The atmosphere at the Texans' game on Sunday afternoon was livelier. The crowd was estimated at 37,000, twice as large as Friday night's, and included more than one hundred men dressed in barber smocks as well as thousands of youngsters who had not paid.

It also included a pair of "spies." With a rare Sunday off, Landry and Gil Brandt quietly drove to the Cotton Bowl, bought tickets, and watched the Texans play the New York Titans. Frankly, they were curious.

They saw an entertaining game. Titans quarterback Al Dorow, who had played in the NFL and Canada, threw four touchdown passes in the first half, shocking the Texans' defense, which had pitched a shutout the week before. But Davidson and the Texans' offense also put up points, never letting the Titans get too far ahead. New York led at halftime, 24–14, and held a thirteen-point advantage early in the fourth quarter before the Texans closed on a long run by Abner Haynes and a field goal in the final minutes. But the Titans ran out the clock to win, 37–35.

Landry and Brandt exchanged worried glances as they walked out. The quality of play wasn't up to NFL standards — the "unstoppable"

Dorow had washed out of the older league — and the Barber Day promotion had flopped. But there were some talented players on the field,
and the all-out offense was fun. The fans had enjoyed themselves.

As they drove home, Landry and Brandt understood that the Cowboys were in a real fight for Dallas's favor. They could laugh about the
"goofy" AFL all they wanted, but honestly, it was no joke.

On Monday at 9:00 AM, the Cowboys reported to the team's executive
offices in the Triple A Building on Central Expressway. They split into
two conference rooms, offensive players in one, defensive players in
another, and watched film until noon. They reviewed their loss to the
Eagles and studied the Redskins, whom they would play Sunday in
Washington.

Assistant coaches ran the projectors, but Landry handled all the
teaching and coaching, shuttling back and forth between the groups.
The atmosphere, as always, was studious. Landry didn't raise his voice
when reviewing mistakes, but firmly explained how to correct them,
zeroing in on the perpetrators with an unsettling focus. The players
had quickly learned to dread these sessions, which could turn humili-
ating.

At noon, the players were given an hour to grab lunch and get across
town to practice at Burnett Field, home of Dallas's minor league baseball team, the Rangers. Located south of town, the rickety wooden
ballpark, built in the twenties, was a depressing place. The locker room
was cramped, damp, and dark. Players hung their clothes on rusty
nails. The showers spit cold water. The outfield grass, where practices
were held, was squishy because the ballpark was situated on the Trinity
River floodplain. The field was often unplayable after a hard rain, forcing Landry to resort to "plan B," which consisted of the players cram-
ming into a yellow school bus and driving to a nearby high school field
to practice. Jimmie Parker, the team's business manager, had come
from the Dallas school district and could pull strings.

Landry's practices were organized, detailed, and long. His fertile
football mind constantly spewed ideas, and he used the afternoon
workouts to install and polish them. The players seldom hit the showers before 5:00 PM.

In many ways, it was a pleasure to play for the Cowboys. The front office helped players find apartments, churches, and schools for their kids; Dick Bielski laughed at the idea of his cranky former team, the Eagles, offering such help. The Cowboys were fun too. Bedford Wynne, the minority owner, often attended practices and games and was around to pick up bar tabs. Few of the players had been to Texas before, and they liked that the beers were big and cold, the Mexican food delicious, and the girls pretty, especially the stewardesses who lived in their apartment complex near Love Field.

But the players were there to play football, and that aspect of the situation was a chore. Bielski only had to practice in the mornings when he played for the Eagles; the players spent their afternoons selling insurance or working retail, needing the extra money because they didn't earn enough from football to support their families. On a typical day with the Eagles, Bielski downed a few beers after a morning practice and worked in the afternoon. But he couldn't now. Landry viewed football as a full-time job, a professional endeavor. Practice was an all-day affair.

Some players didn't care for that. They respected Landry's knowledge, but playing for him was hard work. He handed out a new playbook for each game, sometimes containing as many as 150 plays, with separate sections for special situations. The players who had come from Pittsburgh and Detroit, where the offenses were far simpler, thought the thick playbook was a joke. They couldn't wait to meet for beers and complain.

Plus, Dallas wasn't excited about the Cowboys, to put it mildly. The crowds for the first two games had been sparse. Several days before the opener, the players had been unable to practice at Burnett Field after a rain and then couldn't go to the nearby high school because of a mix-up. They wound up riding around on a bus for thirty minutes, looking for any open space, before ending up in a city park, where they got out, limbered up, and worked out for an hour. The drivers of cars whizzing by paid no attention to the NFL's newest franchise. It seemed no one cared.

For veteran players accustomed to playing in big games before big crowds, this was quite a comedown. They felt like they had been consigned to a fringe outpost on the pro football landscape.

It felt good to get on a plane at the end of that week and travel to

Washington to play the Redskins; this was familiar terrain. The players enjoyed themselves the night before the game, but after receiving a warm reception from the fans of his former team, LeBaron struggled to grip the ball in a chilly rain, threw three interceptions, and missed several open receivers. The Cowboys trailed by six points at halftime and wound up losing, 26–14. The next day, after watching films of the game, Landry told reporters, "Our defense reminds me of a team that has been in training camp for three weeks."

That didn't breed optimism for their next game, against the Cleveland Browns at the Cotton Bowl. Cleveland's offense was a powerhouse featuring Jimmy Brown, the All-Pro fullback, and Bobby Mitchell, a fleet runner-receiver. The Browns had put sixty-nine points on the board in their first two games.

Playing at home on Sunday afternoon for the first time, the Cowboys hoped to draw a larger crowd. "See pro football's greatest back, Jim Brown!" screeched newspaper ads, highlighting a selling point — better-known opposition — that was supposedly the Cowboys' not-so-secret weapon in their attendance duel with the Texans. Also, the State Fair of Texas was in full swing, luring huge crowds to the environs around the Cotton Bowl.

Ten-year-old Mike Rhyner and his sister and parents attended the fair that Sunday, and when Mike heard a crowd cheering and a band playing in the Cotton Bowl, he turned to his father, the ardent Texans fan, and said, "I want to go see the Cowboys. There's a game going on."

Howard Rhyner relented, giving his son a dollar. Mike ran to one of the stadium gates, waving his dollar.

"I want to go in," he said.

The ticket attendant told him a dollar wasn't enough if he wasn't accompanied by an adult.

"This is all I've got," Mike said, "and my father isn't coming."

The attendant looked around to see if anyone was watching, and handed Mike a ticket. "Go on in, son," he said.

In the end, just 28,000 fans attended, and the game itself was equally disappointing. The Browns became the first team to treat the Cowboys like an outclassed expansion squad. Cleveland drove eighty yards to a touchdown on its first possession, and the game went downhill from there. Brown and Mitchell stormed for big gains, and the Browns scored three more touchdowns before halftime, two set up by Dallas mistakes. Meanwhile, the Browns' fearsome defensive front knocked over Dallas's linemen and swarmed LeBaron before plays could develop.

Leading 35–0 midway through the third quarter, Cleveland coach Paul Brown thought about pouring it on Landry, who had bested him in recent years as the Giants' defensive coordinator. But Brown knew it would reflect badly on the league if the score got out of hand, so he pulled his first team. The reserves pushed the score to 48–0 early in the fourth quarter.

Most of the fans were gone by then; they were eating cotton candy and riding rides on the State Fair midway, which was certainly preferable to seeing how far the Cowboys trailed the league's true elite. The Cotton Bowl was virtually empty when the Cowboys finally scored on a pass from Don Heinrich to Billy Howton.

Celebrating the score, a cheerleader jumped on a horse and set off across the field at a gallop, but he lost control of the animal and crashed into a parked ambulance behind the bench. The horse and rider went sprawling in a hilarious highlight, or lowlight, that local television news stations replayed that night, unwanted nongame publicity again overshadowing the game.

Mike Rhyner stayed until the end. The score was lopsided, but at least he owned the football cards of the players in this game — Jim Brown, Bobby Mitchell, even Eddie LeBaron and L. G. Dupre. Mike was excited to see them live, even in a pitiful game.

After the final gun, Mike raced outside and found his family. The Cowboys had played terribly, he said, but he had a terrific time.

In Monday's *Times Herald,* Bud Shrake wrote that Landry had red eyes and an unsteady voice after the 48–7 defeat and seemed in a mild state of shock. "If Brown and Mitchell had played the whole game," Shrake wrote, "we would have needed to send the game films to Cal Tech to get the score computed."

As it was, the game was a brutal statement on the Cowboys' lowly place in the NFL. "We couldn't even get a pass away," Landry lamented. "I guess the only consolation is we don't have to play them again."

That was true. The league had designated the Cowboys as a "swing team" in their first season, meaning they would play one game against

each of the NFL's other twelve teams, "swinging" between the Eastern
and Western Divisions. They would join the East in 1961, playing an
annual home-and-home series with the division's other teams, while
the new Minnesota team joined the West.

For now, it was a relief to know there wouldn't be another game — on
the road, no less — against Cleveland.

Still wobbling from the Cleveland debacle a few days later, the Cowboys' front office asked for a couple of players to go to the State Fair and
man an autograph booth on their day off. McIlhenny and Heinrich volunteered (for twenty-five bucks, the team's standard appearance fee).
They settled into their seats at midday, prepared to chat with fans. But
many of the people who stopped by the booth were fans of the Texans.

"Sorry, but you guys lose and the Texans win," one said.

"We're supporting Mr. Hunt's team," chimed another.

McIlhenny and Heinrich shook their heads. They signed a few au-
tographs, but many of the fans weren't friendly. "It wasn't too far removed from being an animal at the zoo and having people poke a stick
at you. They didn't have nice things to say about the Cowboys," McIlhenny recalled years later. "They liked the Texans. They thought the
Texans were a lot more fun."

Abner Haynes stepped out of the Texans' locker room at the south end
of the Cotton Bowl and was immediately surrounded by autograph
hunters who had been waiting for him. They jabbed pens, programs,
and blank paper at the young halfback, who had just devastated the
Denver Broncos with his running and pass receiving in a 34–7 victory
for the Texans. The date was November 13, 1960.

When Haynes had obliged all of his fans, he walked slowly to his car,
bones aching, and slid into the driver's seat. Wheeling out of Fair Park,
he drove through South Dallas on his way home to his wife and two
young boys. Afternoon sunshine had pulled people out of their dens
and into the parks and streets. When they spotted Haynes at stop-
lights, they waved and exclaimed, "Abner! Great game!" Few actually
had attended the game — the Texans had announced a crowd of 21,000
that was clearly a generous estimate — but they had either listened on
the radio or heard that their local hero had another big day.

Just a few years earlier, he had been a gawky, anonymous teenager in this all-black neighborhood, but now he was the toast of South Dallas — even all of Dallas, perhaps, or certainly its football fans.

No player on the Texans or Cowboys was having a better season. Haynes had put on a typical performance that day against the Broncos: 114 yards rushing, including breakaway dashes of thirty-six and twenty-seven yards; two pass receptions for forty yards, including a twenty-nine-yarder; one kickoff return for twelve yards and a punt return for eleven.

With a series of similar efforts, Haynes had emerged as one of the AFL's brightest stars. It was hard to believe he had sat on the bench behind several other backs in training camp just a few months earlier. Once the season began, he had surpassed them all. Jim Swink, seeing his playing time diminish, had given up on football again and returned to medical school. Jack Spikes and Johnny Robinson had missed several games with injuries. Haynes, meanwhile, had become the AFL's top rusher and one of its most dangerous playmakers.

His teammates, many of whom had come from college programs that didn't recruit blacks, marveled at what he could do. He was like a rabbit dashing across a grassy field, springing forward, shifting weight, cutting back and forth unpredictably as he eluded pursuers. He wasn't the fastest back, but he was eyeblink-quick, hard to pin down, and knew how to use blockers to open running lanes.

"Man," Spikes had gushed to him, "if we'd had you at TCU, we'd have won the Southwest Conference three times."

Haynes laughed lightheartedly at the praise. He knew he was the first African American many of his teammates had played with, as well as the first many Dallas fans had cheered for, and he loved that. But while he relished breaking such barriers, he wasn't hung up on exacting revenge or proving the silly point that blacks could play when they obviously could. His white North Texas teammates had embraced him, not spurned him, and now the whites on the Texans also had his back. Robinson, Spikes, Burford, and others had ventured into South Dallas to eat and drink on his turf, and also taken him into all-white establishments in North Dallas, intentionally forcing the places to drop their policies to let him in.

The entire AFL regarded Haynes as one of its stakes to football legitimacy, along with its other stars such as George Blanda and Billy Cannon of the Oilers, Jack Kemp and halfback Paul Lowe of the Chargers, and receiver Lionel Taylor of the Broncos. When *Sports Illustrated*'s Tex Maule, who had worked in the NFL, haughtily wrote in early November that Haynes couldn't play in the older league — likely parroting his mentor Tex Schramm — AFL personnel responded fiercely.

"That's ridiculous. Haynes is fabulous. He can run and catch as well as anyone in football. Pittsburgh is sick they didn't get him," said Buster Ramsey, coach of the Buffalo Bills, who had played and coached in the NFL since the forties.

The only disappointing aspect of Haynes's fine season was that it hadn't translated into success for the Texans. They had recently lost three straight games, including a road decision to the Oilers, who had emerged as the AFL's top team with a hard-hitting defense supporting the playmaking of Blanda and Cannon. The Texans' overall record was five wins and four losses, but their inconsistency had dropped them behind the Chargers in the Western Division standings.

The inconsistency vexed Stram. His defense pitched a shutout one week, but gave up thirty-seven points the next. The offense was blanketed by the Oilers one week, then scored seventy-nine points in back-to-back games. What was going on?

The injuries to Spikes and Robinson certainly had hurt, as had Cotton Davidson's up-and-down play — he passed for more than three hundred yards in one game, threw five interceptions in another. Perhaps the inconsistency was just a by-product of youth. All eight AFL teams were relying heavily on rookies, but the Texans had more than any — sixteen of their twenty-two starters. Maybe the young guys needed more time to master Stram's offense and defense, which were sophisticated, involving multiple sets and adjustments at the line.

But it could be the problem wasn't the Texans themselves as much as their opposition, which had turned out to be far more formidable than expected. Although *Sports Illustrated* and the NFL looked down their noses at the AFL, it was, in fact, a pretty decent league. Every team had players the NFL had tried to sign. The Oilers had a thumping defense. The Chargers had burning speed and an array of productive black players. Lamar had initially feared that poorer franchises such as the Broncos and Raiders wouldn't field competitive teams, but they had won some games.

The typical AFL game was a lot like the one between the Texans and Titans that Landry and Brandt had watched at the Cotton Bowl — a high-scoring, back-and-forth affair, with passes filling the air. Broncos quarterback Frank Tripucka was averaging more than thirty pass attempts per game. The Titans' Al Dorow wasn't far behind. Offenses in the AFL were producing a lot more points and yards than their NFL counterparts. Games in the older league suddenly seemed slow-paced and old-fashioned. While some of the AFL's players obviously were not up to the NFL's standards, the league's overall caliber of play was respectable.

Its attendance was another story. The per-game average of 15,000 fans was a pittance compared to the NFL's 40,000-plus. The Raiders were being treated as outsiders in San Francisco, drawing under 10,000 a game. The Broncos were faring little better in Denver. The Titans, stuck at the dilapidated Polo Grounds, were being disparaged in New York. The Chargers, despite their winning record, were barely filling one-fifth of the Los Angeles Coliseum. Football fans in Southern California seemingly preferred to stay home on Sundays and watch the NFL's Rams on television.

There were a few mild successes sprinkled in. The Oilers were drawing a solid 20,000 a game. The Patriots, playing at Boston University's dimly lit field on Friday nights to avoid conflicting with the NFL Giants' popular Sunday afternoon television broadcasts, had built a raucous following of some 16,000. And the Texans had drawn an average of 30,000 to their four home games. That led the league. But a small percentage of the Texans' fans actually paid to get in, and fewer were coming as the season progressed. To Lamar's dismay, it seemed that Dallas's fans were either disappointed in their inconsistent team or increasingly bored with the AFL itself.

On the Monday morning after the lopsided victory over the Broncos, the Texans reported to their practice site on North Central Expressway. This was one area in which the Texans had it all over the Cowboys. Lamar had erected a makeshift campus on the former site of his Zima Bat batting cage business — a large corner lot not far from SMU. The all-in-one "facility" had a full-sized field with goalposts and several outbuildings for meetings. It was a whole lot more pleasant and practical than depressing Burnett Field, and the players never had to pile onto a school bus and ride around looking for a city park to practice in.

Stram didn't push the players hard during practice on this Monday, wanting to preserve them for the final month of the season. They had been going strong since July. Five months of practices and games had taken a toll. With AFL rosters consisting of just thirty-three players, as opposed to the NFL's thirty-eight, starters had to play on field goal, punt, and kickoff teams. That increased the wear on their bodies. Many Texans were playing with injuries. Both offensive guards were out with knee problems. Spikes was limping around on a sore ankle.

Several weeks earlier, before the Texans played the Oilers in Houston, Sherrill Headrick and a teammate had both been jarred when they collided during pregame warm-ups. Headrick had played the entire game despite feeling dazed, roaming the field and making tackles as usual. Several days later, he went to a doctor complaining of persistent back pain. The doctor discovered that Headrick had cracked a vertebra in that pregame collision. He had played with a broken back!

Incredibly, Headrick just put a pad on his back and kept playing. He refused to sit out a play, much less a game. His teammates, watching with jaws agape, gave him a nickname borrowed from the popular Alfred Hitchcock movie released that year. They called him "Psycho."

Their next game was in Boston against the blue-collar Patriots and quarterback Butch Songin, the former playground sensation who was enjoying a prolific "rookie" season at age thirty-six. (Or was it thirty-eight?) After practice on Thursday morning, the players showered, dressed, and boarded a flight for Massachusetts. As always, each wore dark slacks, a dark tie, and a bright red blazer with a white-and-gold Texans patch over the breast. Their hair was short, their faces shorn of mustaches and beards. The AFL could be a ragtag affair, but Lamar and Stram wanted the Texans to look like champions and exude class. Lamar had provided the blazers, Stram the no-facial-hair edict.

Trailing the Chargers in the standings, the Texans needed a win and thought they could get it — they had pummeled Boston in the exhibition season — but the red-clad Patriots ambushed them. Boston's normally porous defense stopped the Texans; Haynes found no running room, and when Davidson tossed him a pass, a linebacker slammed into him and drove him to the hard turf as the fans whooped it up.

Meanwhile, Songin threw for a touchdown to put Boston up, and Davidson was pressured into throwing an interception, setting up another Boston score.

Down 20–0 in the second quarter, Stram replaced Davidson with Hunter Enis, the rookie. The switch worked initially as Enis led a long scoring drive shortly before halftime, tossing several completions to Chris Burford and sneaking over from the 1 for the score. He then moved the offense into scoring territory again on the first series of the second half, putting the Texans in position to make the game interesting.

But Johnny Robinson fumbled on a sweep, blunting their momentum, and Songin drove his offense sixty-five yards for a touchdown, moving the ball almost entirely through the air. When Enis threw an interception on the next possession, the Texans unraveled. Pretty soon, the Patriots had a 42–7 lead.

Stram was glum in the locker room after the game, his team back at .500, playoff hopes all but extinguished. "We tried everything. Nothing worked," he said.

The Texans remained on the East Coast to play the Titans at the Polo Grounds on Thanksgiving afternoon. The game was similarly disastrous. With Al Dorow passing to receivers Don Maynard and Art Powell, who were wide open in the Texans' beleaguered pass defense, the Titans rolled to leads of 14–0, 28–10, and 34–13. The only bright spot for the Texans was Haynes, who broke a sixty-seven-yard touchdown run to keep the Texans marginally in the game. They staged a fourth-quarter rally, but the Titans held on to win, 41–35.

The AFL had scheduled the holiday game because the NFL always played on Turkey Day — in Detroit — as did many high school teams across the country, and the new league wanted to find a niche on the holiday most associated with football. It was the perfect opportunity for a national broadcast, with so many people in front of their TV sets at home.

For better or worse, AFL games had become a Sunday afternoon TV programming staple across the country. It was unclear how many viewers were tuning in, but ABC was broadcasting at least one game from coast to coast every week, with booth announcers Curt Gowdy and Paul Christman and sideline reporter Jack Buck describing the action. Regional broadcasts of local teams were also on the docket on many Sundays, enabling fans to watch AFL football virtually all day if they wanted.

If the attendance at games was any indication, the broadcasts were not helping to build a popular brand. It was assumed that NFL broadcasts attracted larger audiences despite being more regional in nature. But if the steady drumbeat of AFL programming had accomplished anything, it had introduced the league's fledgling teams to mass audiences, a feat that prior start-up leagues such as the AAFC had failed to accomplish.

The league had given the holiday game to the big-city Titans and their bombastic owner, Harry Wismer, in hopes of having an entertaining game, and also just to placate Wismer, who had become a pain. He always had a complaint—about a referee's call, some perceived slight, or a mistake he believed Lamar was making. He disdainfully viewed Lamar as a spoiled rich kid whose daddy had bought him a team, but meanwhile, his own burgeoning money problems were keeping the Titans from being taken more seriously in the Big Apple.

Lamar wanted to beat Wismer, but more important, he wanted the game to sell well and look good on national television. Neither wish came true. The announced crowd of 14,000 looked pitiful on ABC, and the Titans knocked the Texans out of the playoff race.

The Texans showered, put on their fancy red jackets, and flew home to a city paying less and less attention.

# 11

## "We've scared off every fan we have"

CLINT MURCHISON JR.'S eyeglasses, small stature, and reserved nature belied the power he wielded. As his NFL team's inaugural season unfolded, he and his brother were seeking to gain control of the Allegheny Corporation, a venerable Manhattan holding company that controlled $5 billion in assets, including the New York Central Railroad and Investors Diversified Services, a financial colossus featuring the world's largest mutual fund. It was a Texas-sized piece of business even for Murchison, but he was accustomed to negotiating deals of a scope that boggled mortal minds.

Murchison was a hard-edged businessman with a soft shell. He had a quick wit, an eye for portrait photography, and loved nothing more than a good prank, like buying George Preston Marshall's fight song and holding it for ransom. FBI director J. Edgar Hoover, a friend and frequent guest in Clint's Dallas home, woke one morning and came down for breakfast only to find a live jackass hitched to the staircase.

Years after the Cowboys and Texans feuded for Dallas, sportswriter Gary Cartwright would recall an early-sixties visit to Lamar Hunt's home that included a game of one-on-one basketball followed by tuna casserole. "Lamar was an amiable sports nut who memorized statistics and challenged friends to name the starters on SMU's 1935 Rose Bowl team," Cartwright would write. By contrast, Murchison was a board-room power broker who enjoyed the trappings of immense wealth. He picked up huge tabs and had a standing reservation at the 21 Club in New York City.

During the Cowboys' first season in the NFL, Murchison and his wife initiated a tradition of hosting brunches at his North Dallas home before the team played at the Cotton Bowl. Bedford Wynne and a handful of Murchison's friends and their wives ate omelets, drank Bloody Marys, and talked about the game or the parties they had attended together the night before.

On November 6, 1960, Murchison's three sons and daughter darted through the brunch crowd, revved up for the day. Clint III was the oldest, an eighth-grader at St. Mark's, an elite all-boys private school in North Dallas. Burk was two years younger, followed by Coke Anne, the only girl, and Robert.

To say they enjoyed having their father own an NFL team was an understatement. They were on the inside, attended team functions, and knew the players. Clint III even sat on the bench during games. Their friends would give anything for such opportunities.

Their father handled their devotion to the team with typical light-heartedness. When they told him about school chums whose parents backed the Texans, he didn't rail against them. He just smiled and said, "Well, they're for the bad guys."

On this morning, the kids gathered around their father and asked him to predict who would win that afternoon. The Cowboys were playing the Los Angeles Rams, and everyone in the Dallas organization was excited because Landry was starting Don Meredith for the first time.

"The good guys are going to win today," Murchison stated.

His brunch guests laughed and applauded. Murchison always picked his team to win. One of these days, he would be right. The Cowboys had played six games so far and lost them all.

Two hours before the scheduled kickoff, the owner and his wife and friends drove off for the game. Murchison hoped to find traffic stacked up around Fair Park, but unfortunately, he glided straight to his special parking spot next to the Cotton Bowl.

The Cowboys had run large ads in the papers all week, hoping to

drum up interest: "See the exciting Don Meredith and his gang of colorful, sometimes thrillingly unpredictable teammates!" But few fans
were buying the pitch. The Cowboys had lost to the Baltimore Colts,
45–7, at the Cotton Bowl the week before. The combined score of their
last two home games was 93–14. That was not "colorful" or "thrillingly
unpredictable." That was just depressing.

One of Murchison's drivers took his children to the game. They met
up with their parents at their seats on the 50-yard line, a few rows up
from the Dallas bench. The weather was ideal, sunny and warm with
a light breeze, but that had not helped bring fans out either. Fifteen
thousand, if that many, were on hand for the kickoff, with the usual
half consisting of kids who had gotten in free.

Landry had turned to Meredith somewhat out of desperation after
the loss to the Colts the week before. LeBaron had played miserably,
completing as many passes to his own receivers as he did to Baltimore
defenders — three apiece. The Cowboys had trailed at halftime, 31–0.
It was time to try something different. Landry knew Meredith probably was not ready to be a full-time starter, but the Rams were a good
opponent for his first real test: they simply lined up and played their
base defense, seldom shifting.

Landry tried to make his young quarterback's job easier by calling
the plays from the sideline, using his halfbacks, McIlhenny and Dupre,
as couriers. They shuttled back and forth to the bench on every other
play, bringing in the coach's call.

Landry tried to sound optimistic before kickoff. "Ordinarily it takes
three years for a rookie to develop, but I believe this boy can do it in
one," he said gamely.

The first half went surprisingly well. Meredith led the offense downfield on the opening possession, completing a pair of passes for first
downs. The drive produced a field goal, and Meredith trotted off the
field to applause. The Rams quickly retaliated with a long touchdown
pass and expanded their lead to 17–3 by early in the second quarter.
But Meredith completed a pass to Bielski, and Walt Kowalczyk set up
a touchdown with a long run. The Cowboys were in it, 17–10. Maybe
Murchison's prediction would be right.

But any such hopes faded quickly. The Rams added a touchdown
just before halftime and broke the game open with a long scoring run

in the third quarter. Meredith disintegrated. He had hit nine of eighteen passes in the first half, but did not complete a single throw to a Dallas receiver in the second half, missing ten in a row. He did throw three to the Rams.

"I looked bad," Meredith said glumly after the game. "I have a long way to go, a lot to learn."

Landry lamented that the young quarterback looked "rusty" and missed some open receivers, "which happens."

Murchison visited the locker room after the game, as was his habit, quietly encouraging the players and Landry and offering a joke to lighten the mood. They had now played seven games and lost them all.

The next day, Murchison received a call from Schramm, who was livid. The *Houston Chronicle* had reported that the Cowboys would pull out of Dallas before the end of the season, following the lead of the NFL's 1952 Texans. They would start anew in Minneapolis in 1961, the paper said.

The story was not true — the idea had never been discussed — and Schramm believed that Lamar had planted it to propagate the notion that the winless Cowboys' future was shaky. Lamar offered a confession of sorts, saying he had heard the rumor "in football circles" and was merely repeating it.

The comparison between Dallas's 1952 and 1960 NFL franchises was not entirely inappropriate: both had lost badly from the outset in front of diminishing crowds at the Cotton Bowl. But Murchison and Bedford Wynne adamantly denied they would skip town like their predecessors.

"I don't know where this stuff comes from. There has never been any thought of leaving," Wynne told the *Times Herald*. "We're looking forward to next season. With the draft, and after our young players get another year's experience, we're going to have a better team. We have not lost any more money than we projected. We knew we wouldn't make any money at first. We counted on it. We're in for the long haul."

Murchison's franchise had a multitude of football assets the 1952 Texans had lacked, advantages that bettered their prospects. They had Schramm's front office savvy, Landry's sharp coaching, and Murchison's financial backing and patience. The 1952 Texans hadn't known what they were doing and didn't have enough money to pay their players by November. They were sad sacks. The Cowboys were just an expansion team in a competitive league.

The Cowboys were so savvy that they had even anticipated this miserable opening season. They weren't about to let it short-circuit their long-range plan to rule Dallas's pro football scene.

Murchison was irritated enough about the erroneous Houston newspaper story to take a shot at Lamar and the new league — in his own inimitable style, of course. "If first-season attendance is any criteria of whether a team is going to move or not, then the Dallas Texans will move to Anchorage, Alaska," Murchison declared, "and the Oakland Raiders will move to Opelousas, Louisiana."

As he stood with his teammates watching the starting lineups get introduced before the Cowboys played the 49ers on November 20, Meredith looked around the Cotton Bowl and shook his head ruefully.

"Well, we've done it. We've scared off every single fan we had," he drawled.

Indeed, from where he stood on the stadium floor, by the end zone tunnel leading to the locker rooms, the stadium appeared empty. A few fans were scattered around the lower bowl. The upper decks were entirely vacant, as if they had been condemned.

The Cowboys had hoped to draw a decent crowd for their final home game of 1960, but they knew what was coming. When Murchison asked Schramm at the start of the week how many tickets had been sold, the general manager gulped and admitted they had sold just seven. Murchison paused, ingesting the news, and replied, "Well, why would anyone buy so soon before the game?"

But the public wasn't buying, period. The Cowboys had chilled what remained of the public's enthusiasm with more discouraging performances, most recently a 41–7 loss to the Green Bay Packers that dropped their record to zero wins and eight losses. Their home crowds had diminished as the harsh reality of expansion life kicked in, and today's opponents, the middle-of-the-road 49ers, weren't much of an attraction.

Borrowing from Lamar's playbook (without admitting it), the Cowboys had tried to drum up interest by offering fans more than just four quarters of football. Half-page newspaper ads touted the opportunity to see the "colorful" Cowboys and "great stars such as Hugh McElhenny" playing in "another National Football League thriller," as well as a circus featuring elephants, llamas, parade floats, and "many exciting acts in the Halftime Show of the Year!"

But that didn't boost sales, and Sunday's cold, drizzly weather didn't help either. Fair Park's streets were empty and quiet before the game except for a few stragglers in yellow rain slickers. The Cowboys announced a crowd of 10,000, but in fact, some 3,000 were inside the gates, huddled under the upper decks in the stadium's shadows, avoiding the rain but leaving the open stands almost completely empty.

"There aren't enough Texans here to defend the Alamo," one San Francisco sportswriter said.

As the game against the 49ers began, Clint Murchison III surveyed the stadium from his usual spot on the bench and wondered if he could count the crowd — one fan at a time. It would not take long. When the game started, he could easily hear the comments of fans in the stands, comments not even uttered loudly. Had an NFL game ever been played in a library?

Clearly, he thought, the city just wasn't going to get behind his father's team until they at least won a few games and gave the public something to rally around, something to believe in.

As usual, Murchison had predicted at brunch that morning that "the good guys" would beat the Bay Area team he had tried to buy in the early fifties. Maybe today they could turn things around.

Stalking the sideline in a dapper raincoat, Landry certainly wanted to prevail. This game probably represented the Cowboys' last chance for a victory in 1960. After this, they would conclude their schedule on the road against the Bears, Giants, and Lions. Those would be tough ones. Landry rued the thought of a winless season, a "feat" the NFL had not witnessed since 1944, when the immortal Brooklyn Tigers and Card-Pitt (a temporary blend of the Cardinals and Steelers forced by the war) both went 0-10. Shoot, even the 1952 Texans had pulled off one win.

To jump-start his struggling offense, Landry tried yet another strategy. He alternated LeBaron and Meredith on every down, sending them in with the plays he called. He hoped this "quarterback shuttle" would confuse the defense while increasing his control of the offense. Neither the rookie nor the veteran was keen on the idea, but they knew better than to challenge Landry.

The shuttle didn't flop. Both quarterbacks made plays and moved the ball. In the second quarter, Meredith finished off a long drive with a short touchdown pass. Meanwhile, the Cowboys' young defense was giving an inspired performance led by Tubbs, who would finish with twenty tackles. Competitive for a change, the Cowboys actually led at halftime, 7–6.

The lead quickly disappeared when rookie Jim Mooty fumbled the second-half kickoff and the 49ers turned the mistake into a field goal, taking a 9–7 lead. But the Cowboys struck back when LeBaron and Frank Clarke hooked up on a seventy-six-yard touchdown pass early in the fourth quarter. Clarke took the ball away from a defender at midfield, stumbled, regained his balance, and sprinted to the end zone to put the Cowboys up, 14–9, with nine minutes left. The few fans buzzed excitedly, thinking they might see their team's first win.

But in fact, they were about to experience one of the season's most tortuous interludes.

The 49ers quickly regained the lead. John Brodie completed a pair of passes to move the offense to the Dallas 29, and a fullback ran through a huge hole and steamrolled a pair of defensive backs to reach the end zone. The Cowboys now trailed, 16–14. But they still had time to rally. Unfortunately, Tom Franckhauser, replacing the benched Mooty, fumbled the kickoff, and the 49ers converted that mistake into a field goal and a 19–14 lead.

The Cowboys were still within one score, but they fumbled yet *another* kickoff, their third in a row — Bill Butler dropped this one — and the 49ers turned that miscue into a touchdown, putting them up 26–14. That was the final score.

Tubbs was so frustrated that he ripped off an opponent's helmet and hurled it in the final seconds, drawing a penalty. He was still furious in the locker room after the game. "We didn't have any poise when we needed it," he fumed. "We should have won this game."

Between fumbled kickoffs and interceptions thrown by LeBaron and Meredith, the Cowboys had lost seven turnovers.

"You can't give a National Football League team the ball as many times as we did today and survive. We've been doing it all season," Landry lamented.

In the visitors' locker room, the 49ers were hardly euphoric about capturing a mistake-filled game in front of 70,000 empty seats. "When you win like that, you feel like you lost — well, almost anyway," coach Red Hickey said.

The last thing Landry wanted to do that night was go to a party. It wasn't that he was morose. He just wanted to spend a rare quiet night at home with his wife and children before moving on to preparing the Cowboys for their next game. As always, he had a lot of ideas. A heavy load of planning lay ahead.

Nonetheless, he took Alicia to the team's holiday party that night. It was a lavish affair for the players, coaches, and staff at a popular supper club. Schramm was determined to continue to set a high standard for organizational class, despite the team's record. Murchison was in lockstep with him on the subject.

At the party, a group of players, mostly veteran survivors of the expansion draft, wound up in a social circle with Landry. Emboldened by cocktails, they vented their frustrations. Like the fans, they had their explanations for what was wrong with the Cowboys. The offense was too complicated. The defense was inexperienced. Don Heinrich was especially vocal, probably because Landry had started giving his snaps to Meredith.

Landry listened with a polite smile. He was accustomed to hearing criticism. As part of the Cowboys' attempt to lure fans, they held a weekly public luncheon at a downtown hotel. Landry interrupted his routine and delayed the start of that afternoon's practice to drive downtown, give a short speech, and answer questions. For a couple of bucks, any fan could eat a meal and ask him anything.

Years later, it is almost unfathomable that a coaching legend-to-be interrupted his game preparation to answer challenging, sometimes insulting questions from fans. *Coach, what in the heck is a quarterback shuttle? Coach, why do we keep fumbling? Coach, are you sure you know what you're doing?*

But with the Cowboys in a fight for survival, Landry had to do more than just coach. That meant putting up with pointed questions from disappointed fans.

When his players voiced similar critiques at the holiday party that night, Landry excused himself quickly. With all due respect, he was operating on a different plane — from the players, from the fans, shoot, even from Schramm. They were all focused on how to fix the current woes, which was fine, but Landry was focused on the bigger picture.

Oh, sure, he wanted nothing more than to win, starting immediately. But since taking the Dallas job, he had devised a master plan that trumped all other issues in his mind — a blueprint for success that, alas, could not be put fully in motion for several years. It involved finding a way to beat the four-three defense he had invented and championed while with the Giants. That, Landry believed, was the Cowboys' ticket to long-range success in the NFL.

The four-three had become the standard base alignment for pro football defenses, an effective antidote to speedy modern offenses. But now that he was a head coach, Landry had to figure out how to beat his baby. His friend Vince Lombardi had turned Green Bay into a winner by pulverizing the four-three with a simple power attack, running straight at it and crushing it with sound blocking and strong running. But Landry couldn't do that. Lombardi had some of the league's best personnel at his disposal, All-Pro linemen such as Jim Ringo and Forrest Gregg and ball-carriers such as Jim Taylor and Paul Hornung. The Cowboys couldn't come close to matching that, not with their roster of journeymen and neophytes.

Landry had to find another way to beat the four-three. One day the lightbulb came on. If he couldn't blast through it, maybe he could fool it. It was a defense that depended on players' ability to read offensive formations, recognize "keys," and adjust. A lot went on just before the snap. If the Cowboys threw up a haze of smoke, Landry reasoned, opposing defenses might have a hard time.

He scratched out the outline of what he called the "multiple" offense, as in multiple formations. The quarterback called a play in the huddle and brought the offense to the line, pausing long enough to give the defense time to read its keys and react. But as the defense reacted, the offense also shifted. The tight end might jump from one side of the line to the other. The backs might change their alignment from an "I" (one behind the other) to a "T" (alongside each other). A back might go in motion. And as those distracting shifts and feints unfolded, the quarterback might call an audible and change the play altogether.

Landry was almost certain it would work. It was so logical — as the defense read you, you changed what it read. But while that made sense, it was a sophisticated strategy. All eleven players in the offensive huddle had to know exactly what they were doing, and what everyone else was doing. They had to know when to throw up smoke, shift, and go in motion, and they had to move precisely, in unison. It would take years of practice to get it right. A long list of things could go wrong.

As Landry's mind whirred, it churned out fresh ideas about putting multiple men in motion, hiding backs behind linemen, even having linemen briefly stand up straight before the snap to distract and confuse the defense. Crazy stuff! Double-reverse passes. Flanker options.

Landry had put a bit of it in play with the Cowboys this year, not to win so much as just to survive. But his players were not talented (or loyal) enough to run the complex offense he had in mind. He was not about to take that on until Meredith could master it and the players around him were smart and talented enough to pull it off.

These fans and players complaining about the offense already being too complicated had not seen anything yet.

When he sat down with Schramm and explained his long-range thinking, Schramm, a forward thinker in his own right, responded enthusiastically. This was precisely why the Cowboys had hired Landry. With his beautiful football mind, he was always ahead of the evolutionary curve.

Schramm, in turn, explained Landry's concept to Murchison, who nodded and smiled, knowing his grasp of football was infinitesimal compared to Landry's. The owner had confidence in the men he had hired. Of course he would let them do their thing.

Nonetheless, waiting for Landry's offense to mature was going to be tough. There was another team in town winning more games, and even though the Texans faced inferior competition, Dallas's fans seemingly weren't nuanced enough to understand that. To them, a losing team was a loser, period. The Cowboys' dismal reputation was work-

Abner Haynes on the sideline, ball in hand, uniform caked in mud. It is not an exaggeration to say he carried the Texans.

*Courtesy of The Dallas Morning News*

Tommy Brooker is carried off the field after kicking the game-winning field goal in the 1962 AFL championship game in Houston.

*Courtesy of The Dallas Morning News*

Clint Murchison, the Cowboys' owner in their early years.

*Courtesy of The Dallas Morning News*

The Texans' Chris Burford (88) leaps to catch a pass before a lot of empty seats at the Cotton Bowl. *Courtesy of The Dallas Morning News*

Lamar Hunt (tie askew) and Hank Stram (overcoat on) celebrate with players and fans at Love Field after the 1962 AFL championship game. *Courtesy of The Dallas Morning News*

The Texans pour champagne on each other in the locker room after defeating the Houston Oilers in overtime in the 1962 AFL championship game. *Courtesy of The Dallas Morning News*

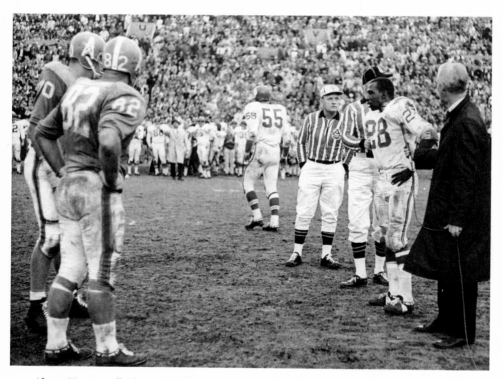

Abner Haynes tells the officials and a national TV audience that the Texans will "kick to the clock" to start overtime at the 1962 AFL championship game.

*Courtesy of The Dallas Morning News*

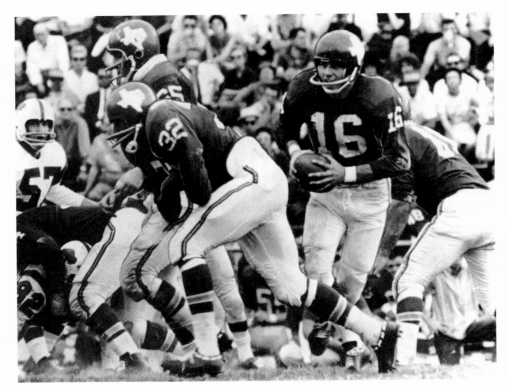

Len Dawson (16) pulls away from center with the ball against the Buffalo Bills in 1962. His career was almost at an end before he joined the Texans. *Courtesy of The Dallas Morning News*

The Kansas City Chiefs donned these "throwback" helmets when they played the Dallas Cowboys on October 11, 2009.

*Courtesy of Ridell Sports, Inc.*

Tex Schramm (left) and Tom Landry as they set out to build a football team from scratch in 1960. *AP Photo/NFL Photos*

Cleveland's Ray Renfro reels in a touchdown catch over the Cowboys' Tom Franckhauser in the Browns' 48–7 win at the Cotton Bowl in 1960. The Cowboys were not a big draw.

*AP Photo*

Tom Landry at the outset of the Cowboys' second training camp at St. Olaf College, in Northfield, Minnesota, in 1961. *AP Photo*

Cowboys tight end Lee Folkins, wearing the team's all-white road uniform, is confronted by a pair of defenders after catching a pass against the Philadelphia Eagles at Franklin Field in 1962. *AP Photo/Bill Ingraham*

Pete Rozelle (center) is flanked by Tex Schramm (left) and Lamar Hunt as they announce the AFL-NFL merger in New York on June 8, 1966. *AP Photo*

The AFL's original owners, who called themselves "the Foolish Club." Houston's Bud Adams is seated on the left. Buffalo's Ralph Wilson is standing, third from the left. Lamar Hunt is standing, in the middle of the back row.

*AP Images/Pro Football Hall of Fame*

Don Meredith, fresh from SMU, where, he confessed, the offense was a lot simpler than Landry's. *AP Photo/NFL Photos*

Lamar Hunt, founder of the AFL and the Dallas Texans. *AP Photo/NFL Photos*

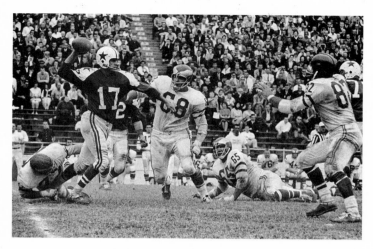

Meredith in familiar circumstances, under duress.

*Bettmann/CORBIS*

George Halas, the NFL's legendary "Papa Bear," whose behind-the-scenes manipulations brought the Cowboys to Dallas. *Bettmann/CORBIS*

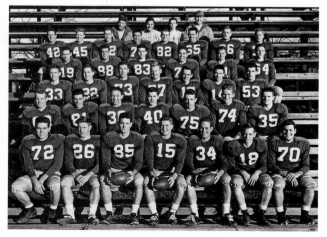

SMU's undefeated 1951 freshman football team, with Lamar Hunt (35) in the second row, all the way to the right.

*Courtesy of SMU Heritage Hall*

Don Meredith with his first pro contract in hand, after Lamar Hunt (left) and Tex Schramm (right) battled over his rights in the fall of 1959. It is not hard to tell who won.

*Courtesy of SMU Heritage Hall*

The Texans hoped that halftime shows featuring petting zoos, marching bands, and pretty girls would help draw fans.

*Photo by James T. (Brad) Bradley of Bradley Photographers*

Abner Haynes breaking into the Denver Broncos' secondary during the Texans' 34–7 victory at the Cotton Bowl on November 13, 1960.

*Photo by James T. (Brad) Bradley of Bradley Photographers*

ing against them, keeping them from becoming more popular. That would obviously have to change at some point in the not-too-distant future.

But the losing was tougher on no one more than Landry himself. Schramm and Murchison were not perched on the sideline every Sunday, presiding over defeat after defeat. They weren't having their acumen openly challenged, even mocked.

Landry could take it for the most part. He could close his eyes and see a better future developing, even if no one else could now. He was confident in his coaching and certain he could take the Cowboys where everyone wanted them to go.

But he also had doubts about the frustration and impatience festering in the stands, in the locker room, perhaps even in the owner's mind. Dallas liked winning teams and college football. That was a potentially dangerous backdrop for a losing pro team. Landry had wondered from the outset whether the Cowboys actually would survive.

He had faith and a vision, but this was going to take patience. If the people around him did not have as much, well, the "smartest coach in football" could always sell insurance.

The Cowboys made it ten in a row a week later, losing to George Halas and the rugged Bears, 17–7, on a windy afternoon in Chicago.

Having come into existence largely because of the influence wielded by Papa Bear, the Cowboys now experienced the darker side of his power. Several dubious officiating calls went Chicago's way, including one infuriating whopper. It was Rick Casares Day at Soldier Field, as the Bears honored their Pro Bowl fullback, but Casares fumbled as he headed for the end zone on a first-quarter run. The Cowboys clearly recovered, yet the referee waved off the fumble and signaled touchdown, offering no explanation. The Cowboys were down early again. Welcome to Papa Bear's NFL.

The Cowboys managed to keep the score close. After LeBaron went down with broken ribs, Landry turned to Heinrich, fearing what might happen to Meredith on the road against such a daunting opponent. (Halas used twenty-five different defensive schemes.) Heinrich moved the offense into scoring range several times while the Dallas defense, suddenly opportunistic, forced five turnovers. The Cowboys pulled within a touchdown when McIlhenny took a screen pass sixty-three yards for a touchdown in the third quarter.

In the end, they fell short because Cone missed three short field goal attempts and the Bears stopped them on a fourth-and-inches play at the Chicago 20 with the game on the line. But they were upbeat after giving the Bears such a good game. "We had a good feeling out there today," said Mike Falls, an offensive guard, in the locker room. "Everyone had confidence and no one lost his poise. I can see now that we have the nucleus of a pretty good club."

Despite the improved showing, the Cowboys were given little chance against the Giants in Yankee Stadium on December 4. Although the Giants had been set back by injuries and were not going to win a third straight Eastern Division title, they were still tough to beat, especially at home. No one knew that better than Landry.

Fifty-five thousand fans — the largest crowd the Cowboys had played before — saw the Giants take a 21–7 lead in the first twenty minutes as quarterback George Shaw passed the Cowboys dizzy. But the Cowboys didn't fold. Landry had planned to start Heinrich against his former team, but switched to LeBaron on a last-minute hunch. The little quarterback's damaged ribs were heavily taped, but he loosened up in the second quarter. Mixing short passes and runs, he drove the offense the length of the field and found Dupre open in the end zone for a twenty-one-yard touchdown pass. After another drive resulted in a Cone field goal, the Cowboys were only down four at halftime, 21–17.

The Giants added a field goal early in the third quarter, but LeBaron's offense motored upfield again. Throwing to Doran and Howton, he moved into New York territory, then spotted Dupre open again in the secondary. The veteran back caught LeBaron's spiral at the 5, took a hit, and twisted into the end zone for a twenty-three-yard score — tie game, 24–24.

Given the Cowboys' brief but unfortunate history, it was hardly surprising when the Giants regained the lead midway through the fourth quarter. Shaw lobbed a pass toward Bob Schnelker, their Pro Bowl end, in the corner of the end zone. The Cowboys had solid coverage, but Schnelker stuck out a hand, reeled in the ball, and held it as he hit the ground to complete a spectacular touchdown.

The Giants' fans figured that would probably quell the upset bid.

Seven minutes remained. But LeBaron exuded confidence when the offense gathered around him in the huddle to start the next possession.

"We're moving on these guys. Let's just keep doing what we're doing. Come on!" he said.

The offense rolled downfield. LeBaron passed to Doran for a first down and hit Howton for another. McIlhenny swept around left end for twelve yards. The ball was on the New York 11. Howton broke open on a crossing pattern and grabbed LeBaron's line drive spiral just before he slammed into the goalpost and went sprawling. But he held on for the touchdown, and Cone's extra point tied the score at 31–31.

Shaw tried to pull the game out for the home team, but a Dallas interception quelled the Giants' final drive, and the game ended in a tie. When the gun echoed in the suddenly quiet stadium, the Cowboys raised their arms triumphantly. They hadn't won, but for the first time, they hadn't lost.

With huge smiles, Murchison and Bedford Wynne walked the aisles of the plane that evening, congratulating the players during the flight back to Dallas. The alcohol and jokes flowed freely as the players slapped each other on the back and reviewed their big plays. "It was like we had won the world championship," Jerry Tubbs would recall.

For the first time, fans came to Love Field at midnight to meet the team's plane — two fans, to be exact, holding aloft a sign that read WELL DONE, COWBOYS.

Before practice on Tuesday, each Cowboy player received a large brown box adorned with a personal card from Murchison. Pulling out elegant leather cowboy boots — their Christmas gift from the owner — they laughed and tried them on.

"What in the hell am I supposed to do with these?" asked Nate Borden, a defensive end from New Jersey.

Dick Bielski, a self-proclaimed "thick Polack," couldn't fit his wide foot into the sleek boot. He asked Clint Huoy, the team's trainer, what he should do.

"Just give them to me. I'll work it all out with Mr. Murchison," Huoy said.

A few days later, Bielski received a call from a custom bootmaker in Fort Worth. "Ah hear ya'll cain't fit into your boot," the bootmaker drawled. He took Bielski's measurements and off-season address and promised to send another pair.

Two months later, in the middle of a snowy New Jersey winter, Bielski was summoned by his mailman to a nearby post office, told only that he had a package. He hurried over, curious. When he pulled his new boots out of the box, he laughed out loud. Those damn Texans were something.

On December 11, the Cowboys closed out their season with a 23–14 loss to the Lions in snowy Detroit. There were few positives. The defense yielded easily, allowing bulky Lions fullback Nick Pietrosante to break a pair of long touchdown runs. LeBaron tried to lead a rally, but it went nowhere.

No fans were waiting for them at Love Field that night — not even the two die-hards from the week before. The Cowboys had ended 0-11-1, the NFL's worst record since 1944. Other than the tie with the Giants, it had been a season to forget.

Standing at midfield a few minutes before kickoff, Lamar surveyed the sparse crowd for the Texans' final home game. They would announce 18,000, but 10,000 was more like it. There were knots of fans near midfield and in the end zones. The upper decks were empty. It wasn't much of a crowd for a sunny December Sunday, perfect for football. And less than half of the fans had bought tickets, Lamar guessed.

The small crowd was no surprise. Both the Texans and visiting Buffalo Bills had been eliminated from playoff contention, rendering this finale meaningless. Yes, the Texans had rebounded from their depressing failures in Boston and New York to win two straight, including one against the Oilers, and a victory today would give them a final record of eight wins and six losses, good for second place in the division. But their ups and downs had frustrated fans and, if the size of this crowd was any indication, chased many away. They had 4,000 paying customers for this game, if that many. Talk about discouraging. The night before, some 68,000 fans had watched Texas and Alabama play in the Bluebonnnet Bowl, a second-tier postseason college game in Houston. The disparity between that crowd and this one was as clear as the Texas sky: pro football remained a lesser attraction in Dallas and an especially tough sell when a team did not live up to expectations on the field.

But Lamar refused to get too down. That simply wasn't his nature. And he was on the field before kickoff because it was "Lamar Hunt Appreciation Day," with a pregame ceremony honoring him. The other AFL owners had devised the idea and sent signed proclamations. Lamar had reluctantly consented to have them read to the crowd.

Dressed in his red team blazer, he listened as Charlie Jones, the Texans' radio announcer, read the proclamations extolling his vision, toughness, and persistence. Lamar acknowledged the compliments with a smile and a faint nod. He was, in fact, immensely proud of the AFL as its first season neared an end. Countless problems remained, but all eight teams had survived, with almost one million fans passing through the turnstiles at games. The TV audiences had been larger than expected. The league was being taken seriously by the public, if not by the NFL.

After the ceremony, Lamar returned to his seat in the lower bowl, accepting congratulations from fans as he walked up the concrete steps. Jack Spikes kicked off, and the Texans' defense quickly stopped Buffalo, forcing a punt. After being picked apart so miserably in Boston and New York, the defense suddenly had come together, registering back-to-back shutouts. Perhaps Sherrill Headrick had inspired his teammates by playing a game within days of having hemorrhoids removed. More likely, the young defense had finally just started to fulfill its potential.

Buffalo's defense also was stout, and the first half unfolded with few scoring threats for either side. Spikes booted a field goal early in the second quarter, and Bills quarterback Richie Lucas, a rookie, replied with a twenty-yard touchdown run. Buffalo had the lead at halftime, 7–3.

But the Texans fared better after halftime. Haynes swept left for twelve yards. Robinson gained eighteen on a swing pass. On a second down at the Buffalo 33, Davidson faded back as Burford ran downfield, faked inside, and headed for the corner of the end zone. Davidson arched a pass before the receiver's final move, and the ball sailed to Burford just as he turned to look. He held on as he fell, completing a scoring play. With Spikes's conversion, the Texans had the lead, 10–7.

On the second play of Buffalo's next series, Texans safety Don Flynn leveled Lucas on a blitz just as the quarterback released a pass. The throw fell incomplete, and Lucas remained down. A trainer helped him to his feet, but he was too woozy to stay in. On the next play, Smokey Stover blitzed the replacement, knocked the ball loose, and Headrick recovered. The Texans converted the break into a touchdown, with Spikes bulling across from the 1.

A few minutes later, Robinson took a screen pass seventy-three yards for a touchdown, weaving through the defense as blockers cleared his path. The Texans had a 24–7 lead, and that was the final score.

Lamar came to the locker room to congratulate Stram and the players, some of whom could reflect back on seasons of personal triumph. After starting his long-odds journey at the tryout camp in July, Stover had started every game. Headrick, offensive guard Bill Krisher, and defensive end Mel Branch would make the Associated Press All-AFL squad, as would Haynes. The rookie back had ranked first in the league in rushing and all-purpose yards (combined rushing, receiving, and return yardage), tied for second in touchdowns, and finished fifth in pass receiving. The media would select him the AFL's Most Valuable Player by a wide margin.

Lamar sought out Haynes and shook his hand in the locker room as the young halfback dressed.

"Just a great season, Abner, a great year," Lamar said.

"Thank you, sir," Haynes replied. "I wish we had won a few more ball games. We will next year."

The comment set Lamar's mind in motion. Next year? Yes, it was time to start planning. While league affairs would remain his priority, he would focus more on the Texans. They had lost over a half-million dollars in their first year. Lamar needed to make changes, reconfigure operations. The Associated Press had reported that the AFL's teams would combine for $2 million in losses in 1960. The actual total was higher, Lamar knew.

A reporter called Lamar's father, H.L., for a comment about the Texans' losses, noting that his son's team might have lost a million dollars.

"Well," H.L. replied, "at that rate, he can only make it for another hundred and fifty years."

# PART III

PART III

# 12

★

# "They should play each other"

WHEN CLINT MURCHISON hosted a Christmas party at his home in December 1960, shortly after the end of the Cowboys' first season, his guests arrived with great expectations.

At the same party the year before, his friends had arranged for him to receive an enormous gift, larger than he was, in "the biggest box I've ever seen," he said later. Everyone roared as the present, wrapped and adorned with a ribbon, was dragged into the living room and positioned in front of him. As he looked at it, wondering how to open it, the top suddenly flew off. Out popped Candy Barr, Dallas's best-known stripper.

An admirer of the well-turned prank, Murchison readily admitted this was a classic. His guests wondered if there would be an encore at the same party a year later. Sure enough, after drinks and dinner, another giant box was rolled in and set before Murchison. He smiled, told a few jokes, and started to pull the ribbon. Suddenly, the top flew off as it had a year ago and out popped . . . Lamar Hunt.

"Merry Christmas, Clint!" the owner of the Texans shouted.

Murchison started to laugh and could hardly stop. His friends had outdone themselves.

Try as they might, the young owners of the Cowboys and Texans could not muster genuine antipathy for each other. Although Lamar and Murchison were almost a decade apart in age and different in many respects, they actually enjoyed each other's company. They had a lot in common and could certainly exchange stories about life with strong-willed, successful fathers.

They also liked to have fun. A few months after Murchison's holiday party, Lamar was conducting a meeting of the Spur Club, his season-ticket group, when the door creaked opened and in stepped, of all people, the owner of the Cowboys, wearing a red Texans blazer. Murchison waved, said hello, and darted back out the door.

Now Lamar could not stop laughing.

"Lamar and I actually get along fine in between lawsuits," Murchison joked to a reporter that spring.

But although they were personally amicable, their teams couldn't stand each other. The Texans viewed the Cowboys as haughty. "We openly rooted for them to lose," Stram said later. The Cowboys just wished the Texans would go away.

Was it possible to make that happen? A newspaper letter to the editor written shortly before Christmas 1960 by Curtis Sanford, the sports-loving oilman who had started the Cotton Bowl game, suggested a way to lessen the city's bounty of pro football teams by one.

Sanford, now sixty-three years old, directed his letter to Lamar and Murchison and sent it to the sports editors of the *Morning News* and *Times Herald*. Printed in the afternoon paper under the headline "To the Death," it was, in a way, more interesting than anything that happened on the field to the Cowboys or Texans during their inaugural seasons. It certainly gave the fans something to talk about over the holiday season.

Dear Clint and Lamar:

I am sure you will agree with me when I say that the City of Dallas has just experienced a rather hectic professional football season. Likewise, I am sure you will agree that Dallas is a major city and will be successful in pro football with one team. I, as a football fan, hate to see a pro football war here.

Under such circumstances, everyone loses, [starting with

the] prestige of the great City of Dallas. Football interest at SMU, no doubt, is injured under such circumstances. The fine people, the owners of both pro teams here, are losing substantial sums of money, which is not good.

Realizing that the owners of both pro teams are financially able and are determined to continue this struggle for many years, that still does not remedy this current football problem here.

In an effort to remedy this situation, may I suggest a game to be staged here in the Cotton Bowl between the Cowboys and Texans on January 8th or thereabouts, with the winner of such game to remain in Dallas, the loser to go elsewhere.

If the owners of both teams would agree to such a game, I would be happy to promote the game with the help of other civic leaders here. I would be agreeable to making a firm guarantee of $100,000 to be distributed as agreed by the owners of both teams.

I would suggest that the profits from such a game be given to the Dallas Community Chest. There would definitely not be any charge or compensation of any kind to myself or anyone connected with me.

I am hoping you will interpret this letter as intended. I assure you it is my sole wish that the professional football situation here be straightened out and that pro football in the City of Dallas can continue on a successful and profitable basis, as it should be.

May I have your thoughts about my suggestion?

J. Curtis Sanford

Exploiting the reader-friendly angle that had been dropped in its lap, the Morning News sent Sam Blair out to interview people "on the street" about the possibility of such a game. He gathered comments from fans and ran a story headlined "Fans Favor Cowboy-Texan Clash." L. R. Winborn, a lawyer, said, "I'm for the Texans because they're winning, and I would love to see them play the Cowboys." R. T. Dryk, a policeman, said, "I saw all of both teams' games at the Cotton Bowl this season. I like them both. I'd like to see them play a game. They should play each other. It would be a good game."

Would it?

The Texans had fared better on the field in 1960, winning eight of fourteen games, while the Cowboys flopped miserably, going winless. But the Cowboys' opposition had been much tougher, and the Cowboys had a roster of hardened NFL veterans with far more pro experience than the Texans' youngsters.

Ruminating about such a game was all anyone would do. The Cowboys believed they had nothing to gain and everything to lose by playing the upstart Texans, who desperately wanted to prove they belonged on the same sporting plane. Cowboy management blithely dismissed the possibility. "It's utterly preposterous, simply impossible," Bedford Wynne told the *Morning News,* noting that the Cowboys' players had scattered to their off-season homes and that asking them to return to play a game would be unpopular, to say the least. The Texans' players wouldn't care for it, either.

NFL commissioner Pete Rozelle was downright acerbic when asked about his Dallas franchise possibly taking on an AFL team. "I don't think we should be doing business with the same people who are suing us for ten million dollars," Rozelle said, referring to the antitrust suit Lamar and the AFL had filed in June.

Privately, the Cowboys were furious that the idea had received any public airing at all. They smelled a setup. Sanford had supported Lamar from the outset. He was on the Texans' "advisory board" and was a charter member of the Spur Club. The Cowboys believed that Lamar had asked him to write the letter, knowing it would put the Cowboys in the awkward position of having to turn down a game the fans wanted. This had Lamar's fingerprints all over it, the Cowboys believed.

Lamar made the most of it. Initially, he agreed with Wynne that it "would be difficult" to play a January game, but then he formally issued a challenge to the Cowboys through the papers, suggesting they play an August exhibition at the Cotton Bowl.

When Schramm, always one to take the rivalry personally, was asked about the idea, he coolly replied, "We need stronger competition than that to get ready for the National Football League season."

Lamar kept up the pressure. "The public is demanding the game take place," he said, pointing to stories running in both papers. That comment drew a gentle rebuke from Blackie Sherrod in the *Times Herald.* "Dear hearts, the way the 'public' turned out for both the Texan and Cowboy games last season, it could ill afford to demand anything, even mustard for hot dogs," Sherrod wrote.

With the Cowboys refusing to play along, the story eventually waned. But it circulated in the football industry, and John Breen, general manager of the Houston Oilers, couldn't resist taking a shot at Lamar. The Oilers had just won the first AFL title, beating the Los Angeles Chargers in the championship game before a packed house in Houston. Breen could look down his nose at Dallas, where attendance for both teams had lagged.

"It would be great to see the Texans play the Cowboys, but I think the winner should get to leave Dallas," Breen said. "I think the loser should have to stay."

In the months after the Cowboys' first season, Murchison paid little attention to his team. His attempt to gain control of the Allegheny Corporation took up most of his time. He and his brother owned large stakes in Allegheny's assets but disliked its dour chief executive, Allen Kirby, an East Coast blueblood. The brothers had worked to arrange for a proxy vote to be held in the spring of 1961, and now they were lobbying Allegheny's shareholders to give them power over Kirby. The national business press was eating up the battle between new and old money, Texas oil and New York finance.

John Murchison moved to New York to lead the fight, and Clint Jr. commuted between Dallas and New York to help while also stepping in to lead whenever John needed a break. In the end, the brothers gained the support of enough shareholders to win the proxy vote and wrest control of Allegheny from Kirby, a major upset considering that many of the voters were Wall Street investors more likely to align with Kirby than with young Texas upstarts.

The brothers' triumph landed them on the cover of *Time* magazine on June 16, 1961, under the headline "Making Money Work: A Texas Technique." On the cover, an artist depicted John (in a blue suit, seated) and Clint (wearing glasses and a brown suit, standing, with his left hand on his hip) in front of an aerial view of lower Manhattan. A cowboy lasso was poised around the island in the background, insinuating that Texas money was about to capture Wall Street.

Nine years earlier, in 1954, their father, Clint Murchison Sr., had appeared on the cover of *Time*. Until now, only the English royals and American political families such as the Kennedys and Roosevelts could brag that two of their generations had made *Time*'s cover. But now the Murchisons of Texas — a new form of royalty — had done it.

*Time*'s article recounted the brothers' spectacular history as investors and stated that they symbolized the new generation of Texas tycoon who was "more apt to wear a Brooks Brothers suit than Texas boots" and to focus on electronics, real estate, insurance, and shipping rather than oil. According to the article,

> lean, hawk-faced John is quiet and reflective, quick to charm friend and foe with his affable reasonableness. Before making up his mind, he likes to walk around a proposition and look over and under it — but acts with steely decision once he has set his course. Clint Jr., brush-haired and fierce-eyed behind his glasses, is more aggressive, and often intimidates people with his acerbic wit and brusqueness.

Clint Sr. described his sons as "vice and versa" in the article, but despite their differences, they were a formidable team. Given an estimated $75 million by their father, they had doubled it by investing in over one hundred businesses, including hotels, banks, insurance firms, publishing houses, and some of the nation's largest residential builders. "Even without Allegheny, they own or direct enterprises worth more than one billion dollars," the article stated.

Their ownership of the Cowboys went unmentioned; the team constituted a minuscule percentage of their sprawling empire. In their first season, the Cowboys had earned $391,704 in ticket sales, $150,000 from television rights, $35,000 from radio rights, and $3,898 on game program sales, and the team had spent $712,000 on salaries, $120,985 on travel, and $28,718 on training camps. Overall, the Cowboys had lost more than $700,000 — a lot of money unless you had more than a billion dollars in assets.

But despite their meager finances, the Cowboys were a priority for Clint Jr. He loved going on road trips, flying with the team, talking (or listening) to Schramm about decisions, and just being involved in pro football. He was committed to developing a winning franchise.

Losing so much money in the first year didn't please him, but the year before, when he had suggested he might lose $250,000, Schramm had told him to brace for losing even more. So he was ready. And as usual, Schramm had been correct.

Although the Cowboys had failed to win a game in 1960 and had been overshadowed by Lamar's promotions, Murchison believed they were on the right road. He had faith in Schramm, who had faith in Landry, who had devised a brilliant long-range blueprint. They were spending money on scouting players rather than bringing in bands and circus animals. Gil Brandt was traveling the country, studying players, and building a network of scouts. The Cowboys were well ahead of the Texans in that crucial aspect of the football business. Schramm had insisted that they focus on it, and Murchison believed it would pay off.

After the 1960 season, when sportswriters called him for a reaction to the possibility of the Cowboys and Texans playing a game, Murchison declined to comment. He didn't see the need to dignify what he believed was a ridiculous idea. Others viewed the Cowboys-Texans conflict as a complex battle, but Murchison thought it was simple. He didn't care about the Texans. The Cowboys weren't going anywhere. They had joined an established league and embarked on a plan to grow. Their financial losses were no surprise. Murchison had more than enough money to continue feeding the franchise until it turned a corner and started to win.

*Time* had called him "aggressive," but in this case he was willing to be patient and let his team develop. The Cowboys' time would come. Eventually, Lamar would have to choose between staying in Dallas and losing money or going elsewhere. Murchison was going nowhere.

Shortly before the Texans' first season ended, Lamar abruptly fired his general manager, Don Rossi, having deduced that the feisty former sporting goods salesman didn't really understand pro sports. Rossi had worked hard to sign players, but he had complained about Lamar's preoccupation with promotions, and the two butted heads over a financial arrangement with a sponsor from which Rossi was discreetly profiting.

For a replacement, Lamar sought out Jack Steadman, chief financial officer for Penrod Drilling, the oil company that H. L. Hunt had set up for his sons. A circumspect, devoutly religious father of three, Steadman had worked for Lamar's brothers for a decade, rising through the ranks to a prominent management position. He had taken Penrod's net profits from $600,000 to $6 million in two years as chief financial officer.

When Lamar announced in 1959 that he was starting the AFL, he had asked Steadman to help him set up the business end of both the league office and the Texans' front office. Steadman did so while continuing to work for Penrod. A self-described "football nut," Steadman enjoyed talking about the game with Lamar.

But when offered Rossi's job, Steadman declined; he had worked hard at Penrod and was skeptical about starting over at a new venture with such a dubious future. Lamar accepted that rationale.

In late October, while visiting one of Penrod's rigs in St. Charles, Louisiana, Steadman received an urgent message to call Lamar.

"Jack, I have to make a change. I want to talk to you again about coming to the Texans. Can we do it tomorrow?" Lamar asked.

"I'm in Louisiana, Lamar," Steadman said.

"I know. Just get back here to Dallas as soon as you can," Lamar said.

"Well, I'll have to drive all night," Steadman said.

"Fine, just get here when you can and we'll talk," Lamar said.

When they met, Lamar asked him to reconsider becoming the Texans' GM in place of Rossi. After obtaining a personal guarantee from Lamar that he could return to his job at Penrod if the Texans folded, Steadman agreed to come on board.

With Steadman in charge, the Texans' business-side operation became more professional. Lamar had wanted someone who understood how the Hunts ran a business. Steadman had been mentored by Johnny Goodson, a Hunt estate trustee and one of H.L.'s longtime associates.

Lamar also brought in someone new to run the football side of the front office. Will Walls had done a fine job of targeting players such as Sherrill Headrick and helping the Texans sign them, but Lamar believed he needed someone younger and more energetic, with a broad view of the overall college football scene. Basically, they needed their Gil Brandt. They fingered Don Klosterman, a thirty-one-year-old scout for the Chargers.

Klosterman had been a superb college quarterback a decade earlier, leading the nation in passing as a senior at Loyola in Los Angeles. Drafted by the Cleveland Browns, he couldn't crack the lineup, was traded, and wound up sitting on the bench for his hometown Rams. After a military stint, he came back to play in Canada, but while on a ski vacation in Banff in 1957 he smashed into a tree, broke his ribs and back, and was paralyzed from the waist down. A doctor told him he would never walk again, but he was back on his feet in a year. His playing career was over, but he became a scout. Lamar had met him and liked his spirit and upbeat personality. Klosterman worked hard and clearly knew talent, having helped the Chargers assemble one of the AFL's best teams. The Texans contacted him, interviewed him, and hired him. Maybe now the Cowboys wouldn't have such an edge in scouting.

Upon joining the Texans' front office, Steadman also took some time to study their war with the Cowboys from a business perspective. He had major concerns. A pro football team needed support from the local corporate community to succeed, he believed, but with the Murchisons having as much influence as the Hunts in Dallas, the city was dangerously divided. People who did business with the Hunts ignored the Cowboys, and the Murchisons' allies disdained the Texans. As a result, neither team had enough corporate support. And for the same reason, support from the local government — another key to success, Steadman believed — also was not forthcoming. Dallas's political leaders couldn't support either team for fear of alienating one of the city's wealthiest families. Paralyzed, they just ignored pro football.

Yet as he settled into his new job, Steadman was encouraged. Lamar's passion and energy were infectious. It was clear he was driven to establish himself in sports and become his own man, apart from his father and brothers. In that way, Lamar was just like H.L., who had built an empire from scratch. The son was similar to the father in many respects, Steadman believed. Lamar could recount names, dates, and events going back years and put them to use when arguing a point; his memory, like H.L.'s, was remarkable. He was just as relentless too, always devising ideas and schemes, from "Barber Day" to the two-point conversion. He could exhaust you right away when he came into the office in the morning with ideas he had concocted.

Steadman arrived with a mandate to put more of a Hunt stamp on the Texans. He hired a family attorney to oversee the constant legal maneuvering, and he borrowed two of Hunt Oil's best "land men," Mack Rankin and Jim Beaver, to help recruit and sign players.

Rankin, whose office was across the hall from Lamar's at Hunt Oil, had already done some work for the Texans during their inaugural season, mostly policing the guys who really liked to party, such as Sherrill Headrick. Rankin identified their favorite late-night haunts and tipped bartenders to let him know when he was needed to come down at closing time and get everyone home. He practically wore out the pavement in front of their favorite spot on Cedar Springs Avenue.

After "dragging them out by their ears," as he recalled years later, he also had to make sure they were up and on their way to practice the next morning. He didn't mind. Although his background was in accounting, he had grown up around sports in Longview, Texas, where his father was a sportswriter for the local paper. Like many people in the Lone Star State, Rankin was a huge football fan.

Lamar and Steadman gave him more responsibility as the Texans entered their second year. Working his way up the ladder at Hunt Oil offices in Louisiana and Mississippi, Rankin had been in charge of putting drilling deals together, keeping wells pumping. He had gone into the countryside and befriended farmers so they would lease their land to Hunt. As a former Army procurement officer, Rankin was also used to negotiating contracts. Those skills could be a major help in the AFL-NFL war, Steadman realized. With teams battling fiercely for players, it was crucial to build relationships with players' families and also to be able to negotiate deals. Steadman vowed to put him and Beaver to work.

The AFL held the early rounds of its 1961 draft by phone in November 1960, trying to get an edge on the NFL, which held its draft in December. Believing the Texans were sufficiently stocked with skill-position stars, Klosterman sought to bolster the team's interior play while still adhering to Lamar's preference for local stars. In the first two rounds, the Texans selected E. J. Holub, a rugged center from Texas Tech, and TCU's Bob Lilly, whom TCU coach Abe Martin called "the best tackle I ever coached." Klosterman then took another tackle, Ohio State's massive Jim Tyrer, in the third round; Jerry Mays, a fiery

SMU defensive tackle, in the fifth round; and Fred Arbanas, a tight end from Michigan State, in the seventh round.

It would turn out to be a sensational draft class, full of players who would have long pro careers. But would they play for the Texans? Rankin and Beaver went to work, Rankin taking on Lilly while Beaver went with Holub. Rankin met with Lilly several times in Fort Worth, explaining that Dallas's AFL team could pay more than the NFL and that the AFL was an exciting enterprise. Beaver spent days at the Holub family's kitchen table in West Texas, seeking to convince them the AFL was right for E.J.

The entire Hunt family became recruiters. After hearing repeatedly from Rankin, Tyrer and Arbanas agreed to come to Dallas and check out the Texans. Lamar and his father arranged to meet them at baggage claim at Love Field. They greeted the youngsters, plopped ten-gallon cowboy hats on their heads, and headed for the car, carrying the players' bags. The players were awestruck about meeting H.L. and received another shock in the parking lot when the Hunts opened the doors to a 1953 Hudson, a modest car hardly befitting the family's financial standing. Then Lamar couldn't open the trunk. Tyrer yanked it open and put the bags inside.

After that inauspicious start, the Hunts dazzled the two players from the Midwest, showing them opulence and pretty women as only Texas could. Arbanas, a Detroit native, was especially excited. One of his uncles had been stationed at a military base in Texas a decade earlier and had come back wearing cowboy boots and a cowboy hat, talking about "the Wild West." That fired Arbanas's imagination as a boy. He loved the Texas myth, and loved the idea of moving to Dallas from the moment the Texans drafted him. Maybe he would see John Wayne leading a cattle drive. He agreed to sign, as did Tyrer.

The NFL had not even held its draft yet, and the AFL was piling up players.

A month later, Schramm, Brandt, Landry, and Bedford Wynne represented the Cowboys at the 1961 NFL draft in Philadelphia. Although they were thrilled to participate in a draft for the first time, they were frustrated about their chances of bagging any big-name players, having traded away their picks in four of the first ten rounds. They were especially sorry not to have their first-round pick, which had gone to the Redskins for LeBaron and was now the draft's second overall pick.

The Cowboys weren't scheduled to pick until the second slot in the second round — the sixteenth overall choice — so while they also loved Holub and Lilly, they had little hope of coming home with either.

But as the draft began, Lamar, of all people, indirectly helped the Cowboys' cause. Teams were interested in Holub and Lilly but didn't draft them because Rankin and Beaver had been courting them so heavily. The NFL teams didn't want to waste high picks on players they couldn't get.

The Cowboys had a different view of the situation. Brandt also had been courting Holub and Lilly, and Lilly, whom the Cowboys liked more, had told them he was unsigned and open-minded. The only public statement Lilly was making about his pro career — made because Cleveland's Paul Brown had expressed interest — was that he was going to play in Dallas one way or the other. He was from Throckmorton, west of Fort Worth, and determined to play near home.

In other words, Paul Brown shouldn't bother drafting him because he would just sign with the Texans.

As the first round unfolded, the Cowboys watched anxiously as college stars such as Tommy Mason, Norm Snead, Mike Ditka, and Tom Matte were selected. Lilly and Holub remained available. When it was Cleveland's turn later in the first round, Paul Brown deliberated. He wanted Lilly, but having been discouraged from taking him, selected Jim Tyrer, whom the Texans also had signed.

Brown phoned Tyrer to give him the news, but the big tackle was so noncommittal that Brown immediately suspected the player already had signed. Before the next team picked, Brown asked to withdraw his pick. Pete Rozelle relented. With the league at war, the commissioner wanted his teams to be able to sign their picks.

As Brown sat at his team's desk deciding how to proceed, Tex Schramm saw an opening. He rushed over to Brown and proposed a trade. The Cowboys would take Cleveland's first-round pick in return for some future picks and players. Brown was interested, but the two couldn't agree on what the Cowboys would give up in return. They haggled for a half-hour, holding up the entire draft.

Finally, they agreed to terms. The Cowboys would get Cleveland's first-round pick in exchange for Paul Dickson, a guard, and Dallas's first-round pick the next year.

The Cowboys immediately announced they were taking Lilly. They were confident they could sign the big tackle.

It was their turn again just two picks later, as the second round began. Although they weren't as confident about signing Holub, they took him, believing they could land him.

The Cowboy delegation was ecstatic. After doubting that they would obtain any top players, they had landed their two favorites — a pair of Texas boys, no less. But they couldn't celebrate for long. Drafting Lilly and Holub pitted them squarely against Lamar and the Texans. Both teams had taken the same players with their top two picks and wanted desperately to sign them. The battle of Dallas truly was on.

Lilly and Holub were in San Francisco for the East-West Shrine Game, an annual all-star game featuring the nation's top college seniors. In fact, the two young Texas natives were rooming together. In the hours after the NFL draft, they suddenly had company. Brandt flew out from Philadelphia to try to sign both. Lamar came from Dallas with Rankin and Beaver. Having lost Don Meredith to the Cowboys a year earlier because of a naive lack of aggressiveness, he wasn't going to make the same mistake again.

With the all-star game still several days away, Lilly and Holub spoke to representatives of both teams until 4:00 AM. Both teams made contract offers to both players. The Cowboys topped Hunt's offer by enough to convince Lilly to sign with them. His contract's terms included a $5,000 signing bonus and a first-year salary of $11,500.

A few hours later, Lilly and Holub joined their West squad teammates for a morning practice. So many pro scouts were buzzing around that the game's organizers barred them from coming inside the stadium to watch. The scouts had to wait until practice ended to speak to the players.

Lamar, not being a scout, strolled right into the stadium and watched the West squad work out. The other scouts were furious, but

Lamar, typically unflappable, downplayed the incident when he spoke to an Associated Press reporter. "No, there wasn't any trouble," he said. "They just opened the gates and I walked in. There were a couple of scouts there. I think they were letting people in."

But if Lamar took pleasure in beating the system, he was brought back to earth later that day when the Cowboys announced they had signed Lilly.

Charles Burton of the *Morning News* broke the news to Lamar on the phone. Lamar disputed it initially, telling Burton, "I spoke to Lilly just a few hours ago and he didn't put it that strong." Burton told Lamar the Cowboys had issued a press release. The deal was done.

Lamar replied, "Well, I'm very surprised at the offers the NFL teams have been giving to linemen, $13,000 or $14,000. They seem to be offering 40 or 50 percent more than a year ago. I don't know what they offered Lilly, but I know what we offered. He will be getting as much as most any lineman. I think NFL teams are going to have problems when word gets out that some rookies are making as much or more than proven stars."

The Cowboys were euphoric about locking up their first outstanding young college player. "Needless to say, we're thrilled to have a player of his caliber," Landry told reporters.

Now the pressure was really on Lamar. He *had* to sign Holub. If the Cowboys landed both, the Texans might as well leave Dallas.

The Cowboys had been wining and dining Holub in Palo Alto, where the players were staying, and felt they were close to landing him. Lamar put the heavy rush on. He went to dinner with Holub, Rankin, and Beaver, and then the four went back to their hotel by the Stanford campus. Holub's room had a porch with a swing and two chairs on it. The four men sat outside and talked until well after midnight. Holub wanted specifics, asking what the Texans were offering. Lamar talked in generalities.

Rankin took drastic action. "Lamar, I think it would probably be okay if you went on to your room and got some sleep," he said. His young boss was a wonderful person, but not as adept at closing a deal as Rankin himself, the veteran land man and former Army procurement officer.

Shortly after Lamar left, Rankin and Beaver struck a deal. Sitting on a hotel porch swing in the middle of the night, Holub agreed to sign with the Texans. He had always preferred them, he later admitted, naively believing they were more likely to remain in Dallas than the Cowboys because they had won more games in 1960.

Holub signed on the eve of the Saturday night all-star game. Lamar phoned the Dallas papers to make sure they printed the news. He wanted fans in Dallas to know the Texans could outduel the Cowboys. In fact, with the Hunt Oil land men, Klosterman and Steadman, now on his side, he believed the Texans were readier than ever to do battle.

The Cowboys refused to indulge Lamar's optimism. "We got the guy we wanted," Schramm said — a comment that would look prescient twenty years later when Lilly was inducted into the Pro Football Hall of Fame.

# 13

☆

# "Did you wear mouse ears or a helmet?"

O N OCTOBER 8, 1961, Dallas's pro football war moved to a new battleground — the living rooms of North Texas. For the first time, the TV broadcasts of the teams' games would go head to head on different channels. The Cowboys' game in Minnesota, against the Vikings, would be shown starting at 1:30 PM on channel 4, the CBS affiliate. The Texans' game in Denver, against the Broncos, would kick off an hour later on channel 8, the ABC affiliate.

With the teams on television simultaneously for several hours, fans would have the rare opportunity to sit in their dens and watch both, provided they were perched close enough to their sets to flick between channels. (The TV remote wouldn't become popular for another two decades.) Which team would draw more viewers? That race was drawing less attention than the duel to draw bigger crowds at the Cotton Bowl, widely regarded as a key metric even though both teams were "papering" their houses, rendering any lessons somewhat moot. But the battle to attract TV viewers was just as important. In the future, the ability to lure eyeballs to TV sets would become a crucial skill for teams in all sports as television rights fees developed into a major income source.

Lamar was ahead of that learning curve. In Denver with the Texans, he was mindful of the TV audience back in Dallas. Each viewer was a potential customer, a potential Spur Club member. Perhaps the Texans would pick up some new loyalists today, he thought. They were off to a strong start in their second season, having won two of their first three games. Maybe their game against the Broncos would be more exciting than the Cowboys' game against an expansion team.

The Texans' core was unchanged for the most part from 1960, with Davidson at quarterback, Haynes at running back, Headrick at middle linebacker, and familiar names such as Stover, Spikes, and Burford filling key roles. But there were new faces too. E. J. Holub, the prized rookie, was starting at linebacker and also taking snaps on the offensive line, making him a two-way player — one of pro football's last, it would turn out. Jim Tyrer, the hulking young tackle from Ohio State, also was playing.

One lineup change had been mandated when the Texans lost their long legal battle with the Cowboys over Jimmy Harris. In April 1961, a judge ruled that the veteran cornerback had violated his NFL contract by not giving an NFL team an "option year" when he came out of retirement to play for the Texans in 1960. To his dismay, he was ordered to change leagues and suit up for the Cowboys in 1961.

When Harris joined his new team, some of the Cowboys' hardened veterans gave him a hard time. "How was it over in that Mickey Mouse league? Did you wear mouse ears or a helmet?" one asked. Everyone got a laugh out of that as Harris shrugged. They stopped teasing him soon, but Harris wished he were back with the Texans. (His play would reflect his unhappiness. He would lose his starting job by November and retire again after the season as the only player to suit up on both sides of the battle for Dallas.)

Schramm delighted in disrupting Lamar's plans. The Texans suddenly had a hole in their secondary when Harris changed sides. But the Cowboys helped them fill it. Late in the exhibition season, Stram received a call from Gil Brandt about an undrafted rookie defensive back from Oregon named David Grayson. He had played well for the Cowboys during training camp and the preseason, but Landry thought he was too short, so the Cowboys were cutting him.

Brandt really liked him, though, and wanted to help him get into pro ball.

"Hank, why don't you take this guy? He's a good player, and he's already in town," Brandt said on the phone.

Stram took the call in stride. Although he disliked what the Cowboys represented and rooted for them to lose, he liked Landry, Schramm, and Brandt personally. When they ran into each other around town, they were cordial. Stram knew this wasn't a stunt. He talked to Lamar and Klosterman, and the Texans went ahead and signed Grayson, who, as advertised, came in and immediately earned a starting spot.

For once, the Texans owed the Cowboys thanks.

Wanting to cut costs, Lamar had held training camp in Dallas that summer instead of in Roswell, New Mexico; he had a nice practice facility on Central Expressway, so why not use it? The players were thrilled. It was miserably hot in August, but bunking at SMU's modern campus of brick buildings in the upscale University Park neighborhood was a lot nicer than eating unidentifiable slop and jumping into irrigation ditches at the New Mexico Military Institute.

The Texans had opened the 1961 season with a big game at the Cotton Bowl against the Chargers, who had moved to San Diego after averaging fewer than 12,000 fans per game at the massive Los Angeles Coliseum. Stram hoped for a strong performance against the defending Western Division champs, but the Texans fell flat in a 26–10 loss as Davidson threw four interceptions, all but one tipped by the Chargers' towering defensive line, which included rookies Earl Faison and Ernie Ladd. The crowd, announced at 24,000, was a disappointment.

The Texans rebounded nicely the next week, beating the Raiders, 42–35, in a wild game in Oakland, and then beating the Oilers, the defending league champions, before an announced 28,000 at the Cotton Bowl. The Oilers took an early lead when Billy Cannon took a pass seventy yards for a touchdown, but the Texans dominated after that. With their line cracking open holes, Spikes ran inside for 146 yards and Haynes sped outside for 117 as the Texans won, 26–21.

Now they were in Denver to play the Broncos, who were off to a poor start with just one win in four games. Lamar hoped the game would draw a large viewing audience back in Dallas with the Texans coming off that big win over the Oilers.

Although he was disappointed in his ticket sales, Lamar believed more people were following the Texans than their modest attendance figures suggested. He kept meeting people who knew the names and statistics of the players, yet seldom actually attended the Texans' games. Clearly, Lamar felt, the team's weekly TV broadcasts were enabling them to keep up.

Lamar believed strongly in TV's ability to develop fans. One of the reasons he thought a new league might work was his experience watching the 1958 NFL championship game between the Colts and Giants. That overtime classic had translated magnificently onto the small screen, bringing the hard hits and suspense into his den.

Yes, Major League Baseball was still the "national pastime," but its long-standing hold on the country's sports public was beginning to wane — largely because of TV, Lamar believed. Football was more compelling on the small screen. You could actually see the football, as opposed to a baseball on some sets. For convenient entertainment, it was hard to beat sitting at home and watching a violent, athletic contest that took your breath away.

Lamar had made it a priority to get AFL games on TV as the new league lurched into existence. The more popular networks, CBS and NBC, already had ties with the NFL and weren't interested, but fortunately ABC, the lesser major network, was looking to add sports programming.

Negotiating on behalf of all eight AFL teams, Lamar had agreed to a five-year, $8.5 million contract with ABC before the 1960 season. Each team would get $170,000 from the network in 1960 and slightly more in subsequent years. In exchange, every AFL game would be on ABC. There would be weekly local broadcasts and a national "game of the week." Hours of AFL football would be available to millions of fans across the country on Sunday afternoons.

The NFL's owners were startled, to put it mildly, when AFL teams elected to share their payout from ABC. Each NFL team cut its own TV deal every year. Popular large-market teams such as the Giants and Colts commanded hefty rights fees and didn't want to share with small-market teams such as the Packers, who commanded far less. In 1959, nine NFL teams had contracts with CBS, all individually negotiated, with payouts ranging from a high of $175,000 for the Giants to a low of $75,000 for the Packers. The Colts and Browns had their own mini-network on NBC, which televised a national game featuring one of them every week. The Colts earned a whopping $600,000 a year through this arrangement.

This sizable revenue disparity was feeding a growing competitive imbalance in the NFL. The Packers and other perennial also-rans such as the Cardinals and Steelers didn't have as much money to pay players and, not coincidentally, didn't win as many games. That gap was only going to widen as the war with the AFL drove up the price of talent.

The idea of a league sharing its television revenue had bounced around the fringes of the sports world for a decade. Baseball's outspoken Bill Veeck had once said the game would benefit if teams split their revenues instead of having the lordly Yankees earn five times as much as anyone else. But Veeck was blithely dismissed. The Yankees were too powerful, and the idea smacked of socialism, his fellow owners said.

More recently, Branch Rickey, another iconoclast, had suggested that teams in his proposed third major league share their TV revenue to level the playing field and keep the league balanced. But that league never got off the ground.

The NFL had always resisted sharing television revenue, partly because the "haves" didn't want to share, and also because the owners believed that Congress wouldn't allow them to negotiate as one with a network because that would be an antitrust violation. When Lamar chose that route and pulled it off, Pete Rozelle and the NFL owners took notice. They would never give Lamar credit for the idea, but some now believed that their league could benefit if every team received the same amount from this growing revenue stream. Political strings would have to be pulled, and it would be a task to convince Giants owner Wellington Mara and Colts owner Carroll Rosenbloom to give up some of their TV revenue, supposedly for the good of the league. But the idea was gaining momentum.

Lamar wasn't interested in the revenues TV generated as much as the exposure it provided, both in Dallas and across America. Although the Texans' home games were blacked out in Dallas to encourage fans to come to the Cotton Bowl, the road games were always on, often when the Cowboys were playing at the Cotton Bowl. Fans had to choose between staying home to watch one team and watching another in person.

It was hard to say how that competition was going. But regardless, Lamar was so convinced of TV's power that he had changed his marketing strategy, taking the money that had paid for halftime zoos in 1960 and redirecting it into television ads.

He still pulled his share of stunts to sell tickets, but his eyes were increasingly fixed on the little screen.

Tom Landry wasn't worried about people in Dallas watching on TV on this Sunday. Unlike Lamar, he didn't care that the Cowboys' game in Minnesota started an hour earlier, giving the Cowboys a chance to grab viewers with a strong first-half performance. Landry was only concerned about winning. The Cowboys were playing better early in 1961 than they ever did in 1960. A win would give them three wins and one loss and leave them tied for first place in the Eastern Division.

Such success had been impossible to envision in 1960, but the Cowboys had become more competitive. They had opened the season with their first-ever win, beating the Steelers in Dallas, 27–24, on a last-second field goal by their new kicker, Allen Green, before a crowd of 23,500. Then they beat the Vikings, 21–7, in a matchup of the NFL's two newest teams before 20,500 at the Cotton Bowl, giving them a 2-0 record heading into a game at Cleveland. Although the Browns stuffed them, 25–7, they held up better than when Cleveland destroyed them in 1960 and their mascot crashed into an ambulance.

The Cowboys had undergone substantial changes. The grouchy veterans from the expansion draft were mostly gone, replaced by a younger, more eager group. Landry had cut the older players during training camp at St. Olaf College in Northfield, Minnesota. As they walked up a hill from practice to their castlelike dorm, they were tapped on the shoulder and told to report to Landry with their playbook. The Cowboys no longer needed them. Jerry Tubbs, Dick Bielski, Frank Clarke, and a few others had survived, but not many.

The biggest change was in the offensive backfield. A year earlier, recycled veterans such as L. G. Dupre and Don McIlhenny had handled the ball-carrying duties, but now that job belonged to a pair of promising youngsters, Don Perkins and Amos Marsh. Dupre had been released and McIlhenny relegated to the bench.

Perkins, the former University of New Mexico star who had missed the 1960 season with a broken foot, was a dark-skinned African American with deep-set eyes and a senatorial speaking voice. He had returned for his second season in excellent shape and claimed a starting spot. Although he was just five-foot-ten and 190 pounds, he consistently gained yardage up the middle, hitting holes with his quick first steps.

Marsh, a rookie fullback, was a classic Gil Brandt "find." A brawny handful for tacklers at six-foot-two and 230 pounds, he had focused on track at the University of Oregon, enjoying success as a sprinter; on the football team he had caught just ten passes as a senior wide receiver and had not been selected in either the AFL or NFL drafts. But Brandt signed him, intrigued by his blend of speed and size. When Landry switched him to fullback in training camp, Marsh startled the coaches by blasting through holes for gains.

At quarterback, Don Meredith had progressed enough to share the first-team duties with Eddie LeBaron. Landry shuttled them in and out repeatedly during games, sometimes letting one stay in for several consecutive series, sometimes alternating them from play to play. Their receiving targets included Clarke, Billy Howton, and the two young running backs. Suddenly, the Cowboys had playmakers.

Their defense had a stronger spine after having allowed a staggering 31 points per game in 1960. Bob Lilly, the big rookie, filled one end spot, and Chuck Howley, an athletic young linebacker obtained from the Bears, was starting alongside Tubbs. The secondary was still led by Don Bishop, an agile cornerback who had led the Cowboys in interceptions in 1960, but otherwise the unit was entirely new, featuring Warren Livingston, a rookie cornerback from the University of Arizona; Dick Moegle, a veteran safety (and former star halfback at Rice), whom Brandt had obtained from the Steelers; and Jimmy Harris.

Howley, a former first-round pick, had spent the prior season at home in West Virginia after suffering a broken leg that seemed to have ended his career. He didn't want to go back and play for Halas, so the ever-helpful Papa Bear had handed him to the Cowboys. Howley had already made several big plays in the first three games.

As the Cowboys warmed up in Minnesota, dressed in white pants, white jerseys, and white helmets, the Vikings made noise at the other end of the field. Wearing purple jerseys, the NFL's newest team wanted to exact revenge after losing in Dallas several weeks earlier.

"You better watch out — we're going to clock you," warned running back Hugh McElhenny, the former 49ers star who had come to Minnesota in that team's expansion draft.

The Vikings had already fared far better in their inaugural season than the Cowboys in 1960. They had opened with a home game against the Bears and, in a shocker, won easily, 37–13, as a crowd of 32,236 shouted in disbelief. The win had grabbed the attention of fans throughout the Upper Midwest. Coached by Norm Van Brocklin, who had quarterbacked the Eagles to the NFL title in 1960 and then retired to the sideline, the Vikings were more exciting than the Cowboys, with a lively offense featuring a rookie quarterback named Fran Tarkenton. A third-round draft pick from Georgia, he had thrown four touchdown passes against the Bears in his debut and exhibited a knack for dropping back to pass, tucking the ball under his arm, and scrambling for gains.

Although they had lost twice since their opening win, the Vikings had been ferociously competitive; the week before they had gone into Baltimore and almost upset the Colts before a packed house, leading for much of the game until a fifty-two-yard field goal at the final gun beat them, 34–33.

But despite the Vikings' success, Landry expected to beat them as he spoke to the Cowboys' players before kickoff. They had dominated the Vikings at the Cotton Bowl, and Landry had concocted a special defense for Tarkenton. He was certain it would confuse the young quarterback.

Ever the scholar, Landry didn't exhort his players to go whip those Vikings; he just reminded them to heed what they had worked on in practice during the week. That would carry them to victory, he said calmly.

The crowd of 33,070 cheered excitedly as Allen Green's opening kickoff sailed through the air at Metropolitan Stadium on a warm, cloudy afternoon. The cheers waned when the Vikings' kick returner fumbled and the Cowboys recovered at the 29-yard line.

Perkins ran between the tackles twice, picking up a first down, and then Meredith hit Howton on a timing route in the corner of the end zone; the young quarterback released the ball before Howton cut and turned to look for it, and it sailed right to him. The Cowboys had the lead barely a minute into the game.

Tarkenton hurled a pair of incompletions on his first offensive series when Landry's defense blanketed his favorite receivers — in fact, he wouldn't complete a pass until the final minutes of the first half. After a punt, the Cowboys picked up a pair of first downs with Meredith and LeBaron alternating plays, running on and off the field with plays called by Landry. That drive was halted, but another produced a touchdown in the second quarter, giving the Cowboys a 14–0 lead at halftime.

The Cowboys' defense continued to dominate in the third quarter, with Lilly and Nate Borden pressuring Tarkenton from the edges of the line and Tubbs and Howley blitzing unexpectedly. The Dallas offense sputtered but benefited from good fortune. LeBaron threw a sideline route that should have been intercepted at midfield, but the Minnesota cornerback dropped the ball, and four plays later LeBaron hit Clarke on a crossing route for a twenty-three-yard score.

Desperate to get going, Tarkenton forced a pass into heavy coverage and was intercepted by Don Bishop near midfield. Clarke ran a streak route, straight ahead at full speed, and Meredith hit him as he broke past the safety. The fifty-two-yard scoring play gave Dallas a 28–0 lead. Ten minutes remained, but many fans were filing out of the stadium. This game had been a profound disappointment.

When Jimmy Harris intercepted Tarkenton, Van Brocklin pulled the rookie in favor of George Shaw, a veteran who had come to Minnesota in the expansion draft. But Harris also intercepted him, and the Cowboys ran out the clock on their most lopsided triumph ever.

The players saluted Landry in the locker room, ascribing the victory to his masterful defensive plan. The coach was still a hot topic on the flight home that evening. After takeoff, a group of players gathered in the galley to drink beer and discuss their success. They were tied for first in the NFL's Eastern Division.

"Nobody knows more about football than Tom. It's uncanny how much he knows," Dick Bielski told the group, which included Gary

Cartwright of the *Morning News*. "There was one game where he stood on the sideline and called five straight plays the other team ran. He named them right on the nose. Maybe he ought to suit up again and get on the field and tell the other ten guys what is coming."

Bielski paused, smiled at a thought, and shook his head as he continued: "If we could absorb just 75 percent of what he says in practice during the week, we wouldn't lose a game."

As Lamar and Bob Howsam, owner of the Broncos, chatted before their game in Denver, both nervously eyed the stands at Bears Stadium, the minor league baseball park where the Broncos played. The sun had shone in Denver all week, and Howsam had predicted more than 20,000 fans would attend his team's home opener. But the weather had turned nasty on Sunday, the temperature falling into the low forties as rain fell intermittently. Lamar could see the crowd was going to be small.

It was disappointing, but not surprising. There were several budding success stories across the AFL — Houston averaged 25,000 fans per game, and the Chargers fared almost that well in San Diego — but the Denver and Oakland franchises were struggling, Oakland averaging just 8,000 a game and Denver doing little better.

Privately, the Denver players wondered if fans didn't want to support them because of their hideous uniforms. The Broncos wore mustard-colored jerseys, brown pants, brown helmets, and hideous socks with vertical brown-and-mustard stripes. They were almost ashamed to be seen in public. At the end of the season, they would burn their socks in a public bonfire.

Lamar had known that some franchises would fare better than others. He always preached patience to Howsam, Bud Adams, and the other owners. If they were doing well, terrific, but if not, it wasn't surprising for new teams in a new league to need time to mature. Just hang in there, he said, and remember, television is bringing our games to more people than it appears. There's reason to think those viewers will become customers, Lamar said.

As Jack Spikes's opening kickoff sailed into the gray sky, Lamar envisioned what Dallas viewers would see if the Texans beat the Broncos. Their record would improve to three wins and one loss, keeping them near the top of the Western Division. That was a nice advertisement. Maybe their next game at the Cotton Bowl would draw more fans. That would be a welcome change.

From the outset, the Texans were in control of the game. It almost seemed like the small crowd depressed Denver's players. Playing in those awful socks certainly did. And the Broncos just weren't much of a squad. They had won only five of eighteen games in their brief history, lacking offensive consistency and defensive mettle. They could score with quarterback Frank Tripucka throwing passes all over the field, but they seldom did enough right to win.

In a coincidence only viewers of both games could have noticed, the Texans recovered a fumble on the opening kickoff precisely one hour after the Cowboys recovered a fumble on the opening kickoff of *their* game. On the Texans' sideline, Hank Stram turned and shouted for the offense to get onto the field.

Cotton Davidson called the huddle together and ordered a pitch to Abner Haynes running right. The Texans had stuck to their ground game the week before and run up record yardage totals, so why stop now? The offensive line, led by guard Billy Krisher, an All-AFL selection in 1960, seemed on top of its game. Jerry Cornelison had come on strong at right tackle, and Jon Gilliam, an unheralded 240-pound rookie, was the new starting center. The Texans had signed him away from the Packers.

Two runs by Haynes and a pass interference penalty moved the ball to the 1, and backup fullback Bo Dickinson, playing because Spikes had a shoulder injury, blasted into the end zone. The score remained 6–0 when Spikes's extra point was blocked by Wahoo McDaniel, the full-blooded Choctaw-Chickasaw Indian who had been in the Cowboys' first training camp before being cut. He was now a linebacker for the Broncos.

Tripucka tried to match the score, but an interception returned the ball to the Texans. After the offense went nowhere, Spikes booted a twenty-one-yard field goal for a 9–0 lead.

It turned out that Denver coach Frank Filchock had spent the week installing a new offense, which the *Times Herald*'s Bud Shrake would characterize as a "Canadian-brand double-wing, unbalanced line, fly-back extravaganza." Filchock had tired of trying to win with an all-out passing attack, so he was trying something new. His timing wasn't great — the crowd at the home opener had hoped to see fireworks — but Denver's offense stumbled through the first half as Filchock shuttled Tripucka and another quarterback in and out, hoping one would provide a spark. The fans began to boo; sitting in the rain, they were feeling cranky.

In the second quarter, the Texans went on a long drive. Stram's strategy was simple — cram it down Denver's throat. Haynes ran left and right with pitches, as did Frank Jackson, a rookie halfback from SMU. Dickinson slammed up the middle.

Haynes, who led the AFL in rushing, delivered the big play. He swept around left end, cut back toward the middle of the field, and weaved through the secondary, picking up sixty-four yards by the time he was brought down at the Denver 11. A clipping penalty moved the ball back fifteen yards, but the Texans soon made that up. On first down at the 24, Davidson appeared to hand off to Dickinson, drawing the defense up, but Davidson pulled the ball back and looked upfield. Chris Burford was open near the goal line, having shed his defender. Davidson hurled the ball at him, and Burford grabbed it and stepped into the end zone.

The Texans led 16–0 at halftime and continued to dominate in the third quarter, controlling the ball for all but six plays as their offense moved steadily. A pair of fumbles kept them from adding points, but the Broncos couldn't rally without the ball.

Finally, in the fourth quarter, Filchock scrapped his new offense and ordered Tripucka to start flinging passes again. The Broncos immediately drove eighty yards to a touchdown, then intercepted a Davidson pass and scored again on a twenty-six-yard pass from Tripucka to Lionel Taylor. The Broncos went for two points and failed after both touchdowns, leaving them seven points behind.

The small crowd cheered for Denver's defense to make a stand, but the Texans ran out the clock with handoffs to Haynes, who finished with 139 yards rushing. Final score: Dallas 19, Denver 12.

As the players showered and dressed for their flight back to Dallas, Lamar stood with Stram in a corner of the locker room, discussing the game. Stram jabbed his finger at a piece of paper with the game stats. Davidson had attempted seventeen passes and completed just five. The veteran quarterback was struggling. He had misfired on 60 percent of his passes through four games. The Texans were winning because of Haynes and the ground game, but they would need a better passing game.

Wearing his red blazer and a dark tie loosened at his collar, Lamar nodded, acknowledging the team might have an issue if Davidson didn't pull himself together. But he didn't let that prospect ruin his mood. The Texans had put on a good show for the TV audience back home. Haynes, the homegrown star, had been at his best, dodging tacklers and breaking long gains. The Chargers had won the night before to remain unbeaten, but the Texans, with three wins and a defeat, were right behind them.

Lamar wondered whether the Texans or Cowboys had drawn the larger viewing audience. Both teams had won. Both had winning records. Although there was a method for measuring TV audiences, Lamar doubted its accuracy. No one would know which team had won their square-off. Only in time, as they continued to battle for fans, would it become clear which was doing a better job of invading dens across North Texas and becoming a topic of conversation.

# 14

★

# "They shouldn't be able to do this to us"

EDDIE LeBARON ROLLED to his right, looking for Billy Howton or Jim Doran in the end zone. The New York Giants' defensive backs scrambled to cover them. The crowd of 41,000 screeched, generating an ear-rattling din that had often been heard at the Cotton Bowl on Saturday afternoons, but never on a Sunday.

The five-foot-seven LeBaron kept rolling with his arm cocked, surveying the receivers and defenders zigzagging in front of him, the dark-shirted Cowboys trying to escape as the white-shirted Giants clutched and grabbed them. It was an electric moment for the home team, startlingly rich in potential. The date was October 15, 1961. The Cowboys trailed by a touchdown early in the third quarter. They were looking to tie the Giants. First place in the Eastern Division was on the line. Could it be that Landry's team, in just its second year, really was ready to compete with the big boys?

Their fast start (three wins in four games), the Giants' visit, and a golden October afternoon in North Texas had helped lure their largest crowd ever to the Cotton Bowl. "There was even a traffic jam before the game," one sportswriter wrote. Then the Cowboys jumped out to an early lead when Don Meredith hurled a touchdown pass.

But the savvy Giants responded. With Kyle Rote and Alex Webster leading the offense, the Giants tied the score before halftime and went ahead in the third quarter when Webster bulled into the end zone on a short run, completing a drive prolonged by a fake punt. The big crowd fell silent.

Suddenly, though, as if insulted by the quiet, the Cowboys awakened near the end of the third quarter. With LeBaron and Meredith shuttling in and out, the offense moved across midfield. Perkins ran behind the left guard for six yards and charged up the middle for eight. Meredith found Doran eluding a linebacker and hit him for eleven. LeBaron hit Howton on a square-out for thirteen, moving the ball near the end zone. This was impressive. The Cowboys were rising up, showing fortitude, an inner spark they had seldom exhibited.

As LeBaron rolled right and looked to throw, Landry watched from the sideline, Schramm from the press box, and Murchison from his prime seat in the lower bowl. It was hard for them not to consider what hung in the balance. If LeBaron threw a touchdown, the game would be up for grabs, tied with twenty minutes left. The Cowboys might come of age and do away with Lamar Hunt's Texans in a single afternoon. If beating the Giants to jump into first place before 41,000 fans didn't signify that Dallas belonged to the Cowboys and the NFL, nothing would.

With the Giants' hulking defensive end Jim Katcavage on his heels, LeBaron saw Howton pivot in the corner of the end zone and break open. Just before he reached the sideline, the little quarterback released the ball. It spiraled toward Howton amid the din.

And then everything fell apart. The rally, the Cowboys' early-season momentum, and their prospects for taking over the town — all flitted away.

Erich Barnes, a young Giants cornerback, read LeBaron's mind and stepped into the ball's line of flight. It never reached Howton. Barnes grabbed it a yard into the end zone.

As the cheers subsided, Barnes weighed his options. He could down the ball for a touchback, giving the Giants' offense a first down at the 20. Or he could run the ball out.

He elected to run. At the moment when he had to decide, no Cowboy was near him. So he took off.

A third-year player, Barnes was known as a hard hitter, but he had

been a sprinter on the track team at Purdue. He started to run, crossing the 5-yard line, then the 10. Expecting Cowboys to pursue him, he
didn't accelerate to his highest gear, thinking he would soon be dodging tacklers. But none came. LeBaron was sprawled on the ground
after a shove from Katcavage. The receivers were in the middle of the
field. The linemen weren't quick enough to catch him.

Barnes crossed the 20, 25, 30. He looked around and finally saw a
Cowboy coming toward him — Don Perkins, angling across the field at
full speed as he sought to blunt the unfolding disaster. Barnes sped up,
his legs churning faster. He crossed the 30, 35, 40. Perkins didn't have
enough of an angle to catch him. Barnes passed midfield and crossed
into Dallas territory with no Cowboy near him.

The stunned fans watched with blank expressions, their exhilara-
tion having instantly morphed into a nightmare. Instead of scoring to
tie the Giants, the Cowboys were going to fall two touchdowns behind.
It was a staggering reversal.

Barnes practically skipped toward the end zone, crossing the 30, the
20, the 10. In the coming days, statisticians at the NFL offices in New
York would review film of the play, seeking to determine just how far
he had run with the ball. It would go into the books at 102 yards, the
longest interception return in league history.

To say it deflated the Cowboys would be understating its effect. It
crushed the Cowboys.

They probably would have fallen back to earth soon anyway, given
their youth and inexperience. But the process sped up exponentially
after Barnes's big play.

The Giants went on to win that afternoon, 31–10, scoring another
touchdown in the fourth quarter as the Cowboys lost all enthusiasm
and LeBaron threw another interception, his third.

"Of all the games we've played, this was the most disappointing,"
Landry said. "We knew the Giants well. When the game started, we
became optimistic. If we don't make mistakes at the wrong time, we're
right with them. But we made those mistakes, too many."

The next week, 25,000 fans returned to the Cotton Bowl to see them
play the Eagles, who had beaten the Packers in the league title game
nine months earlier. The Cowboys were emotionally flat, lacking the
toughness and playmaking verve they had exhibited the week before

until Barnes's interception. The Eagles scored twenty-two points before the Cowboys reached the end zone.

In the final moments of a 43–7 defeat, safety Dicky Moegle sat on
the Dallas bench, shaking his head. "I can't believe it. They shouldn't
be able to do this to us," he lamented. Most of the fans had departed,
leaving the Cotton Bowl virtually empty. Murchison, standing with reporters as the game ended, smiled and shrugged. "I guess it's a moral
defeat. Any team that can beat Green Bay can probably beat us," he
said.

The loss left the Cowboys with three wins and three losses heading
into a rematch with the Giants in New York. "No matter what happens,
I'm really proud of what you've accomplished this year," Landry told
his players. It sounded as if he feared the worst, but as 65,000 fans
watched at Yankee Stadium on a cool, windy afternoon, the Cowboys
battled the Giants evenly.

There was a reason why Landry's new team played his former team
so well. He knew the Giants' personnel and tendencies. The Cowboys
went up by two touchdowns before the Giants rallied to lead by two
points in the fourth quarter. A long pass from LeBaron to Howton put
the Cowboys in scoring range, and Allen Green booted a thirty-two-
yard field goal with two minutes left to put Dallas ahead, 17–16. When
the Cowboys' Don Healy, a 280-pound defensive tackle, tipped a pass
at the line and intercepted it to end a final New York drive, the Cowboys celebrated an unexpected victory.

But the uplifting result proved to be a tease. The decline that started
with Erich Barnes's interception not only reappeared but accelerated.
The Cowboys lost their next two games, including a 37–7 battering in
Pittsburgh, and tied the Redskins at the Cotton Bowl — a result even
worse than a defeat, as the Redskins had not won all season, George
Preston Marshall's stubborn refusal to use African American players
having left them plainly outmanned. A crowd of 23,000 watched the
28–28 game, during which Meredith suffered a separated shoulder
and was lost for the rest of the season.

In a desultory final month, the Cowboys lost to the Eagles, Browns,
Cardinals, and Redskins to finish the season with a record of four wins,
nine losses, and a tie. Palpably coming apart, Landry's defense reverted
to its 1960 form, allowing more than thirty points in each game.

Landry's mood darkened with each defeat. He barely spoke to reporters after the team's grim season-ending loss to the Redskins on a thirty-degree afternoon in Washington. The pitiful Redskins had played twenty-three straight games without recording a victory, but the Cowboys let a veteran back named Dick James run wild, scoring four touchdowns.

Flying back to Dallas, Landry reflected that the season hadn't been entirely wasted — at least he had found a star runner. Don Perkins had gained 815 yards on the ground during the season, repeatedly blasting through the line for gains despite mediocre blocking. He would finish second in the league's Rookie of the Year balloting behind Bears tight end Mike Ditka. Cowboys center Mike Connelly likened Perkins to "a guy running through a straw fence — he hits it and straw goes flying everywhere."

But even Perkins had done little in the season finale as the Redskins' defense, which had allowed fifty-three points to the Giants a few weeks earlier, seemed a step ahead of Landry's offense.

The day's most entertaining moments took place at halftime. Marshall had arranged for an elaborate holiday "spectacular" featuring a band, chorus, floats, and Santa Claus. Murchison sought to upstage it. The Cowboys' owner loved pulling pranks on Marshall, as when he bought the rights to "Hail to the Redskins," Marshall's beloved fight song. Now Murchison had an even more elaborate stunt planned. As the owner watched from the stands, his friend Bob Thompson, the same Washington lawyer who had slyly purchased the fight song, sought to unleash three crates of chickens on the field while the band played.

Thompson had sneaked the poultry into the stadium by convincing a security guard that they were part of the halftime show, but a supervisor sniffed out the ruse and locked up the crates. The Redskins were furious when they discovered what had happened. "It wasn't funny, and it could have been disastrous," their general manager said. "We might have had to forfeit if the field had become unplayable."

LeBaron tried to rally the Cowboys, throwing a pair of touchdown passes, but James and rookie quarterback Norm Snead kept the Redskins ahead as they secured their first victory in fifteen months. The Dallas papers focused on the halftime controversy. The Cowboys'

34–24 defeat "was kind of an anticlimax," Blackie Sherrod wrote. Live chickens and a foiled halftime plot were a lot more fun to write about than the depressing ending to the Cowboys' once-promising season.

As the Texans fell further behind the Chargers before a packed house of 33,000 fans at Balboa Stadium in San Diego on November 19, 1961, Lamar experienced deep conflict. Sitting in the stands in the sunny cool of an autumn afternoon in Southern California, he didn't know whether to be happy or sad.

The Chargers were an exceptional team, the best the AFL had produced in its brief history. They had won ten straight games without a loss heading into this contest, and now, wearing their power-blue home jerseys with gold lightning bolts on the shoulders, they were beating the Texans with ease. Quarterback Jack Kemp and receiver Dave Kocourek had hooked up on a long touchdown pass to set the tone, and defensive linemen Paul Faison and Ernie Ladd had harassed Cotton Davidson into a pair of interceptions. The halftime score was 17–0.

From the outset of the AFL's existence, the league's unstated but overarching goal had been to develop teams that measured up to the NFL's more established squads, and the Chargers seemingly had pulled it off in two years. Thanks to sharp scouts such as Don Klosterman, now working for Lamar, and a feisty assistant coach named Al Davis, the Chargers had assembled a team that surely could compete in the NFL — not that the older league would admit it. Ladd and Faison were dominating in the interior. Paul Lowe, a young runner, was as speedy as any NFL back. All three were African Americans, as were a handful of other Chargers. Kemp was solid under center, Kocourek a sure-handed all-league end.

A debate about the Chargers had erupted among football experts as the team sprinted from September to November without losing. *Sports Illustrated*'s Tex Maule expressed doubts about the fledgling league in his magazine, but Otto Graham, the quarterback who had led the Cleveland Browns to seven league championships, was impressed.

"The Chargers could make a fine showing in the NFL right now," Graham said.

What about the AFL as a whole?

"It's not as strong defensively as the NFL, but that aspect of the game takes time to develop," Graham said. "There's talent on offense, a lot of scoring, which the fans enjoy. If they can last a few more years, they'll make it."

Lamar was encouraged by Graham's assessment and excited to see the Chargers being embraced in San Diego. Their shift from Los Angeles, where few fans had cared, looked like the best move the AFL had made. Fans in San Diego relished having a team, especially a winner. They were filling the stands at the Chargers' oval stadium near downtown. It was a huge step in the right direction for the league.

But Lamar couldn't enjoy the celebratory atmosphere in the stadium on this Sunday. The team on the wrong end of the score was his, and unfortunately, losing had become the Texans' nasty habit. After starting the season promisingly, they had lost five straight games. This would be their sixth. Their season was in ruins. No one thought they could compete in the NFL.

Stram, worried that Lamar thought the coaching was the problem, believed the ax was falling when Lamar summoned him for a conversation after the fifth straight loss. Stram entered Lamar's office cautiously, fearing the worst, already thinking about what other coaching jobs he might be able to land. But it turned out that Lamar merely wanted to discuss several players.

"So you're not firing me?" Stram sputtered.

Lamar looked surprised. "Absolutely not, Hank," he said.

Some of the team's problems were easy to pinpoint. Davidson was struggling, throwing too many interceptions, completing less than half of his pass attempts. His arm just wasn't that accurate. Abner Haynes was having another strong season, but the Texans lacked offensive balance. That had cost them repeatedly.

They also had experienced some bad luck. Of their five straight (going on six) losses, most had been by small margins, in games decided late.

At Buffalo, they had fallen behind by seventeen points early, then rallied to within three and forced a punt, which gave them a chance to take the lead in the fourth quarter. Haynes returned the punt six yards before being tackled, leaving the ball on the ground as he rose. Inexplicably, a referee ruled that he had fumbled and gave the ball to the Bills, who quickly drove to a touchdown. Furious, Haynes returned the ensuing kickoff for a touchdown, but the Bills held on to win.

The next week the Oilers dealt the Texans a lesson in humility. If they had previously thought they rated with the AFL's better teams, they knew now that they didn't. Avenging a defeat at the Cotton Bowl in September, Bud Adams's team stomped Lamar's, 38–7, before a sell-out crowd at Jeppesen Stadium in Houston. Haynes was roughed up, and the Oilers' George Blanda and Billy Cannon made play after play. When Stram pulled Davidson, the veteran had missed on fifteen of twenty-one passes.

Returning to Dallas to play Boston the next week, Lamar resorted to his bag of tricks to try to boost the gate, announcing that there would be an "exploding scoreboard" with pyrotechnics greeting each score. But the promotion was a bust. In the wake of the brutal loss in Houston, the game drew a sparse crowd, announced at 14,000 but actually far smaller. And the exploding scoreboard turned out to be nothing more than a line of Army mortars buried in a picnic ground outside the stadium. Set off after every score, they "didn't inspire either team but almost made South Dallas surrender," Gary Cartwright wrote.

As for the game, the Texans fell behind when their forty-one-year-old kicker, Ben Agajanian, missed three field goal attempts. (Agajanian and Jack Spikes would convert just seven of twenty-four attempts during the course of the season.) Stram briefly pulled Davidson in the first half, but put him back in when backup Randy Duncan fared no better. Davidson threw for a pair of scores to give the Texans a 17–7 lead, seemingly locking up the win as the fourth-quarter clock wound down. But the Patriots drew close with a touchdown and two-point conversion, then won the game on a field goal as time expired.

As the Texans' fans filed quietly out of the Cotton Bowl, Lamar's mortars fired one final time, a depressing and forlorn sound.

Now, after two more losses had stretched their losing streak to five, the Chargers were pummeling them in California. Down by seventeen at the half, the Texans briefly fought back in the third quarter when Haynes ran for twenty-six yards, Burford caught a pass on the sideline for thirteen, and Davidson finished off the drive with a one-yard quarterback sneak. But the rally didn't last. The Chargers drove back to midfield, and Kemp lobbed a long touchdown pass. The fans roared, a band played, and the Chargers celebrated on their sideline, knowing their eleventh straight win was locked up.

On the flight back to Dallas that evening, Lamar reviewed his team's depressing circumstances. The Texans' record stood at three wins and seven losses. Fans in Dallas were being driven away from the Cotton Bowl, not drawn to it. And Lamar had again backloaded his schedule with home games in the final month, thinking a team in contention for a division title would be a draw. But the crowds would be paltry. Lamar would have to give away tickets to get anyone to come. If he had learned anything in two years of running a team in Dallas, it was that fans there wouldn't support a losing team.

This was no way to win the war with the Cowboys. When Lamar looked around the AFL, he saw budding success stories. The Chargers and Oilers had winning teams and growing fan bases. The Buffalo Bills were developing a constituency in western New York, averaging almost 20,000 fans a game. But his league was taking off without his own team. The Texans were piling up losses on and off the field.

Lamar always preached patience to his fellow owners, but if the Texans experienced another season like this, his own patience with Dallas might run out.

The AFL held a clandestine draft by phone in November 1961, seeking an advantage in the looming "signing season." The college coaches' association had asked both leagues to delay their drafts until December because they didn't want scouts crawling around campuses with contracts in hand during the season, as had been the case the year before. But AFL teams, anxious to get a head start, selected six players apiece during a private conference call around Thanksgiving.

The Texans' top picks were Ronnie Bull, an All-American fullback from Baylor; Bill Miller, a split end from Miami; and Eddie Wilson, a quarterback from Arizona.

When Gil Brandt heard about the draft from a coach and tipped off the Dallas papers, the college coaches were furious. At first, Lamar and Joe Foss denied that a draft had occurred, but one college coach told the *Times Herald,* "They are L-Y-I-N-G." Lamar and Foss then tried to dismiss the event as a "dry run." Finally, they agreed just to nullify the whole exercise.

Brandt sat back with a satisfied smile. That would teach those guys, he thought. But it didn't. While the AFL was embarrassed, its owners privately agreed that their "nullified" selections would still be honored, and as planned, they set out to obtain signatures.

With NFL teams also going all out once they held their draft, another free-for-all ensued. Players still signed with both leagues, content to let the courts decide their future. Salaries took another leap. The Texans lost Ronnie Bull to the Bears, but signed Eddie Wilson and, in a satisfying episode, stole Bill Miller from the Vikings. Miller was in an Arizona hotel suite the Vikings had rented when Lamar reached him by phone and started talking contract terms. Miller abruptly left the suite, took a cab to the airport, flew to Dallas, and signed. Lamar had come a long way as a recruiter and negotiator.

His biggest coup of the year was signing Curtis McClinton, a wingback from the University of Kansas whom the Texans had selected as a "future" a year earlier. A "future" was a player who had eligibility left but could be drafted because his class had been in college for four years. Most had either taken a "redshirt" year because of an injury or, as in McClinton's case, interrupted their college years to serve in the military. Teams in both leagues were drafting such players — the good ones — to obtain their rights even though they wouldn't go pro until they used up their eligibility.

McClinton was six-foot-two, 220 pounds, and had won the Big Eight hurdling title. Klosterman loved his combination of size and athleticism, but so did the Rams, who also drafted him as a future. The Rams went all out to recruit him, flying him to Los Angeles and introducing him to movie stars Sidney Poitier and Paul Robeson. McClinton was impressed but not swayed; a thoughtful young man, he noticed that NFL teams were suiting up few blacks. Meanwhile, Lamar worked on McClinton's mother, a native Texan, meeting with her to sell her on the AFL. She came away impressed. "Son, he's a good man," she told McClinton. That sealed the deal.

Lamar was waiting, contract in hand, after Kansas defeated Rice in the Bluebonnet Bowl in Houston on December 17. McClinton signed with the Texans. His teammate, quarterback John Hadl, also signed with the AFL that evening, right on the 20-yard line, opting for the Chargers over the Lions.

Although the AFL lost top picks such as quarterback Roman Gabriel, defensive tackle Merlin Olsen, and running back Ernie Davis to the NFL, Lamar was excited about his team's young additions. He hoped they would help in 1962. The Texans certainly needed it. They had ended 6-8 in 1961 and, with salaries rising, lost more money in their second season than they did in their first — nearly a million dollars.

The price of playing football in Dallas was going up.

The Cowboys had also lost money, around $600,000, in their second season. Between his original purchase price and two years of losses, Murchison was now $2 million in the hole.

But the Cowboys weren't discouraged. Their booster group totaled more than a thousand members, including many of Dallas's business elite. Their attendance had risen 11 percent in 1961 to a per-game average of 24,571, although that figure included freebies. The team may have collapsed in the final month of the season, but it had made enormous strides overall, going from zero wins to four.

Most important, the Cowboys' revenues were about to jump. Following the AFL's lead, the NFL teams had banded together and signed a collective network television contract for the first time, in January 1962. The Cowboys had earned $150,000 per season in television revenue in their first two years, but that figure would more than double beginning in 1962.

The NFL had actually signed such a deal with CBS before the 1961 season, the large-market owners having come around on the idea that sharing revenues would improve competitiveness and make their product better. But the U.S. Justice Department had nullified the deal, claiming that it violated antitrust laws. The teams had eliminated competition among themselves for television rights, the government said. It had warned the AFL about that in 1960 but never acted. The NFL wasn't so fortunate.

Rather than go to court, Pete Rozelle went to Washington, where the House Judiciary Committee had been debating a "Sports Bill" to exempt pro leagues from antitrust laws when selling their TV rights. Urged by Rozelle, the committee agreed on a bill that also upheld the rights of pro teams to "black out" local broadcasts of home games.

When the bill reached the House floor in September, it generated only a brief discussion. One representative wanted to know if the bill would help the woeful Redskins win a few more games. It quickly passed, and the Senate also passed it a few days later.

Shortly after President John F. Kennedy signed the bill into law in September 1961, the NFL negotiated a two-year, $9.3 million deal with CBS. Each team would receive more than $300,000 annually in 1962 and 1963.

The news was celebrated in the Cowboys' offices. The rise in TV revenue would help stabilize their finances and put them on increasingly solid ground. Although they still depended heavily on ticket sales, they now had a revenue stream that was impervious to wins and losses. Quite simply, they would lose less money. If they could just win a few more games and draw more fans, they might come close to breaking even or — gasp — turning a profit.

While the Cowboys celebrated the news, the Texans cursed it. Although the AFL's original five-year deal with ABC had been a godsend when the league was kicking off, it posed a problem now. The Cowboys' TV revenues were going up while the Texans were stuck with the terms of an old deal providing just $100,000 a year.

The Cowboys also had another financial edge because of the NFL's rule about visiting teams receiving 40 percent of the gate at every game. The Cowboys were struggling to attract paying customers at home, but when they played in Cleveland or New York before 70,000 fans, they came home with their pockets full. The Texans had never played before more than 30,000 paying customers — far fewer usually.

It was becoming difficult for the Texans to compete with the built-in advantages the Cowboys enjoyed as part of the NFL. Both teams were struggling, but one had a surer future.

Murchison had never wavered on his pledge to back the Cowboys until they became winners, no matter the cost. His unflinching stance was intimidating. Meanwhile, the Texans were sinking so far into the red that Lamar sold the lot on North Central Expressway where the team practiced. When an associate of Murchison's bought it, it wasn't a stretch to say that the Texans now leased their practice field from the Cowboys.

Taking in the whole picture early in 1962, Lamar began to believe that the AFL's antitrust suit represented his last chance to knock out the Cowboys. The AFL was seeking not only $10 million in damages but also an injunction halting pro football competition in Dallas. If the AFL won, the Cowboys would have to vacate Dallas at least in 1962 and possibly forever.

According to the lawsuit, the NFL had "monopolized, sought to monopolize and conspired to monopolize the metropolitan areas in which pro football teams could successfully operate, the signing of players, and the sale of television rights." Foss and Lamar had worked on the case for more than two years, and the AFL's lawyers believed they had better than a fifty-fifty shot at winning.

When the trial opened in February 1962 in a U.S. District Court in Baltimore, Maryland, Rozelle stated, "We deny all the material allegations of the complaint." Fully grasping the event's significance, the commissioner had hired one of the nation's top antitrust lawyers to represent the NFL.

Operating without a jury, Judge Roszel C. Thomsen listened to testimony for two months; the trial's transcript would cover almost three thousand pages. Lamar painstakingly recounted his failed effort to bring an NFL team to Dallas, explaining how Halas and Bert Bell had told him the NFL was in no hurry to expand, then reversed course as soon as they knew Lamar was starting a league with a Dallas team.

Lamar, Foss, and other AFL figures pressed their case in media interviews, making strong claims. "We feel we proved conspiracy on the part of the NFL. Can you think of any business reason for the NFL to expand?" Lamar crowed when he finished testifying.

But the NFL's attorneys devastated the AFL's case. They unearthed a 1956 interview with Halas in which he outlined a timetable for expansion in the early sixties — claims he had made to keep Congress off his back. They came in handy now.

Murchison aided the cause. Called to testify in mid-March, he said that Halas had told him in February 1959, before Lamar conceived the AFL, that the NFL would expand to Dallas and Houston in 1961. "Halas was definite about expanding into those two cities," Murchison said.

He also recounted his crucial meeting with Lamar in September 1959, when he offered to share ownership of a Dallas NFL team. "I told him we had known since the first of the year that we would be getting a franchise and asked him to join us," Murchison said, adding that Hunt declined, citing his commitment to the AFL.

On May 21, 1962, Judge Thomsen dismissed the suit with a thirty-seven-page opinion, stating that the NFL obviously didn't monopolize pro football because it hadn't stopped the AFL from getting off the ground. Using research Lamar had provided during the trial, the judge pointed out that the NFL was in less than half of the country's thirty-one metropolitan areas of at least 700,000 residents that could potentially support teams, so it certainly wasn't monopolizing the sport.

Thomsen also denied that the NFL had conspired to put the Texans out of business by having the Cowboys start in 1960 rather than in 1961, writing simply that the NFL had legitimate "business reasons" for moving up the franchise's start date to compete with Lamar's team. Thomsen did note that "interest and attention at both AFL and NFL games in Dallas has been disappointing, and may indicate the city is not as good a location for a professional team as was generally believed."

Rozelle triumphantly called the decision "a complete vindication of the NFL." A smiling Murchison added, "The verdict was the only one I expected. Rather than argue in the press, we argued in the courts."

Lamar was disappointed, fearing his best chance to oust the Cowboys from Dallas had been denied. But ever the optimist, he soon recovered and turned his focus to fielding a winning team in 1962. If the Texans couldn't knock out the Cowboys in court, maybe they could on the field.

# PART IV

# 15

## "Let's beat their asses"

N O ONE WHO WAS present at Murchison's Spanish Cay party in the Bahamas in the spring of 1962 would ever forget the sight of Landry sitting cross-legged under a palm tree on a pristine white beach, intently studying a loose-leaf binder open in his lap.

The rest of the partygoers were in boats just offshore, skiing and fishing under a deep blue sky as Murchison's native staff plied them with rum and coconut drinks — truly a snapshot of the perfect life. But Landry had work to do. He spent the afternoon with his Cowboy playbook.

"To most of us stunned onlookers, it was almost unbelievable that a healthy male animal, in the midst of exotic Eden, would forsake the pleasures of the adventure to concentrate on drab X's and O's. Surely there was time for this in a drearier time and setting," Blackie Sherrod would later write.

Murchison had invited a luminous group to his elegant private retreat for several days of fun: Schramm, Brandt, Landry, Bedford Wynne, Bob Thompson (the lawyer of chicken-plot fame), Pete Rozelle, CBS Sports president Bill MacPhail, Fort Worth newspaper publisher Amon Carter Jr., and Dallas-area sportswriters such as Sherrod and

Gary Cartwright from the *Times Herald,* Bob St. John from the *Morning News,* and Frank Luksa of the *Fort Worth Star-Telegram.*

The basic idea, thinly veiled, was to curry favor with the writers whose papers devoted equal time to the Texans and Cowboys. Maybe they would write more favorably if you showed them a good time. Making a similar attempt that spring, in the downtime between the 1961 and 1962 seasons, Lamar flew a group of scribes to Las Vegas for an evening. "The early sixties were salad days for sportswriters in Dallas," Cartwright later wrote. Murchison, quietly living large in the Texas oil tradition, topped the Vegas junket with his Spanish Cay stag party.

The writers who covered Landry initially feared being around him on Murchison's island, a stately if mildly depraved social setting fueled by alcohol. The coach was a deeply religious straight arrow; this was not his scene. But he had joined in the fun on the first day, participating in a fishing expedition and, ever the teacher, offering tips on how to get out of the water on skis. Murchison, an avid amateur photographer, took photos of him looking relaxed in a white swimsuit and yellow fishing hat, chest bare, fishing rod in hand. Landry even mixed himself a stiff martini that night, surprising the others.

But the next day he let them go out to sea while he focused on his playbook. ("Don't read it; everyone gets killed in the end," Cowboy tight end Pete Gent joked years later.) "As us amateur psychologists learned quickly," Sherrod would write, "this was simply the Landry sanction. The theme. This was his modus operandi. He had relaxed, and now it was time to punch the clock, pay the piper."

This was especially true as the Cowboys' third season neared. Landry believed it was time to unfurl the complex "multiple" offense he had spent the past two years designing. He had shared his long-range vision with Murchison, Schramm, and LeBaron, but refrained from installing the offense because the Cowboys lacked the talent to pull it off, he believed. But now Meredith, in his third season, might be coming of age, and backfield stalwarts such as Don Perkins and Amos Marsh also had been around. The pass-catching corps included Frank Clarke, Billy Howton, and Lee Folkins, a lanky tight end picked up from the Packers. The offensive line had been upgraded with Dale Memmelaar, a guard, and Monte Clark, a tackle, joining Mike Connelly, the center, and Andy Cvercko, a guard.

Landry put it all in motion later that summer at the Cowboys' training camp at Northern Michigan University in Marquette, Michigan. Offensive practices became a blur of feints and surprises. Players went in motion before the snap. The linemen kneeled, then bolted upright for a moment before buckling down into their stances. The process was painful at times, featuring as many mistakes as successes. Landry lost his patience more than once, sternly lecturing the players on the importance of focusing.

The ensuing exhibition season didn't improve anyone's mood. Struggling to adapt, the Cowboys played five games and lost them all, managing just a single touchdown in three of the defeats as their new offense sputtered badly. The Packers pounded them, 31–7. The 49ers crushed them, 26–7. The younger Vikings sent them reeling, 45–26. Some Cowboys grew discouraged, harboring doubts about this "soft" football Landry envisioned. They were running around trying to fool defenses while the other teams were bashing in heads.

As they prepared to open the 1962 season, they feared they might never win a game.


Lenny Dawson was living in Pittsburgh when he signed with the Texans in late June 1962. A month later, the veteran quarterback packed up and drove twelve hundred miles to Dallas for training camp.

Fred Arbanas, the Texans' young tight end, would always remember Dawson pulling up in a convertible at SMU, his windblown dark bangs falling lightly across his forehead. It was as if a Hollywood star had arrived. As a youngster in Detroit, Arbanas had listened to radio broadcasts of Big Ten games when Dawson was an All-American at Purdue.

*Wow,* thought Arbanas, eyes widening, as Dawson grabbed his bags and strode up the steps of the players' dorm at SMU.

But the Dawson who arrived in Dallas was, in fact, a fallen star. He had practically vanished from the football radar since graduating from Purdue and joining the NFL as the Steelers' first-round pick (and fifth overall selection) in the 1957 draft. The four players drafted before him — backs Paul Hornung and Jon Arnett, quarterback John Brodie, and tight end Ron Kramer — were big names now, and the player taken right after him, Jim Brown, was the best back in football. But Dawson had been a bust.

He had sat on the bench for three years in Pittsburgh, his future doomed when the Steelers hired Buddy Parker as their coach and traded for Bobby Layne; Parker and Layne were Texas drinking buddies who had won titles together in Detroit. Dawson was finally traded to Cleveland after the 1959 season, but he continued to sit on the bench, unable to beat out another young quarterback, Milt Plum. After five years in the NFL, he had started just two games.

After the 1961 season, Hank Stram went to Pittsburgh for a coaching clinic and ate lunch with Dawson. As a Purdue assistant a decade earlier, Stram had recruited Dawson out of Massillon, Ohio, convincing him to play for the Boilermakers instead of Ohio State. Then Stram had helped turn Dawson into one of the finest passers in college football history.

Dawson wondered if his former coach could revive his career, and Stram also considered a reunion. "If you ever get released, give me a call," Stram said as they parted.

Like many NFL players, Dawson had given the AFL little respect. His coach in Cleveland, Paul Brown, had disparaged the new league when it started. "Don't pay attention to the AFL. It's not gonna make it," Brown told Cleveland's players. "It's being run by a bunch of rich kids whose parents have a lot of money. They don't know anything about the game. They won't last a year."

But Dawson figured the AFL, now two years old, might represent his last chance to have a decent pro career. He asked Brown for his release, and Brown obliged.

When no teams in either league called him at first, Dawson feared he had fallen so far down the football chain that no one wanted him. But it turned out that late June was when the assistant coaches who monitored the waiver wire were on vacation. The Buffalo Bills and Oakland Raiders soon called. Then Stram called.

Anxious to see what his former coach could do for him, Dawson signed with the Texans. He knew he would have to compete for a job. Cotton Davidson had been the Texans' quarterback since their inception, and the team had used a high draft pick on Arizona's Eddie Wilson. Dawson knew he would have to shine or his career might be over.

As he settled into the Texans' camp, the other players didn't know what to make of him. He was a little older, quiet, and unemotional.

And he was terrible during the first practices under a broiling sun, slow dropping back, slow setting up, slow releasing the ball — as rusty as an old car after five years on NFL benches. His rainbowlike tosses looked almost amateurish compared to the hard line drives Davidson fired at receivers.

Noticing Dawson's struggles, Stram took him aside and worked with him on fundamentals. Dawson's feet sped up, and his passes began to find their targets. Receivers started talking about how easy it was to catch his rainbows.

One of Stram's goals for the 1962 season was to get more dependable play from his quarterback. Davidson ran the offense well, but he had completed just 45 percent of his pass attempts in 1961 and averaged almost two interceptions per game. For Stram, a proponent of the passing game, that was not good enough.

Davidson and Dawson split playing time during the exhibition season as the Texans barnstormed from Lithonia, Georgia, to Midland, Texas. Dawson inched ahead in the exhibition finale, completing thirteen of nineteen passes in a 34–31 loss to the Oilers in Miami, Florida. Stram liked Dawson's accuracy and saw that he could make a range of throws, from deep down the middle to long sideline "outs." He thought Dawson would keep improving. He named Dawson the starter for the regular-season opener against Boston at the Cotton Bowl.

Davidson was disappointed but not shocked; he had almost expected the demotion, knowing Stram and Dawson were close. He resigned himself to contributing as a punter.

The season opener, played on a warm Saturday night, attracted an enthusiastic crowd of 32,000 — one of the Texans' best crowds. Stram drove the team hard in anticipation; the Patriots were a nemesis, having swept the Texans in 1961.

From the outset, it was clear that the Texans had improved, especially offensively. Dawson threw accurate passes to Burford and Bill Miller, a sure-handed rookie. Arbanas, sidelined in 1961 because of a back injury, blocked fiercely and also caught a long pass. Abner Haynes, Jack Spikes, and Frank Jackson, a fleet second-year back from SMU, darted through holes and around tacklers. The team had so many playmakers that Stram had turned Johnny Robinson into a defensive back.

Haynes was almost unstoppable. He opened the game with a short touchdown run and later led a long drive that ended with a scoring pass to Burford. In the second quarter, Haynes swept twenty-five yards for a score around left end. The Texans had a 21–14 lead at halftime and remained ahead as Haynes crossed the goal line twice more in the second half, on a thirty-yard run and a nine-yard pass reception.

In the locker room after the 42–28 win, Haynes, a team cocaptain, held a ball aloft and spoke to the squad. He had rushed for 122 yards and scored four touchdowns.

"Ordinarily, after we win the season opener, we give the game ball to coach," he said, nodding at Stram. "But tonight we want Len Dawson to have it."

Haynes tossed the ball to the new quarterback, who grabbed it, raised it in thanks, and smiled. He had completed sixteen of twenty-three pass attempts for more than two hundred yards without throwing an interception.

"It's the first game ball I've ever gotten," Dawson told reporters as he dressed. "It doesn't seem like I deserve all this. Abner was fantastic, and there were a lot of great catches out there."

Anyone could see that the Texans were better off at quarterback. Even Davidson graciously offered a compliment, saying, "Len played about as well as any quarterback I've ever seen. I'm really happy for him, and for us. I like to see us win."

Two days later, the Texans traded Davidson to Oakland.

The Cowboys' winless exhibition record chilled the public's enthusiasm for the team's third season. Just 15,730 fans came through the Cotton Bowl's new turnstiles for the 1962 season opener against the Redskins. (The turnstiles, which would provide a much more accurate attendance count, had been installed since the Texans announced an estimated crowd of 32,500 for their home opener. Schramm huffed that Lamar probably had drawn half that many.)

Spread around the Cotton Bowl on a sunny afternoon, the fans didn't provide much of a home-field advantage. But they saw an entertaining game.

After the Cowboys scored an early touchdown, the Redskins came back to take the lead. The visitors were suiting up their first African American player, halfback Bobby Mitchell, obtained from the Browns, and he quickly demonstrated what the Redskins, in their ignorance, had been missing all these years. He scored his team's first touchdown on a run and set up another score with a long catch.

But just when it seemed the day might disintegrate, Landry's multiple offense began to roll. As LeBaron and Meredith alternated possessions, the coach's vision came to life on the field. With the Redskins' defense anticipating a run, Clarke sprinted through the secondary into the clear, and Meredith arched a long pass that hit him in stride. He crossed the goal line for a fifty-six-yard score. After halftime, LeBaron and Meredith each led a touchdown drive to put the Cowboys up, 28–14. When Mitchell returned a kickoff for a touchdown, Meredith came right back with another long scoring pass to Clarke.

Many in the small crowd were on their feet. The Cowboys were piling up points! But just when they seemed to have the win wrapped up, they botched it. They let Mitchell get loose again; he caught a short pass and weaved through their defense for an eighty-one-yard score. Then the Redskins made a stop, got the ball back, and drove to a tying touchdown. When a last-second field goal attempt by the Cowboys' Sam Baker flew wide, the game ended in a 35–35 tie.

Landry was disconsolate, eyes cast downward, as he walked off the field. It was encouraging to see his offense take flight, but the Cowboys should have won.

Their burst of offensive excitement generated a slight uptick in their gate the next Sunday — 19,478 came to watch them play the Steelers on another warm, sunny afternoon at the Cotton Bowl. The Cowboys fell behind early, 21–7, but their offense cranked into gear again after halftime. Meredith moved the ball into scoring range with completions to Folkins and Howton, and Perkins burst through a hole up the middle for a touchdown. LeBaron took over on the next possession, which started at the Dallas 1. He retreated into the end zone and hurled the ball far downfield to Clarke, who had maneuvered into the clear near midfield. Clarke grabbed it and raced to the end zone as the fans thundered. A ninety-nine-yard touchdown!

But the cheers waned as fans spotted a referee's flag lying on the ground in the end zone, near where LeBaron had flung the ball — an entire field away from where Clarke had scored. The side judge had spotted Cowboys guard Andy Cvercko holding a Pittsburgh defender.

Not only was the touchdown nullified, but the referee, to the astonishment of both teams and the fans, clasped his hands over his head, awarding a two-point safety to the Steelers.

The normally stoic Landry raced onto the field with his arms in the air, asking for an explanation. This was ridiculous! How could a touchdown for the Cowboys end up as a safety for the Steelers? Emil Heintz, the referee, was ready with an explanation. The rulebook (page 65, to be exact) stated that a safety is awarded "when the offense commits a foul and the spot of enforcement is behind the goal line."

The call was 100 percent correct.

Landry shuffled back to the sideline, shaking his head. "I've been in football for thirty-three years, and I've never heard that one," he said later. Steelers coach Buddy Parker agreed that he had never heard of the rule, "but it was a good time to find out about it."

When the public-address announcer explained that the Steelers were being awarded a safety, the fans began to boo. They didn't care what was in the rule book. This smelled fishy. Their boos cascaded down so loudly that the Steelers couldn't hear Bobby Layne's signals, forcing the officials to halt play when Layne threw up his hands, unable to get off a play. Boos returned every time the Steelers tried to restart the game. The game was delayed fifteen minutes until Layne finally got off a snap.

The Cowboys rallied with two touchdowns in the final twenty minutes, one on a pass from LeBaron to Clarke that was the receiver's fourth score in two games. But the Steelers held on to win, 30–28, and all anyone wanted to talk about afterward was the controversial safety.

In a perverse way, Schramm was happy to see the Cowboys' fans so passionate. That was a first. But to lose a game on such a bizarre call was frustrating, especially when Landry reviewed the play on film, checked the rule book, and admitted the refs had gotten the call right.

As if things weren't tough enough already, the Cowboys were now inventing ways to lose.

Lamar usually stayed out of personnel matters, leaving them to Stram and Klosterman. But he overruled his football experts (for the first and last time, it turned out) to make the Cotton Davidson deal. Stram wanted to keep Davidson, who was a capable backup quarterback and superb punter, but Lamar pulled the trade himself. The Raiders desperately needed a quarterback after Don Heinrich, the former Cowboy, misfired on nineteen of twenty-nine pass attempts in their season-opening defeat. When they dangled their first-round pick in the next draft, Lamar grabbed it.

Coincidentally, the Texans' next game was against the Raiders in Oakland, and Davidson started. The game was played before just 12,500 fans, but also a national television audience on ABC, and the performances of the quarterbacks validated the Texans' decision to go with Dawson. Davidson passed for more than two hundred yards, but also threw four interceptions, while Dawson coolly connected on fifteen of twenty-three attempts, with three going for touchdowns. The Texans won, 26–16. They were off to a good start in 1962.

The Texans knew it was a big game when Sherrill Headrick vomited on the field in the first quarter, right in the huddle. The linebacker they called "Psycho" retched into a locker room toilet before every game, but he only unloaded on the field when the stakes were high.

"Damn, Sherrill!" E. J. Holub shouted as the linebacker spewed into the grass at Nickerson Field at Boston University on the evening of October 12, 1962.

When Headrick finished, he wiped his mouth with his right hand and called the alignment for the next play. Then he looked around the huddle, his eyes glistening in the dim stadium lights. "Let's beat their asses," he said with unnerving calm.

Boston's players and fans were as excited about this game as any in their team's short history. Since losing their opener in Dallas, the Patriots had won three straight, scoring almost forty points per game. Having the Texans in town for a rematch was enough to stoke the fans' passions, but the Patriots' general manager further incited them by suggesting that Lamar handpicked the officials for key games, bringing his own from Dallas when he chose. Although it wasn't true, the infuriating image of a rich, young Texan getting his way sent Boston's fans into a frenzy.

The Patriots had developed a loyal cadre of rowdy supporters in three seasons, and for the first time — and just the second time in AFL history — every ticket was sold in advance of a game. More than

23,000 fans had filed inside the old college stadium when the Texans kicked off on a cool, windy autumn evening in New England.

Boston's fans as well as the Patriots themselves believed they were destined for big things in 1962. Like the Texans, they had found a star quarterback on the NFL's discard pile—thirty-two-year-old Babe Parilli, who had bombed out with the Green Bay Packers but was now tossing a slew of touchdowns to receivers Gino Cappelletti and Jim Colclough. The Patriots had won ten of thirteen games going back to the middle of the previous season, and with their snarling fans stoked for revenge, they expected to pound the Texans.

But Headrick, Holub, and the rest of Dallas's defense were primed for the challenge. The Patriots gained little ground on their first possession as Jerry Mays fended off blocks and held up ball-carriers for Headrick to level. On third down, Dallas's secondary, featuring rookie Bobby Hunt and Cowboy castoff David Grayson at the corners and Robinson at safety, blanketed Parilli's receivers, forcing the quarterback to throw the ball away. That quieted the crowd.

The Patriots' coaches had drawn up a blitzing defense to take Haynes out of the game, and it was effective early; Haynes found little running room. But the Texans scored first after Bobby Hunt recovered a fumble, setting up Dawson and the offense near midfield. With the defense focused on Haynes, Dawson threw to Chris Burford for twenty yards. When the drive stalled, Tommy Brooker, a rookie tight end who could kick, booted a thirty-three-yard field goal.

Parilli tried to get Boston's offense going, but Headrick, seemingly reading the quarterback's mind, roamed the field making stops. Boston's running game was thwarted, and its receivers couldn't get open. In the second quarter, Dawson led a long drive, again hitting Burford as the defense focused on Haynes. Finally, Abner took the ball over the goal line from the 2. After Brooker's extra point, the Texans led, 10–0.

The fans were restless, and their team finally awakened early in the second half. Parilli completed a pass to Cappelletti to move the ball to midfield, then eluded a blitz and tossed to a halfback who slipped away from Holub and sprinted to the end zone.

Down by three, the Patriots seemed to swing the momentum their way when they quickly regained possession. But Headrick slammed a ball-carrier to the turf for no gain on third down, forcing a punt.

Dawson went to work. He passed to Burford for sixteen yards, and when the Patriots finally reshuffled their coverage to account for the receiver, Haynes was left alone when he circled out of the backfield and ran down the right sideline. Dawson, under pressure from a blitz, spotted the lapse and hurled the ball downfield. The crowd groaned when it saw Haynes so open. He grabbed the pass and sprinted to the end zone, completing a sixty-three-yard scoring play.

Dawson then led another time-consuming drive in the fourth quarter, hitting Burford for twenty-nine yards and handing off to Haynes for gains. Using a new power alignment Stram had devised, featuring two tight ends, with Arbanas and Brooker on either end of the line, the Texans controlled the interior and maintained possession for eight minutes. The drive culminated with a field goal by Brooker, putting the Texans ahead, 20–7, with nine minutes to play.

The fans began to leave, grumbling about the game. A few even booed when the Texans' defense stopped Parilli again, forcing another punt. Dawson ran down the clock with short passes and a couple of runs and then, finishing a satisfying night with a flourish, lofted a thirty-yard touchdown pass to Burford on the game's final play. Final score: Texans 27, Patriots 7.

The Texans celebrated in their cramped locker room. They had never played a better game. Bobby Hunt had picked off two passes, the defensive front had stomped Boston's running game, and Smokey Stover had almost knocked out Parilli on a blitz, hitting the quarterback so hard he gave himself a concussion. Meanwhile, Dawson had picked Boston apart, Burford had caught ten passes, and Haynes had delivered the big play. To say they had throttled Boston was an understatement.

"I'm really proud of the guys. They gave an outstanding all-around performance in a tough situation," Stram said.

When you peeled away the layers of the performance, you found Headrick at its core. The maniacal linebacker had played through a broken back, hemorrhoids, and other injuries, but he was just smart and tough on this night, controlling the game as a symphony conductor controls an orchestra, with guile and emotion.

Off the field, he was a bundle of contradictions, a bridge player and a drinker, smart but wild. Without his pads on, he looked too small and slender for pro football. But he anticipated plays, delivered hits, and discouraged opponents. Parilli, who had played against famous NFL tough guys such as Sam Huff and Joe Schmidt, offered him the highest praise. "That guy is as tough and good as any of them," Parilli said.

Headrick was gone from the locker room by the time reporters came looking for him, seeking his response to Parilli's compliment. As usual, he had hurriedly showered, dressed, and hit the door, looking for a bar. The team's charter flight to Dallas didn't leave until the next morning. Headrick would have a hell of a night, happily tipping beers with the Boston fans who had cursed him during the game.

The weather in Denver had already gone from snowy to sunny to rainy that day, and now, as the fourth quarter began at Bears Stadium, sleet was bouncing off the players' helmets. The Texans and Broncos were sliding around the muddy field, taking cartoonish pratfalls as they tried to make plays. It was impossible to distinguish one team's players from the other's. Everyone was caked in the same mud.

The date was November 18, 1962. The Texans had the lead, 10–3, with ten minutes to play, hoping just to escape this miserable situation with a win. But that seemed in doubt after a Denver punt wobbled through the sleet, plopped in the mud, and improbably rolled for fifteen yards, stopping inside the Dallas 10. Len Dawson and the rest of the offense exchanged worried glances in the huddle. They knew they had better not drop the ball and blow this game.

Dawson called a surprise play — a pass to Tommy Brooker, the rookie tight end. The quarterback would fake a handoff in an attempt to draw Denver's defense in as Brooker blocked, released, and headed downfield. The Broncos certainly would not expect the play to go to him.

Brooker had feared a letdown when he joined the Texans for training camp before the season. For a country boy from Demopolis, Alabama, there was no higher honor than playing football for Paul "Bear" Bryant at the University of Alabama, and Brooker had done just that. As a senior, he started on a Crimson Tide team that went undefeated, defeated Arkansas in the Sugar Bowl, and won a national championship. Coming to the Texans as a seventeenth-round draft pick, he was initially unsure if he would make the thirty-three-man squad.

"So you're . . . one of Bear's boys?" Abner Haynes asked as training camp opened. The other players were curious, and Brooker didn't disappoint, playing his way onto the roster. He was a rugged blocker with decent hands, and Stram had put him in play as part of a "double wide" formation with two tight ends; Arbanas lined up outside the tackle on one side, Brooker in the same slot on the other side. The Texans had passed and run effectively out of that all year.

Brooker also made the team because he could kick. Other guys on the roster were penciled in for the job initially, but Durward Pennington, a highly touted rookie from Georgia, missed several field goals and lost the job, and Jack Spikes, the backup, went down with an injury a month into the season. Brooker knew he was taking over when the team went out and bought him a pair of kicking cleats, investing all of twenty dollars.

He had performed his kicking duties pretty well so far. In fact, he had just booted a short attempt through the uprights a few minutes earlier in Denver — no easy thing in this weather — to extend Dallas's lead to 10–3. But now Dawson was calling on him to make a play with his hands, not his feet, in the kind of heavy sleet that seldom fell in Alabama. Brooker took a deep breath, knelt down at the line, dug his hand in the mud, and lunged forward as the ball was snapped. The Denver fans were on their feet, imploring their defense to force a turnover. Brooker took a passing shot at a linebacker, shed the guy, ran into the secondary, turned back, and looked for the ball. Sure enough, here it came. Dawson had found him.

Brooker reeled the ball in and looked ahead. There were no Denver players in front of him. No Denver players anywhere near him, for that matter. Boy, the fake handoff had *really* worked. No one would ever accuse Brooker of having sprinter's speed, but he started to chug and built up some steam. For some reason, no Bronco defenders challenged him. Maybe they all had fallen. He rolled past midfield and headed for the end zone as the sleet-soaked fans fell quiet.

The players on the Dallas bench went wild watching their thick-legged teammate rumble downfield. Brooker crossed the 30, the 20, the 10, palpably slowing down, his lungs on fire, the long run taking its toll. Finally, a defender reached him and slammed into him from behind, sending him stumbling. But he kept his feet long enough to cross the goal line before splashing to the ground with the ball in hand. His slide carried him through the end zone with the defender draped on his back. Touchdown!

It sounded impossible, a ninety-two-yard touchdown pass to Brooker in a sleet storm. But it really had happened.

Brooker slowly rose and trotted to the bench, where his teammates mobbed him, almost laughing more than celebrating. *Way to run, Jesse Owens!* Brooker was in no mood to smile. His lungs felt as if they were about to burst in the thin Rocky Mountain air. A trainer told him to grab some oxygen from the tank on the bench. Brooker walked over, put the cup on his mouth, breathed in deeply, and vomited. Stram saw him doubled over and shouted, "Spikes, you're kicking the extra point."

Brooker needed a few minutes to gather himself, but Denver's return man fumbled the ensuing kickoff, giving the ball back to Dallas.

"Okay, Brooker, get in there!" Stram shouted.

The rookie rose from the bench and put his helmet on as he raced onto the field, his lungs still feeling as if they had been torched. He retched again in the offensive huddle, eliciting snickers. *Hey, Lenny, throw it to Brooker!*

The rookie from Alabama looked around the huddle and smiled. Strangely enough, he had never felt better.

# 16

★

## "We are staying"

NANCY NICHOLS'S CLASS at Arthur Kramer Elementary School
in North Dallas was divided into two groups — kids who cheered
for the Texans and kids who cheered for the Cowboys. Nancy, the
young daughter of the president of the Spur Club, led the cheers for
the Texans.

But while her team certainly was winning more as the 1962 season unfolded, her group was a distinct minority. She was a general in
charge of a small army, with few allies on the playground. The Cowboys
had more support.

Perched in between several desirable neighborhoods, Kramer Elementary attracted the children of affluent families, many of whom
seemed to have allied themselves with the NFL team instead of the
plucky upstart. Nancy had deduced that rich people liked the Cowboys.
And their kids were bullies.

A dedicated loyalist, she took out her frustrations on the tetherball
court, where she ruled with her special shot, an open-palmed topspin
whack that sent the round ball soaring in the air, beyond the reach
of her leaping opponent, as it wrapped the rope around the pole and
brought her closer to victory.

"Texans!" she cried when she hit the ball.

"Cowboys!" her opponents wailed when they hit back.

"Texans!" she cried again.

"Cowboys!" they responded.

Over and over, she slapped the ball to victory in the name of her beloved team. Nothing in the world seemed more important.

The Cowboys fared better as they waded into the heart of their schedule in 1962. After opening with a tie and that bizarre loss to the Steelers, they scored their first victory of the year over the Rams in Los Angeles, then routed the Eagles, 41–19, before 18,645 at the Cotton Bowl, as their multiple offense generated three scores, Marsh returned a kickoff for a touchdown, and Mike Gaechter, a rookie safety who had run track in college, returned an interception 101 yards for a touchdown. The Cowboys now had two wins, two losses, and a tie, and no one could say they were dull.

Their roll continued over the next few weeks. LeBaron, in one of his finest performances, threw five touchdown passes as the Cowboys exacted revenge for the "safety game," beating the Steelers in Pittsburgh, 42–27. Three of the scoring tosses went to Clarke, now regarded as one of the league's most dangerous deep threats. After a close loss at home to the Cardinals, the Cowboys pounded the Redskins in Washington, 38–10, with LeBaron and Meredith each throwing a pair of touchdown passes.

Just as Landry had imagined, opposing defenses were struggling to recognize their keys amid the Cowboys' feints and shifts.

After the win in Washington, they had a record of four wins, three losses, and a tie and had gained more yards and scored more points than any team in the NFL other than Lombardi's undefeated Packers. Next up was a home game against the Giants, who were leading the Eastern Division. A victory by the Cowboys would leave them just a half-game out of first with five to play.

Tickets sold briskly. Customers lined up at the team's box office on North Central Expressway throughout the week leading up to the game. More than 40,000 fans would be coming, and many actually were buying tickets. Dallas, it seemed, was finally discovering its NFL team.

The Cowboys had fared well against the Giants in their brief history, so expectations were high, but as Schramm lamented later, "We sure picked a bad time to stink it up." A lively crowd of 45,000 greeted the opening kickoff, but LeBaron pulled a calf muscle early, so Landry couldn't use the quarterback shuffle. It was left to Meredith to try to beat the Giants, and he stumbled badly, completing just eleven of twenty-seven passes. The Giants rolled to a 41–10 win. The fans left early.

A week later, just 12,692 were at the Cotton Bowl for a game against the Chicago Bears. George Halas was making his first trip to Dallas to face the team he had ushered into existence. On the field before the game, Papa Bear joked with Murchison about the small crowd. Privately, he found it troubling. A franchise should be drawing better in its third year.

A strange game unfolded under a blanket of dark clouds. With LeBaron still unable to play because of the calf injury, Meredith took all the snaps again, and he struggled for much of the day against the Bears' complex defense, failing to see several open receivers. Some fans took to booing the young quarterback, frustrated with his lack of development. But Meredith also tossed three touchdowns, drawing cheers.

Bears quarterback Billy Wade put on a clinic all afternoon, showing what Meredith should aspire to; he passed for almost five hundred yards. The Cowboys still seemed in line for a win when Amos Bullocks dashed seventy-three yards for a score midway through the fourth quarter, putting Dallas up by nine; Meredith audibled at the line on the play, spotting a hole in the defense. But Wade countered with a flurry of completions and the Bears rallied to win, 34–33, on a field goal in the last minute.

Meredith faced reporters with a grim expression after the game. Usually lighthearted in interviews and able to find the humor in almost any situation, he was upset about being booed.

"I can't help it if they want to boo. I do as well as I can. That's all I can do," he said.

Playing the Eagles in Philadelphia the next week, the Cowboys fell three touchdowns behind a struggling team they had routed earlier in the season. With LeBaron still sidelined and Clarke also out with a pulled hamstring, Meredith had his worst game, sailing many passes high and away in a strong wind.

Finally, he drove the offense to the Eagles' 1-yard line late in the second quarter. On first down, he rolled right and had an open path to the end zone, but inexplicably pulled up and fired a pass over receiver Glynn Gregory's head.

"I don't know what I was thinking," he admitted later.

Marsh bulled into the end zone on the next play, saving Meredith embarrassment, but the Cowboys lost, 28–14, in what Landry called "by far our worst performance of the season."

Meredith's mediocre play was a hot topic in Dallas during the week leading up to an early December game against the Browns at the Cotton Bowl. Framing the debate, Blackie Sherrod wrote, "The jury is still out. Usually a quarterback is supposed to 'arrive' in his third season, and a super rookie, as Meredith was painted, might make it in less. But the tall SMUer hasn't set the woods ablaze. He's had his good plays and his bad plays."

Fairly or not, more and more fans saw him as a carefree natural talent who didn't try as hard as he should. "His natural looseness and active sense of humor are sometimes interpreted as carelessness," Sherrod wrote. A national sports magazine had gone so far as to accuse Meredith of nonchalance. The critics "are becoming louder and louder," Sherrod wrote, and the Cowboys are "getting rather touchy on the subject."

Meredith remained mum as the debate swirled. He had enough to worry about as he sought to satisfy Landry and master the coach's complex offense. The truth was that Meredith and Landry were opposites in many respects. Landry was serious about football, a driven perfectionist, while Meredith thought it was just a game, nothing more. Meredith liked to improvise and let his natural talents carry him, while Landry wanted every step orchestrated.

The coach was a straight arrow who taught Sunday school, and the quarterback was a budding hipster who liked a good joke, a good song, and a good beer. That they would clash was almost inevitable.

But their football fates were married, and they shared a desire to see their partnership succeed. Despite Meredith's ups and downs, Landry still saw the potential in his strong arm and nifty touch. And though Landry's micromanaging drove him nuts, Meredith could see the brilliance in the coach's ideas. Meredith was, in the end, a competitor. He wanted to silence the boos, quiet the fears, and, most of all, satisfy his coach.

A Cotton Bowl crowd of 24,226 let Meredith know exactly what it thought of him when he was introduced along with the rest of the starting offense before the Cleveland game on December 2, 1962. A single, angry sound rained down as Meredith jogged from the tunnel to midfield: "Booooo!"

His days of owning the town as a popular All-American seemed a lifetime ago. He was a well-paid pro now, in his third year, and fans wanted him to win games and earn his paycheck. In the minds of many, he wasn't. Never mind that the Cowboys had been exposed in the past month as an inconsistent also-ran lacking talent at many crucial positions other than quarterback. Meredith was the issue, many fans believed.

The fans had few expectations as the game began; the Cowboys had lost four games to Cleveland by a combined eighty-nine points in their history. This wasn't one of Paul Brown's better teams, but it had Jim Brown and a winning record, and that figured to be enough.

From the outset, the Cowboys looked sharper. LeBaron was back to share the quarterbacking duties, and so was Clarke. The first time it touched the ball, the offense drove seventy yards to a field goal, with Perkins and Marsh picking up big gains on the ground and Meredith hitting Folkins on a long pass. After the Browns scored a touchdown, the Cowboys came right back. Perkins gained twenty yards with a screen pass. Marsh ran for eighteen. At the 2, Meredith rolled right and looked to the end zone, reprising the play he had bungled the week before in Philadelphia. This time he spotted Clarke open in the end zone and softly tossed him the ball for a touchdown.

Later in the second quarter, Meredith ran the same play on the goal line yet again and hit Folkins for a touchdown. The Cowboys led at halftime, 17–14, and remarkably, they came out for the second half and blew away the Browns, putting together four touchdown drives. Meredith was nearly perfect, hitting short and long passes and dissecting the defense with audibles at the line. LeBaron was almost as sharp.

When LeBaron hit Clarke for a touchdown early in the fourth quarter, the Cowboys led, 45–14. Boos had been replaced by cheers and standing ovations. Meredith had missed only two pass attempts. The final score was 45–21. On the heels of three straight defeats, the unpredictable Cowboys had played their finest game ever.

"A lot of people around here don't realize it, but people around the league know Dallas has a fine team," Cleveland's Paul Brown said. "This team, with a few lucky stabs, could have gone all the way." (In a shocking move a month later, Brown would be fired by Browns owner Art Modell, who had bought the team the year before. Modell would cite this late-season loss to lowly Dallas as an example of why a change was needed.)

Reporters spoke to a smiling Meredith in the locker room. Asked to explain how he could play so poorly one week and so brilliantly the next, he shrugged and said, "I try to play the same all the time. It'll all come out in the wash, I guess."

Meredith's teammates were delighted to see him give such a strong performance after being criticized. Folkins walked across the locker room to point out to reporters that Meredith had thrown two touchdowns on the same goal-line play he botched in Philadelphia.

"Everyone was down on him last week. He was great today," Folkins said.

No one was tougher on Meredith than his coach, but no one was happier now than Landry. "Meredith has had tremendous pressure on him these past weeks. He has done a good job all the time. The other boys didn't play [well] the last couple of weeks, but they all did today," Landry said.

In the *Times Herald* the next day, sportswriter Frank Boggs wrote that Meredith "very likely drove his hecklers to drink" by "calmly making them eat their boos." In the same paper later that week, sports cartoonist Bob Taylor summed up the situation with a classic sketch, depicting "The Unpredictable Don Meredith Doll," which had a toy key in the side of its head and directions listed below:

Wind it up — and it throws a football over your head . . .
Or wind it up — give it a razzberry and it makes you eat it!
Comes equipped with (1) effigy hanging rope, (2) voodoo sticking
   pins, and (3) a pedestal.

Meredith, who appreciated a good laugh even in trying times, threw his head back and laughed when he saw it.

A week after their snowy win in Denver, the Texans were obliterating the Raiders at the Cotton Bowl. The date was November 25, 1962. Up by two touchdowns early in the third quarter, they were on their way to their third straight victory and ninth in eleven games. They had become the exciting, winning team Lamar had always wanted, and with the Chargers falling off badly because of a quarterback controversy (veteran Jack Kemp or rookie John Hadl?) and injuries to several key players, the Texans were running away with the Western Division title.

A year earlier, Dawson had been on the bench in Cleveland, Curtis McClinton had been at Kansas, and Fred Arbanas had been out with a back injury after being selected in the 1961 draft. (The Texans tried to cut him, but he hired a lawyer who told the team it was obligated to treat his injury.) Now Dawson was throwing passes to Arbanas, Burford, and others, and McClinton had emerged as Abner Haynes's backfield mate. The Texans, quite simply, were loaded.

Dawson mostly handed off to Haynes or McClinton on the team's first offensive possession against the Raiders on this humid November afternoon. Haynes went for six yards around left end, McClinton for nine off right tackle, Haynes for fifteen around right end. Haynes had been devastating defenses for three years, and he was enjoying his best season yet in 1962, but it was McClinton's emergence that had put the Texans over the top, giving them a fearsome one-two punch.

McClinton was four inches taller and forty pounds heavier than Haynes, with sloping shoulders that made him look like a speeding bullet. Haynes had taught him the fundamentals of carrying the ball, how to use blockers and open space, how to square his shoulders and attack defenders. It seemed incredible now that he had mostly blocked for other players at Kansas.

Spikes had immediately seen that McClinton was likely to take the starting fullback job, but Spikes had still helped him learn Stram's playbook. That's what happened on a winning team. And Spikes didn't have to tell McClinton anything twice. The young man was intelligent and worldly, having spent two years in Singapore in the Army Reserves. He planned to attend grad school and get into banking or government.

Spikes had started through the first month of the season, but when he suffered a thigh injury, McClinton stepped in. Now, six weeks later, McClinton was gaining as many yards as Haynes, even more on some Sundays. Haynes was one of the league's most valuable players, but defenses were paying *less* attention to him because McClinton could burn them just as easily.

When the Texans' initial drive reached the Raiders' 5-yard line on this November afternoon, Dawson faked to McClinton, drawing in the linebackers, and rolled right. Arbanas blocked a defensive end, slipped into the secondary, and angled for the corner of the end zone. A safety picked him up, but Dawson's pass led him perfectly. He lunged for the ball, grabbed it, tumbled, and came up holding it high, showing the referees he had possession.

The touchdown catch was Arbanas's fifth of the season. Most coaches in both pro leagues were still using their tight ends primarily as blockers, but a few, including Paul Brown, Halas, and Sid Gillman, were utilizing them as receivers, seeing the advantage of giving their quarterbacks an extra target. Stram certainly had seen the light. Arbanas was big, mobile, and sure-handed, a tough blocker nimble enough to run pass routes. Dawson loved throwing to him, especially near the goal line.

After the Texans' defense stopped the Raiders, Dawson started another drive. The Raiders' defense couldn't match the Texans' speedy personnel. Haynes burst off right guard for seven yards. McClinton ran around left end for eleven. Dawson faked to Haynes, dropped back, and fired a sideline route to Burford for twelve. A twenty-six-yard run by Haynes moved the ball near the end zone, and Dawson sneaked over for a 14–0 lead.

On a drive in the second quarter, Haynes and McClinton alternated big gains and Dawson tossed to Arbanas for another touchdown. The Texans led by fourteen at halftime, and then Haynes took over, leading a pair of drives with twisting, turning runs, putting the ball into the end zone each time himself. The Texans led, 35–7.

Lamar watched with unabashed pride. Although he was worried about the winless Raiders, he was thrilled about his team. The Dallas Texans were damn good. Their offense was dangerous, their defense stout. They were a solid blocking and tackling team, sound and well coached.

But they still weren't attracting many fans.

The crowd for this game against the Raiders was pitiful. The Texans would announce 13,557, their smallest of the season. Fans were sprinkled around the Cotton Bowl's lower tier, leaving vast expanses of the bowl empty — entire sections in some cases. And there was no one in the upper decks. You could fire off a gun up there and not hurt a soul.

Lamar had tried every trick to draw fans in the team's first two seasons, but the Texans had lost too many games. Now they were winning, but the crowds were no better — even worse. Only a few thousand in this meager crowd had actually paid for their tickets.

The game was butting up against a telecast of a Cowboy game in Philadelphia, and as always, some fans surely had elected to stay home and watch the NFL game rather than come to Fair Park and plunk down money. It was the eternal excuse in Dallas's football war, the effect of having another team in town.

Lamar was weary of it. Although he was unconvinced that the Cowboys had more fans — in fact, he knew they didn't — he had to admit the evidence suggested that, as he had feared from the outset, Dallas couldn't support two teams. The Texans still had two home games left on their regular-season schedule, and Lamar hoped crowds would pick up as the Texans kept winning, but deep down he knew nothing would change. The town just wasn't big enough for his team and the Cowboys.

Murchison could barely suppress a giggle on the team charter as it flew toward Washington. The Cowboys' majority owner loved traveling with the team — especially the Saturday nights, when he and his cronies always had fun — but this trip promised to be especially memorable.

Murchison and his friends were always trying to pull pranks on George Preston Marshall. It wasn't a stretch to say that they would try anything after they smuggled chickens into the stadium the year before and almost succeeded in setting them loose on the field at halftime.

Now they were really determined to pull off something as the Cowboys returned to Washington. Decorum prevented Murchison, as a team owner, from leading the operation; he let his cronies handle that clandestinely. But as a top-notch practical joker, he was in on the planning and couldn't wait to see this stunt pulled off.

The failed chicken plot had spawned headlines in Washington, and during the week leading up to the 1962 game, sportswriters speculated about what might unfold. Adding to the drama, a full house of 50,000 fans was expected, as the Redskins were enjoying their best season in more than a decade, and their fans were revved up after watching bad football for so long.

As Marshall's beloved Redskin band played "Hail to the Redskins" before kickoff, four banners were unfurled in the upper deck reading, simply, CHICKENS. Then two men dressed in chicken costumes dashed onto the field, tossing colorful eggs from a sack. Security guards apprehended one, but the other ran around the field during the national anthem, let a live chicken loose out of a sack, and escaped without being caught as Murchison and his friends howled.

When the Cowboys beat the Redskins that day, Murchison flew home experiencing a sense of satisfaction that his other businesses couldn't match. He was having enormous fun. Even after the Cowboys fell into their usual late-season swoon and ended the season with a record of five wins, eight losses, and a tie, he was pleased. The team's record disappointed many fans, but Murchison saw progress. In three seasons, the Cowboys had gone from zero wins to five. Landry and Schramm, his football architects, had taken the pathetic expansion-year Cowboys and remade them into a young, exciting squad. They had beaten the Browns, Eagles, Redskins, and Rams in 1962. It was only a matter of time until they started winning, Murchison believed.

The franchise's bottom line also was improving. The NFL's network television contract with CBS had doubled that revenue stream, and the Cowboys had pocketed 40 percent of the gate after playing before crowds of 62,694 in New York, 58,070 in Philadelphia, 49,888 in Washington, and 44,040 in Cleveland. True, attendance at the Cotton Bowl remained disappointing — the per-game average of 21,781 in 1962 represented an 11 percent decrease from the year before — and that was keeping the team in the red. Murchison had never expected to lose $2.5 million in the first three years, but he didn't mind as long as the future appeared bright.

On the one Sunday when the Cowboys played at home with something on the line — against the Giants at midseason — they had drawn 45,000 fans. The Texans had never drawn nearly that many to any game in 1962, despite enjoying a hugely successful season on the field. They were going to be playing for the AFL championship in late December, but in their last regular-season home game they had drawn fewer than 15,000 fans.

Shortly before Christmas in 1962, Murchison and Lamar sat down separately for interviews with the *Times Herald*. Their answers to the same slate of questions were printed at the end of the regular season in a popular question-and-answer column called "The Witness Stand."

> Q: *Printed estimates claim your team lost $1 million in each of its first two seasons. How accurate is this figure and will it be as high this year?*
> Hunt: Our policy has been to never discuss losses, gains, player salaries, etc. This is not in good taste in any business. I hate to be evasive but our policy will have to remain the same. Our losses this year will be less, substantially less, but I can't give you a figure.
> Murchison: There was a printed report that Dewey beat Truman in 1948. As was that one, this estimate is quite wide of the mark. We have not made a profit but I think we have an excellent chance of doing so next year.
>
> Q: *In terms of your battle with the other side for the fans in Dallas, was there any real test this year?*
> Hunt: Unfortunately we never reached a good test point.
> Murchison: We have never felt that our success depends on what the Texans did but rather upon what we did.
>
> Q: *Will two teams continue to exist in Dallas?*
> Hunt: My personal opinion is that two teams can't thrive here. We're planning on the Texans being here and in operation.
> Murchison: As long as the Texans are here, there will be two teams.

*Q: Would you ever consider moving?*
Hunt: I would have to be blind to say we would never consider moving. We are trying to run this thing as a business, and if someone from another city made an offer which was impossible to refuse, I don't think we would shut our eyes to it.
Murchison: When we have won five consecutive world championships, we may put the team up for bids. However, I am sure Bedford [Wynne], being a real fan, will be the high bidder.

*Q: If the teams played, who would win, and by what score?*
Hunt: I would say, if all things were equal, meaning injuries and that sort of thing, we would win. Two years ago I wrote a letter to Murchison inviting him to play us. I never heard from him. We are willing to play them in an exhibition game next fall, but it is hard to talk to them because they prefer to take the position that we don't exist.
Murchison: I would love to answer, but coach Landry is using my IBM [computer] right now.

It was impossible not to notice the differences in their answers. Lamar took the questions seriously, while Murchison joked. Lamar left open the possibility that he might decide another city was a better place for his team, while Murchison, as had been true from day one, didn't budge.

"We are staying," he told the *Times Herald.*

To Lamar and the Texans, his certitude was intimidating.

# 17

☆

# "We will kick to the clock"

ABNER HAYNES PACED the sideline, fuming as he watched the kickoff sail into the air. *Abner, you fool! How could you do that?*

He had carried the Texans all season—for three seasons, really—but now that they were within reach of a title as the AFL championship game between the Texans and the Houston Oilers moved into sudden-death overtime on December 23, 1962, he had made a gargantuan mistake. He had bungled, of all things, the coin flip. *The coin flip!* It sounded ridiculous. But the Texans just might lose as a result.

The 37,981 fans who had crammed into Jeppesen Stadium sent up peals of noise as the Oilers' offense, led by thirty-five-year-old George Blanda, began overtime at their 34-yard line. The Oilers had won the league title in 1960 and 1961, and now it appeared they might soon add a third. The first team to score would win, and the Oilers not only had the ball first, but also had a stiff wind at their backs. Haynes wondered if the Texans' offense would even get on the field in overtime.

The first half had been played in mild weather conditions, but a classic Texas "blue norther" had rolled in at halftime, sending temperatures plummeting and winds gusting. Dark clouds scudded across the sky, and a siren wailed in the distance. The Weather Service had posted a tornado warning. The Oilers hoped to wrap this thing up quickly, complete a few passes, move into scoring range, and kick a field goal. Having a thirty-mile-per-hour wind at their backs certainly helped.

It was the wind that had caused Abner's confusion at the coin flip. Tied, 17–17, after four quarters, the Texans and Oilers had been forced to play on to decide a winner. While the players rested, Stram counseled Haynes and E. J. Holub, the Texans' captains, on what to do at the midfield coin flip, which would determine which team got the ball first.

With the wind in mind, Stram issued an unusual directive: "If we win the flip, we're going to take the wind rather than the ball."

The team that won the flip usually took the ball, but Stram believed it was more important to have the wind in this situation. He had faith in his defense, believing it could stop Blanda and get the ball to the offense, but he did not trust his punter, Eddie Wilson, a rookie whose per-kick average was not among the AFL's best. The Texans would have field-position problems if the game came down to Wilson kicking into the wind. And of course, if the team needed a field goal to win, Tommy Brooker, the Texans' kicker, would have a better shot with the wind at his back.

The wind was blowing toward the north end of the stadium, the same end where the stadium's clock and scoreboard were located. "If we win the flip, we want to go that way," Stram said, pointing to the clock situated behind the north end zone.

With Stram's orders in mind, Haynes and Holub met at midfield with the Oilers' captains, offensive tackle Al Jamison and defensive end Ed Husmann, the latter an expansion-year Dallas Cowboy now playing in the AFL. Red Bourne, the referee, stood between them with a coin in hand, ready to orchestrate the flip and get overtime going.

Also standing at midfield was a cameraman for ABC, which was televising the game across the country, and Jack Buck, a young reporter who had been relaying dispatches from the sidelines back to play-by-play announcer Curt Gowdy during ABC's broadcast.

The TV audience for the game had swelled during the afternoon as fans across the country came upon it. With Christmas two days away and heavy snow falling in the Northeast, millions of people were nestled at home, looking for entertainment. A championship football game going down to the wire fit the bill. In the coming days, Lamar would be staggered by reports of a television audience of many millions. For the first time, the AFL had elbowed itself to the front of the nation's sporting consciousness. The "little league," as some in the NFL derisively described it, was little no more.

With ABC's on-field camera and Buck's microphone relaying the scene, the coin flip unfolded. Bourne explained to the captains that the teams would play until someone scored, and that if neither scored in fifteen minutes, they would exchange ends and keep going. He then looked at Haynes and Holub and said the Texans, as the visiting team, would get to call the flip.

"You call it while the coin is in the air, and call it loudly now," Bourne said. Then he flipped the coin and barked, "Call it."

Haynes, standing next to Buck and in front of Holub, shouted, "Heads!" Bourne repeated Haynes's call, then inspected the coin lying on the field. "Dallas won the toss," the referee said. "You have your choice, of course, kicking or receiving."

Haynes leaned into Buck's microphone and said, "We will kick to the clock," thinking he had relayed Stram's wishes.

Bourne looked at him. "You're going to kick?" he asked, making sure he had heard correctly.

"Yes," Haynes replied.

"To the clock?" Bourne said.

"Yes," Haynes said.

Bourne turned to the side and gave a kicking motion, signaling the result to the crowd. Holub took off for the bench, thinking the proceedings were over. Buck pulled his microphone away.

But the Oilers' Al Jamison didn't move from midfield. "Mister official, he can't do that," Jamison said.

"Do what?" Bourne asked.

"He can't pick both," Jamison said.

Bourne looked at him.

"They can't decide what to do [kick or receive] and also which side they want," Jamison said.

Immediately realizing Jamison was correct, Bourne asked which end the Oilers wanted to defend. Jamison pointed to the end the Texans had wanted. Bourne never signaled that the Texans would now kick the other way — into the wind. He just told Haynes, Jamison, and Husmann.

The Oilers' captains giddily raced toward their bench, amazed that they would get the ball first and also have the wind at their backs.

"Damn, we've got this game made!" Jamison chirped.

On the other side, Stram was incredulous. How could the Texans have won the toss and ended up kicking into the wind? Jack Buck picked up on the drama, telling Gowdy, "Around that Dallas bench, Curt, they're going crazy, they don't know what's going on."

Gowdy paused, obviously stunned, and then repeated the bare facts, as if to make sure he understood: "They're kicking against the wind."

As word spread on the Texans' bench, Holub, who had been at midfield but left prematurely, stomped around like a bull. "What the hell?! What the hell?!" he shouted.

"I said it, I said what you wanted," Haynes told Stram.

It turned out that Haynes had erred by saying, "We will kick," before stating which goal he wanted to defend. The first half of his reply ("we will kick") became the Texans' choice, rendering the second half of his reply ("to the clock") irrelevant. Once he said the Texans would kick, meaning the Oilers would receive, all the Oilers had to do was pick an end to defend.

Stram shrugged and patted Haynes on the shoulder, consoling his star halfback. "It's okay, Abner, we'll still get them," he said, seeking to remain calm to keep his players' emotions in check. There was nothing anyone could do now anyway.

The crowd cheered when the kickoff teams jogged onto the field and the Oilers' great fortune became apparent. On ABC, Gowdy asked Buck for an update, and Buck replied, "I asked one of the Dallas players what happened, and he said Abner simply made a mistake."

Gowdy repeated the news: "Haynes made a mistake."

Brooker's kickoff was held up by the wind, and the Oilers' Bobby Jancik ran forward, caught the ball, and returned it to the Houston 34. Given that excellent field position, Blanda, who had already thrown for more than two hundred yards, called a play in the huddle and brought his offense to the line. The crowd stood, anticipating a quick knockout.

Haynes implored the Texans' defense to make a stop. "Let's go, guys! Come on, Sherrill!!" he barked.

He glanced around the stadium as the winds buffeted the field and sent hot dog wrappers dipping and dancing, as if possessed by demons. *Damn crazy weather!*

In living rooms across America, millions of football fans went back over the bizarre episode they had just witnessed, repeating a phrase destined for a place in football history: "kick to the clock." Haynes had thought nothing of it when he said it, but it was already haunting him. Back in Dallas, his parents were practically in tears as they heard Gowdy accuse their son of possibly blowing the game.

For most of the day, it had appeared Haynes would be remembered for the right reasons. As usual, he had played brilliantly, finding the end zone twice as the Texans built a 17–0 lead in the first half.

The Texans had reached the championship game after compiling a regular-season record of eleven wins and three losses and easily capturing the Western Division; no other team in the division had finished over .500. Their explosive offense was the key to their success. Len Dawson had passed for almost three thousand yards and twenty-nine touchdowns, emerging as the AFL's most proficient quarterback. Chris Burford had caught forty-five passes, twelve for touchdowns. Curtis McClinton has rushed for more than six hundred yards and would be voted the league's Rookie of the Year, just ahead of Fred Arbanas. Overall, the Texans had scored an astounding fifty touchdowns in fourteen games.

Haynes had been the focal point, as had been the case since the Texans' first game three years earlier. Stram wanted the ball in his hands as often as possible. No one could win a game like Abner. He was durable, productive, versatile, and sure-handed. He had led the AFL yet again with nineteen touchdowns in 1962, rushed for more than a thousand yards, and caught almost forty passes. And his finest attribute was his attitude, Stram believed. Haynes was a wonderful teammate, a true believer in the AFL cause, intensely loyal to the Texans. He would always do what was best for the team.

Knowing that, Stram had approached him before the championship game with an unusual request.

"Can you switch positions?" Stram asked.

"Sure, coach," Haynes quickly replied. "What's going on?"

Burford, the All-Pro end, had gone down with a leg injury late in the season. The Texans had hoped to get him back in time to play in the title game, but it wasn't going to happen. Meanwhile, another injured player, fullback Jack Spikes, finally was healthy again after battling a thigh injury all season. So the Texans had more backs than they needed between Haynes, McClinton, and Spikes, but no dangerous receivers.

Brainstorming, Stram devised the idea of switching Haynes to receiver for the title game. Why not? A terrific athlete and consummate pro, Haynes could do it. He ran great routes and had great hands. The sight of him split wide would send the Oilers into a panic.

Haynes agreed to the idea and practiced for the game as a receiver, with Spikes and McClinton manning the backfield behind Dawson.

On the morning of the game the weather in Houston was cloudy and mild. Several hundred Texans fans had made the trip from Dallas, game tickets in hand, but their cheers would be lost in the stadium. Houston had its sights on a third straight title. The Oilers had started slowly in 1962, falling behind Boston in the East, but seven straight wins to end the regular season had put them back in the title game.

They could match the Texans' firepower with Blanda, Charlie Tolar (a bowling ball of a fullback who had rushed for a thousand yards), Billy Cannon, and receivers Charlie Hennigan and Willard Dewveall — Lamar's former SMU teammate. The Oilers also had more big-game experience. Oddsmakers in Las Vegas favored them by three points.

If the Oilers had a weakness, it was Blanda's habit of taking risks with his passes, throwing into traffic. While he had passed for about as many yards and touchdowns as Dawson during the season, he had thrown forty-two interceptions, a staggering average of three per game. (Dawson, by comparison, had thrown just seventeen.) Blanda was fearless and had a big arm, but that had its downside.

The Oilers had driven into Dallas territory in the first quarter, but when Blanda tried to hit Dewveall in the end zone, Holub stepped in front of the pass, grabbed the ball, and took off the other way. Cutting back and forth, he raced forty-three yards before being tackled near midfield.

Dawson quickly took advantage of having Haynes as a receiver, tossing him the ball on a sideline route for a fifteen-yard gain. Spikes picked up another first down up the middle, and after the Oilers held, Brooker kicked a short field goal to give the Texans a 3–0 lead.

The Oilers drove to the Dallas 40 on the ensuing series, but the Texans held, and Blanda, who also kicked and punted, attempted a forty-seven-yard field goal. When it fell short, the Texans had excellent field position again, taking over at their 40. They moved across midfield and into Houston territory, picking up small chunks at a time on the ground. McClinton slammed into the middle for four yards. Spikes went around left end for three. Haynes, shifting to the backfield for a play, went right for four. A quick pass to Arbanas picked up five.

On second down at the Houston 28, Haynes split wide to the right. When the ball was snapped, he faked inside and slanted out as Dawson rolled right. The pass hit him on his front uniform number, and he reeled in the ball near the sideline. Turning, he quickly cut inside a defender, saw space in front of him, sprinted toward the goal line, sidestepped a defender, and strolled into the end zone, coolly tossing the ball to a referee as he circled back.

"Haynes with the touchdown!" Gowdy shouted on ABC.

The Texans celebrated on their bench as Brooker added the extra point to give them a 10–0 lead. The big crowd had quieted, and it grew even quieter when Blanda tossed another interception, his second of the game, in the second quarter. David Grayson picked it off near midfield, and the Texans, with momentum on their side, drove downfield as Dawson blended runs and short passes. On second down at the Houston 2, Haynes lined up in the backfield, took a handoff, and bulled into the end zone behind tackle Jerry Cornelison. The extra point gave the Texans a 17–0 lead.

It was hard to say who was more surprised, the Oilers or their fans. They had certainly not expected this.

But as the sky darkened, northerly winds began to whip, and the temperature dropped, the Oilers began the second half with resolve and aggressiveness, especially on defense. After sitting back and letting the Texans dominate them in the first half, they started blitzing line-backers on almost every play, disguising who was coming until after the snap, an outside linebacker on one play, the middle linebacker on the next. The strategy worked. The Texans suddenly couldn't move.

McClinton and Spikes had little room to run as linebackers plugged their holes. Dawson was harassed when he tried to pass. His receivers couldn't get open, his pocket collapsed, and he was tackled for losses.

With Blanda leading the way, the Oilers started cutting into the lead. With the wind in their faces, they took the second half kickoff and drove sixty-seven yards to a touchdown, with Blanda blending short, safe passes and handoffs to Tolar. A pass to Dewveall covered the final fifteen yards, and after Blanda's extra point, the Texans led, 17–7.

The score drew the fans back into the game. A din rumbled across the field when Haynes fumbled at the Dallas 20 on the next series and Blanda returned to the field, looking to capitalize. But the Texans' Johnny Robinson read Blanda's eyes and stepped in front of Dewveall on a slant route, intercepting the pass near the goal line.

When the teams switched sides for the fourth quarter, the Oilers had the wind at their backs. The Texans' defense dug in to protect the lead. With Dawson and the offense stymied, it was up to linebacker Sherrill Headrick and the defense to hang on. Blanda came at them relentlessly, probing for openings, desperate for points. Early in the fourth quarter, he led a drive to the Dallas 31 and kicked a field goal to narrow the lead to 17–10.

The fans were on their feet, screaming for the defense to get the ball back. McClinton ran for three yards, Spikes for two. Dawson tried to pass but couldn't find an open receiver and was slammed to the ground for a loss. When Eddie Wilson shanked the punt, giving Houston the ball in Dallas territory, the stadium shook with noise.

Blanda took advantage of the field position, using the wind to sail passes to open receivers. Completions to Dewveall and Cannon moved the ball inside the 20. A run by Tolar pushed it inside the 10. Another pass to Cannon left the Oilers a couple of yards from the end zone, and Tolar bulled through a hole and crossed the goal line. As the Oilers whooped on their sideline and the Texans looked on glumly, Blanda's conversion made it a 17–17 game with five minutes to play.

Fans across the country leaned forward in their chairs, curious to see how this high drama would end. The Oilers had come all the way back and appeared ready to overtake their rivals. Dawson and the Texans' offense tried to get a drive going, but went nowhere yet again, forcing Wilson to punt. Dallas fans wanted to cover their eyes when the rookie swung his leg into the ball. For that matter, so did Stram. The ball sailed crazily into the wind, like a knuckleball from a baseball pitcher, and bounced out of bounds at midfield. Less than a minute remained on the clock.

Blanda completed a pass to Dewveall for a first down, called time-out, and lined up to try a forty-two-yard field goal. Just a few seconds remained. The Oilers would win if Blanda booted the ball through the uprights.

During the time-out, Headrick stood with his hands on his hips, facing the line of scrimmage and the Oilers' huddle. He had never been so disgusted. The Texans had let their big lead slip away, and now they were about to lose. The crowd was screaming. The Oilers were talking animatedly in their huddle. Everything was coming apart.

*Do something,* Headrick told himself. *Don't let this happen.*

The Oilers came to the line and set up, center Bob Schmidt fingering the ball for the snap. Blanda loosened his arms and legs, preparing to kick. Jacky Lee, the Oilers' backup quarterback and holder, knelt down to grab the snap and place the ball down for Blanda. The crowd paused, ready to erupt.

The snap sailed to Lee on a line, and he placed it in the dirt. Blanda moved forward and swung his leg, sending the ball out with a thudding noise. Simultaneously, Headrick burst through the middle of the line, raised his arms, leapt high . . . and deflected the ball before it could sail more than a few feet.

Blocked! The kick was no good!

The crowd fell silent. The Texans erupted on their sideline, mobbing Headrick as he came to the bench. A few moments later, Gowdy leaned into his microphone and told his audience, "That's it. Dallas and Houston are going to overtime to decide the American Football League title."

All Haynes wanted was a chance. *Just get me on the field.* It would devastate him if the Oilers took the overtime kickoff and drove to the winning points with the wind at their backs. Haynes would be responsible, even if he still wasn't sure how he had bungled the coin flip. He couldn't bear the thought of letting down his teammates.

Starting at their 34, the Oilers moved past the 40 on runs by Tolar, and Blanda threw for Dewveall on third down, but David Grayson knocked the ball away. As Haynes exhaled, the Oilers punted. The Texans' offense would have its chance. Haynes, Dawson, and the rest of the unit trotted onto the field. Haynes exhorted his teammates in the huddle, determined to make up for his gaffe. "Let's win this game right now!" he shouted.

But Houston's defense stopped them again, blunting a pair of runs and forcing Dawson to complete a short pass to Haynes for no gain on third down. Haynes twisted and wiggled with the ball in his hand, desperately trying to break free, but he finally submitted as he was buried under light blue shirts.

Forced to punt, Wilson dropped the ball and swung his leg as hard as he could, but the wind took the ball and threw it almost straight up. As players on both sides searched the sky, it came down and rolled to a stop at the Houston 45. The Oilers only needed a couple of first downs to put Blanda in position for a kick. The fans rose again, almost as exhausted as the players, but hoping for a happy ending.

On second down, Blanda dropped back, looked to his right for Hennigan, and fired a line drive at the receiver. The Texans' Bill Hull, a six-foot-eight defensive end, read Blanda's eyes and dropped off the line, thinking he could step into the path of the pass. Sure enough, the ball came at him, just above his helmet. He reached up, tipped it, and grabbed it as it came down. The crowd groaned as Tolar and Al Jamison slung Hull down near midfield. The Texans had the ball — with good field position.

Bourne, the referee, blew his whistle one play later, ending the "fifth" quarter. The Texans smiled at each other on the sideline. Now *they* had the ball and the wind. Ha!

Their offense huddled up, the players' shadows lengthening under the stadium's dim lights as daylight ebbed. The temperature had dropped twenty-five degrees since the opening kickoff. The wind continued to gust. A siren continued to wail in the distance.

"We can do this . . . now," Dawson said.

McClinton picked up four yards around right end. Haynes went the other way for six and a first down. Dawson called for Spikes to go back around left end. He took the handoff and ran left, looking for a hole outside the tackle. A linebacker rushed at him, but Al Reynolds, the Texans' left guard, peeled back and knocked the defender away, springing Spikes into the secondary. Three defenders converged on him, but Haynes, playing receiver, shielded one, and Spikes accelerated between the other two. By the time a Houston cornerback slammed into Spikes and knocked him over, the fullback had gained nineteen yards. The ball was at the Houston 18.

"Dallas is in scoring position now," Gowdy said on ABC.

After three running plays gained little yardage but positioned the ball in the center on the field, Stram ordered a field goal. He put his hand on Tommy Brooker, the rookie from Alabama, as Brooker headed onto the field.

"Keep your head down and kick that thing through there," Stram said with a casual smile, seeking to steady the young man's nerves.

"Don't worry, coach," Brooker said. "I'll kick that thing through there like it has eyes."

Before the Texans lined up, Stram called a time-out, wanting to make sure the kicking team was rested and ready. Dawson, who would hold, strode over to the bench and spoke to Stram as an ABC sideline camera captured Dick Davis, a rookie defensive end for the Texans, with his hands clasped in prayer in front of his face.

The rest of the kicking team remained on the field, gathered loosely in a huddle with their hands on their hips. Brooker would say later that he felt his teammates' eyes on him, checking his readiness for the occasion. "You could hear a pin drop out there, even with the crowd noise," he would recall.

Gowdy set the scene for the millions watching on ABC: "This is to win the game if the field goal is good. The score is tied 17–17 . . ."

Dawson trotted back onto the field, and the Texans broke their huddle and set up for the kick. Holub, the long snapper, crouched over the ball and put his hands on either side. He looked between his legs, preparing to snap the ball back. The quarterback put a knee in the dirt and extended his right hand toward the line.

". . . Dawson is the holder at the 24 . . ." Gowdy continued.

When Dawson called a signal, Holub snapped the ball. It flew straight back on a sharp line to Dawson as Houston sent nine players crashing into the line, trying to pancake Dallas's blockers.

"The big rush is on . . ." Gowdy said.

The fans screeched. Could anyone block the kick?

With all those bodies colliding just yards in front of him, Dawson calmly collected the ball and set it down on a pointed end, exposing the fattest part for Brooker. The rookie took a step forward and swung through with his right leg, his foot sending the ball into the air with a thud.

"The kick is up and the kick is . . . good! Dallas is the champion! Dallas wins it on a twenty-five-yard field goal by Tommy Brooker!"

The crowd's cheers died as the Texans mobbed each other and poured onto the field, shouting and leaping and hugging. Stram jogged with them, smiling broadly. Two players picked up Brooker and put him on their shoulders. Holub and defensive tackle Paul Rochester did the same with Stram. The diminutive coach waved a rolled-up sheet of paper he had held during the game.

"I have to say . . . that has to be . . . one of the finest football games I have ever seen," Gowdy said on ABC.

"Well, that was about the wildest finish we'll ever see," color announcer Paul Christman said.

The Texans and Oilers had played seventy-seven minutes and fifty-four seconds, five periods and the beginning of a sixth. It was the longest game in pro football history, an instant classic destined to be remembered by millions.

Gowdy threw the broadcast to Buck, who had waded into the on-field celebration and set up a line of people to interview.

"I'm here with Hank Stram, the coach of the now-champion Dallas Texans. Hank, congratulations," Buck said.

Stram looked up at Buck with a smile. "Thank you very much, Jack," he said. "I can't compliment the squad enough. To stay in the ball game like they did in the second half and to come back and win it like they did, it's a great tribute to them. We're just as proud as can be that we can win the championship and bring it back to Dallas, Texas."

Buck nodded and said, "Here, let's talk to some players. Who's this, Hank?"

Stram replied, "This is Jerry Cornelison, Jack."

As the camera focused on the tackle from SMU, Buck said, "Well, you had to play a lot of offense today, huh?"

Cornelison nodded. "Boy, I tell you, it was tough. Houston has a tremendous ball club. We were really lucky."

Buck then spoke to Spikes, who had rushed for seventy yards and set up the winning touchdown with an eighteen-yard run.

"Jack, you caught the Oilers on a blitz, and that's what won the ball game for you, other than the winning field goal," Buck said.

Spikes nodded and said, "They'd been blitzing the whole second half, and we knew we were going to catch them after a while, but we were getting worried in that fourth quarter, I tell you."

Buck continued, "Well, you set that last one up for Tommy, didn't you? Congratulations."

Spikes smiled. "Yes, sir, thank you," he said.

Buck turned and spoke to Brooker. "Okay, here's the fellow that kicked the field goal. Tommy, nice kick. Never a bigger one than that. Did you think you were going to miss it?"

Brooker smiled. "Well, you cain't miss it," he said in his thick Alabama twang. He had come a long way in the six months since he joined the team as a seventeenth-round pick, unsure if he would even survive training camp.

Next up was Jim Tyrer, the mountainous offensive tackle.

"Ever been involved in anything like this?" Buck asked.

"Greatest win of my career," Tyrer said.

"What about the coin flip? Was that just a mistake?"

"Yes, sir, I believe it was."

"But it turned out okay. I'm glad for Abner's sake."

"Yes, sir. Me too," Tyrer said.

The players left the field and spilled into the locker room, grabbing bottles of champagne that had been purchased and set up in case they won. They popped open the corks, sprayed each other, doused Stram. Reporters poured in and shouted questions at different players. Haynes found himself surrounded by interviewers.

"What in the world happened on that coin flip, Abner?" someone shouted.

The reporters leaned in to hear his reply. "I knew all along," Haynes said, "that we were going to need the wind in the sixth quarter."

He could joke about it now. The Texans had won, saving him from eternal embarrassment.

With Christmas just two days away, a few players elected not to accompany the team back to Dallas. Brooker, the hero, and cornerback Bobby Hunt, who had gone to Auburn and also lived in Alabama, got in a car and drove all night to get home for the holiday. Brooker stopped to see his parents, stopped again for a haircut, and drove on to Tuscaloosa to see Bear Bryant. (He would receive a stack of fan mail, including a letter from twelve-year-old Mike Rhyner, at the Texans' offices. The team forwarded his mail to him in Alabama, where he was enrolled in grad school, and he responded to each letter.)

The rest of the players showered, dressed, and spilled onto a charter for the short flight from Houston back to Dallas. When they landed at Love Field later that evening, more than four hundred fans were waiting for them, cheering and holding signs. That was a first. The only people who had previously welcomed them home from trips were airport employees. But now there was a joyous scene, the fans calling out the players' names and applauding as they walked through the terminal.

Taking it all in, Len Dawson was struck by a glorious thought. Dallas belonged to the Texans now. Look at these people! Hundreds of them! The Texans had broken through. Winning the title game had vaulted them ahead of their cross-town rivals. The Cowboys couldn't compete with this. The Cowboys couldn't even win half their games.

*Man, oh, man,* Dawson naively thought, *the Cowboys are going to have to leave town!*

# PART V

# 18

✩

# "It's nice to be wanted"

S THE TEXANS CELEBRATED with their fans at Love Field, a
*Morning News* photographer hastily organized a picture on the
runway outside the terminal. Wearing jackets, ties, beige cowboy
hats, and broad smiles, Jim Tyrer and Fred Arbanas raised clenched
fists. Stram stood beside them in a trench coat, smiling broadly, a fist
also raised. A gaggle of kids stood at their feet, gazing up and smiling.

Lamar stood in the middle of them, wearing horn-rimmed glasses
and an enormous, satisfied smile. The collar on his white dress shirt
was loose, revealing a tuft of chest hair, and his dark tie was pulled so
loose that the knot hung at his chest. With his right fist also clenched
and raised, he looked as if he had spent a few too many hours at a party.

This had been one of the greatest days of his life, all thirty years of
it. The football team he had nurtured from infancy had won a championship, dramatically, before millions of TV viewers. If he couldn't cut
loose now, he never would.

He had taken some of the Texans' most loyal supporters to Houston with him. The group included Jim Nichols, the president of the
Spur Club, whose daughter was such an ardent fan. Jim and his wife
hadn't brought Nancy, fearing the game might be too intense, and the
celebration, if one occurred, too unseemly. Sure enough, things had

gotten pretty rowdy on the flight home, and some players had wound up autographing Jim Nichols's wife's arm. A very, very good time was had by all.

Lamar presided over the celebration with immense pride. But as he posed for the *Morning News* picture on the tarmac, he harbored a stunning secret. He had given up on Dallas.

Although he hadn't officially decided to move the Texans, he was pretty sure they would defend their title in a different city. It broke his heart, shattered it, but he had concluded that his only choice was to cede Dallas to the Cowboys and take his team elsewhere.

It was hard to say exactly when he made the decision. Early that fall he had started a conversation with David Dixon, a sports-loving New Orleans businessman who had been denied an original AFL franchise but still believed he could get into the league. Lamar traveled to New Orleans to survey the scene. He never said he was moving, but Dixon could see he was considering it. Tulane Stadium was a concrete colossus like the Cotton Bowl. Dixon could lock in attractive dates. Lamar could see a team playing there. He also met with representatives from Atlanta and Miami, which had been in the original AFL mix.

When the Texans' home attendance at the Cotton Bowl failed to spike despite the team's success, Lamar became increasingly convinced he had no choice. He had always believed his beloved hometown couldn't support two teams, but he had hoped the Texans could survive if they won enough games. Everyone loved a winner, right? Well, apparently not. The Texans had drawn crowds of 13,557 and 19,137 on their way to the title. It was beyond exasperating. *What do these people want?*

When word circulated — not in the press, but in the offices of politicians and sports entrepreneurs around the country — that the Texans might be "in play," Lamar received a call from the mayor of Kansas City, Harold Roe Bennett Sturdevant Bartle, known to all simply as "Chief." Sixty-three years old, rotund, gregarious, a lawyer, banker, second-term mayor, and natural salesman, he wanted a team.

Chief Bartle, who had earned his nickname working with Indians as a young man in Wyoming, talked a good game — loudly. He didn't use a microphone when speaking to groups because his booming voice blistered the walls. On his daily morning radio show, he blaringly updated Kansas City residents on whatever good news he had heard. At night he drove to fires to shout support for firemen. Bullish on his city and anxious to use sports to improve its quality of life, he zeroed in on Lamar.

Kansas City was stuck with one tenant for Municipal Stadium, its modest pro sports venue located in the shadow of downtown. The pitiful Athletics of baseball's American League had played there since moving from Philadelphia in 1955. But the city had never really embraced them. They were perennial losers owned by a cranky Chicago stockbroker, Charles O. Finley, who was always contemplating moving. Finley, in fact, had considered taking the team to Dallas before Chief Bartle stepped in and kept it from happening.

Bartle had seen pro football teams generate excitement — and new revenue — in other cities. It was no secret that Dallas had one team too many. He and Lamar met to negotiate. Lamar said he wouldn't move unless Kansas City sold 25,000 season tickets or guaranteed him the revenue from that many sales. Bartlett agreed to that. Lamar wanted the stadium updated and expanded to a capacity of 45,000. Bartle agreed to that. Lamar wanted the corporate support he had lacked in Dallas. Bartle guaranteed it.

A sweet deal was shaping up. Lamar also was increasingly swayed by significant financial urges. So far, he had been able to deduct the Texans' losses on his income taxes — one hell of a write-off. But according to the Internal Revenue Service's "hobby law," you could only do that for five years if your venture never turned a profit. After five years of red ink, the venture was declared a business, not a hobby, and you not only lost the write-off but also had to pay back whatever you had previously written off.

With no end in sight to the red ink if the franchise remained in Dallas, the tax implications were yet another reason to consider moving.

One morning at his office, Lamar beckoned to Mack Rankin, the Hunt Oil land man who had signed E. J. Holub. Lamar trusted Rankin's opinion and his ability to keep a secret.

"I'm thinking about moving the team, and there are two cities in the running," Lamar said. "I can go to New Orleans, or I can go to Kansas City. Which do you think would be better?"

Rankin had worked for Hunt Oil in and around New Orleans and knew how business was transacted there. Public figures and policemen were sometimes on the take. You had to salt your share of palms with payola to get things done.

In Rankin's opinion, clean-cut Lamar wouldn't fare well in that environment. It was a bad match.

"Kansas City is more of a straight-up place. I think you'll do a lot better there," he said.

"Good," Lamar said. "They're offering a nice deal up there."

The Texans' final regular-season game of 1962 — a week before the championship game in Houston — was against the Chargers on December 16 at the Cotton Bowl. Chargers owner Barron Hilton came in for the Sunday afternoon game. On Saturday night, Lamar and Hilton went to a dinner party at the home of an oilman. As the evening unfolded, Lamar recounted his frustrations. Then he had a wild idea.

An avid sports historian, he recalled an incident from the 1930s in which the owners of two NFL teams, frustrated by lagging ticket sales to an upcoming game, contemplated locking the gates to the stadium and not allowing any fans inside. Their game would be played in front of two fans, the owners themselves, one on each side.

They didn't follow through, but a lightbulb went off in Lamar's head as he sat at the dinner table, aware that fewer than 10,000 tickets had been sold to Sunday's game.

"Why don't we do that tomorrow, Barron? Lock the gates?" he mused.

"That's a great idea! Let's do it!" Hilton exclaimed.

Other people at the table encouraged them, but Lamar couldn't bring himself to do it. An announced 18,364 watched the Texans beat San Diego the next day to finish the regular season. Less than half of the fans had actually paid for their tickets.

It was a pitiful crowd for a team playing so well. The AFL deserved better. The league was taking off in Houston, San Diego, Buffalo, and Boston and wobbling to its feet in Denver. It needed more success stories, not more empty stadiums and tales of woe.

Lamar needed a home that would embrace his team as a split-in-half Dallas never would.

After discussing with Jack Steadman how to deal with the Cowboys,

Lamar arranged a meeting with Murchison. Steadman and Schramm also attended.

"Look, this really isn't working. One of us needs to leave. We'll pay you to go," Lamar said.

"We don't want to leave. We aren't leaving," Murchison replied.

"Well, then, pay us to leave," Lamar said.

Murchison said he would do that. They pledged to negotiate terms after the season.

Lamar knew that no amount would convince Murchison to leave, and he guessed that the Cowboys' owner might pay a "farewell fee." Lamar probably was leaving anyway, even if Murchison balked, but he saw nothing wrong with trying to finagle something from the Cowboys. Battling them had cost him millions. Why not offset at least a little of it?

Lamar put his concerns for the future aside for a week as the Texans prepared for the championship game in Houston and then won it, but all along he knew he was facing a crossroads. He hadn't made the absolute final decision when the Texans brought the AFL title back to Dallas, but he continued to negotiate with Chief Bartle, and the more they spoke, the more Lamar believed that Kansas City was the right place for his team.

There simply was no comparison from a business standpoint. Bartle offered him the use of Municipal Stadium for free for two years (actually for one dollar per year), whereas renting the Cotton Bowl cost thousands per game. Bartle offered the use of a training complex that included an office building and practice field, also for free. The team would receive half of the concessions revenue; they had received none in Dallas.

Negotiations between Lamar and Murchison on their "farewell" settlement unfolded behind doors, leaving no trace. According to sources on either side, Lamar didn't want it known that he received money because he thought it would look bad, even if it didn't factor in his decision. Murchison was happy to oblige. Years later, Murchison's sons said they heard their father paid in the neighborhood of $300,000.

To say no one saw it coming would be an understatement. Basking in their championship triumph, the Texans' players, staff, and fans believed that the Cowboys, if anyone, were the ones on shaky ground.

Lamar fueled their confidence by telling the *Morning News* in January that the Texans would face a true test of their ability to lure fans when they kicked off as a championship team in 1963. It didn't sound like he was leaving. But in early February he slowly began telling his inner circle.

Jim Nichols, the president of the Spur Club, was stunned. "I feel like I've been kicked in the stomach," Nichols moaned, wondering how he would explain this to his daughter.

"I kind of feel the same way," Lamar said, "but it makes sense."

When Lamar explained what Kansas City was offering, Nichols reluctantly agreed there was no choice.

Breaking the news to Stram was especially tough. The coach took the battle with the Cowboys personally, rooting for the NFL team to lose, believing the Texans would prevail if they won enough games.

When Lamar met with him, laid out his plan, and explained the reasoning behind it, Stram was crestfallen.

"What do you think?" Lamar asked.

"I guess we have to be realistic about it," Stram said. "The people there are hungry for a football team."

He paused, thinking, then continued. "It's nice to be wanted," he said.

By early February, reporters at the Dallas papers began hearing whispers that something was up. On Thursday, February 8, 1963, the *Times Herald* ran a story headlined "Rich Offer May Move AFL Kings." The next day's *Morning News* ran a piece titled "Kansas City Texans?"

Lamar refused comment until a Saturday news conference, which he began by reading a statement: "I have always tried to run this team as a business, and in fact, in the long run, it must operate on a businesslike basis. Put in layman's terms, that means there must be enough income to meet expenses."

Among the AFL's eight franchises, he explained, only Oakland and New York, where owner Harry Wismer had declared bankruptcy, had less paid attendance than the Texans in 1962. Buffalo's paid gate was 92 percent higher than Dallas's, Houston's 82 percent higher, and Denver's 69 percent higher. The Texans might be winning on the field, he said, but they were failing at the ticket window.

Hedging, he said the move still depended on whether Kansas City

"It's nice to be wanted" ★ 249

succeeded in selling those 25,000 season tickets he had been promised.

"I have given my word to Kansas City," he said. "If they sell the tickets, we will move there, no matter what happens."

When reporters sought reaction from players and fans, they encountered disappointment and bitterness.

"I couldn't be sicker," said Jayne Murchison, a Highland Park High School gym teacher and original Spur Club member who was not related to the Cowboys' owner. "The [season ticket] situation was really looking good, comparatively anyway. Last year, I struggled all year to sell 142 season tickets. This year, after we won, in just three days I sold 76, and had orders for 86 more definite commitments. A lot of people were increasing their orders."

She continued: "But this was always a business proposition for Lamar. He couldn't sit here and lose money forever. I think it's a case of striking while the iron is hot. The Texans won a title, so he got a good offer. There's no guarantee of a title next year, so any offers might not be as good. That's just good business."

Roger Blackmar Jr., an avid fan who lived in Highland Park, told the *Morning News* that he believed the move was premature.

"I feel very strongly that another season here would have clarified the issue," he said. "There is an opportunity for the Texans to reap the benefits from winning the championship and from the great excitement created by that overtime championship game. I felt there might be some conciliatory move by [one of] the two teams after next year, or the year after. But it is quite a shock to have it come now."

Reporters struck a nerve when they asked fans of Lamar's team if they would now switch their allegiance to the Cowboys.

"That one . . . is going to be a hard pill for me to swallow," Jim Nichols said. "I'm for Dallas and promoting Dallas. I'm in business here and feel that ultimately anything good for Dallas is good for me. Eventually I may back the Cowboys because I love football and love Dallas. A lot of people in the [Spur] Club feel the same way."

His hesitation practically leapt off the page.

Nichols's daughter wept unashamedly when he broke the news to her. Nancy was too young to comprehend the business angles. She was just a fan who loved her team and was already counting the days until the 1963 season, when she could sit in the end zone with her friends on cloudless Sunday afternoons and screech for the Texans — the *champion* Texans.

How could she be denied that unparalleled pleasure? How could her heroes leave her behind?

Well, her father said softly, we'll still have a team in Dallas.

Nancy's eyes flashed. "I am not rooting for the Cowboys," she declared. "I will never root for the Cowboys."

And she didn't.

E. J. Holub was at his ranch near Paris, Texas, when he heard the news. "I can hardly believe it," he told the *Morning News*. "Honestly, I don't care too much at all for this. But I know it must be a good move from a business standpoint. And I'm under contract for two more years, so of course, you go where the club goes. I understand it from the standpoint that we should have drawn a lot more fans after proving ourselves. Those small crowds at those last two home games were really disappointing. But I thought we would at least see how Dallas reacted to a championship."

He paused and asked the reporter, "What are they going to call us now, the Kansas City Mules?"

Abner Haynes took it hard. He was the hometown star, the king of South Dallas, the pride of Lincoln High School and North Texas State. But he understood his city had let his team down.

"Everyone wants to be appreciated. When we won games and nothing happened, it was a big letdown," he lamented. "I'm under contract for another year, so I will go. Personally, I'm not sure there is going to be any pro football here in the long run. The Cowboys may not last more than another year or two."

Chris Burford heard the news at the home he had purchased in Dallas; the receiver had put down roots, enrolling at SMU's law school. "I'm really surprised. My family and I would like to stay. Dallas is a good town," he said. But Burford said he would go to Kansas City.

Jerry Cornelison, the offensive tackle, had also put down roots, buying a home in Richardson, starting a family, and catching on with an insurance company. He was making good money selling health and accident policies. To keep the job while playing in Kansas City, he would have to leave his family in Dallas, rent an apartment in Kansas City, and be away for months. It sounded like a lot to go through.

He called Stram and said, "Hank, I don't think I'm going."

"I hope you'll reconsider," Stram replied. (Cornelison remained in Dallas for the 1963 season, then returned to the team and played two more seasons before retiring.)

Frank Jackson, the halfback, was serving a military commitment when the news broke. His platoon sergeant at a basic training camp at Fort Polk, Louisiana, heard about the move on the radio while Jackson was out marching in a rainstorm, and he passed along the news when Jackson returned. Jackson, who had played at SMU, was speechless.

Walt Corey, the linebacker, was in Miami, Florida, teaching elementary school, as he did every off-season. A teammate called him before the news hit the papers.

"Kansas City?" Corey asked, dumbstruck. "Kansas City?"

Jerry Mays was furious enough to spit. Leave Dallas? *Sheee-it.* The defensive lineman was a born-and-bred Dallas boy. He had played for Sunset High School and SMU and picked the Texans over the Minnesota Vikings because he wanted to stay home. Of all the Texans, he had felt the strongest about battling the Cowboys.

"This news really puts me back," he grumped to the *Morning News.* "The biggest disappointment is the fact that the other team has won the battle. This battle was part of me. It really disappoints me that the Cowboys will stay in the city I love and the Texans will leave."

He was in graduate school at SMU, headed toward a career in engineering. Family business ties beckoned in Dallas. "I guess I'll check on working for a firm up there," he said.

A trade to the Cowboys would solve his problems, it was suggested. Mays didn't care for that idea one bit.

"That, to me, would be like selling my soul to the devil. And you can quote me on that," Mays said.

The Texans' most ardent fans didn't want to take no for an answer. Lamar had left the door open, saying Kansas City had to sell all those season tickets. *We can sell more here and convince Lamar to stay,* Jim Nichols thought. He organized a group that descended on a city council meeting to ask Dallas's mayor, Earle Cabell, for help. When Cabell agreed to form a committee to look into keeping the Texans, the group stood and cheered, disrupting the council session.

Within a week, clip-out coupons appeared in both Dallas papers. "Let's Keep the Dallas Texans. It's Up to You," read the headline. The coupon was a season-ticket pledge form with blanks for a name, address, ticket order, and pledge amount. "We can do it. Fill this out and mail it with a check," it stated. The address was a Dallas bank office.

Nichols also started a postcard campaign, asking fans to put "yes" or "no" on a card, sign their name, and mail it to "Keep Our Champions at Home," addressed to an insurance company.

"If the fans want to keep the Texans here as badly as I think they do, we're going into the fight with all we've got," Nichols said. "But on the other hand, if Dallas is willing to let us lose this great team, we'll say 'good-bye and good luck' to Lamar."

The movement didn't generate much enthusiasm. Lamar had made his intentions clear. Although he had technically left the door open, he had already walked through it. He was on his way to Kansas City. His threat of "25,000 season tickets or else" was really just a ploy to generate sales in Kansas City.

Meanwhile, Chief Bartle and the team's new fans in Kansas City quickly organized their season-ticket drive. A banker was put in charge, and he deputized dozens of businessmen. They fanned out across the city, sales books in hand.

"I assure you we will reach the goal. We are organized and will keep going until we do," a chamber of commerce vice president said.

The drive officially kicked off in early April with a luncheon. Lamar flew Jack Steadman, Stram, Haynes, and several other staff members and players up for the event on his private jet. The players wore their bright red sport jackets adorned with the Texans breast patch; those patches would have to be switched out, Lamar thought.

The Dallas contingent was shocked to see five hundred people fill a downtown banquet room with thunderous cheers and applause. The Texans had never drawn half that many to any luncheon in Dallas.

After the event, some local leaders took the players and staff out to see Municipal Stadium. Haynes looked over the puny stadium and glanced at Bob Halford, the team's director of publicity.

"This is where we're going to play football?" Haynes asked.

"This is it," Halford said.

There was no special parking for the players; they would have to stash their cars on neighboring lawns, just like the fans. It was a dicey prospect in the surrounding inner-city neighborhood.

The reality of moving to a new city was sinking in.

Kansas City's ticket drive started fast, with almost 7,000 sales in a week. After it briefly fizzled and Lamar expressed disappointment, it jumped again. By mid-May the total was up to 13,000 — far more than the team had ever sold in Dallas, but short of the goal.

Lamar had to make a decision. He couldn't hedge any longer if the team was really going to play in Kansas City that fall.

On May 22, he held a news conference in Kansas City. "We're coming," he said. Chief Bartle and the fans of Kansas City sighed with relief.

Lamar had planned all along to move, regardless of how many tickets were sold. Thirteen thousand season tickets represented $600,000 in revenues, and with Chief Bartle's guarantee thrown in, the figure topped $1 million. The team had never generated such income in Dallas.

"As a sports town, there is nothing wrong with Dallas except the [two-team] situation that was created," Lamar said. "The American Football League has taken time and energy to build, and has, for all intents and purposes, arrived. Kansas City has, in my opinion, earned the right to be represented in pro football. I am flattered that Kansas City has chosen the Dallas Texans as the team they want."

The members of the front office who were going with the team had to move quickly, find places to live in Kansas City, and move their families. Training camp was less than two months away. Everything was rushed.

Stram watched them all move, one by one, and went home at night to his house on Northaven Road, where he lived with his wife and their five children. He didn't want to go. He loved Dallas. He had established himself as a pro head coach there. His wife and kids were settled. Every night he told them, "Maybe something will happen. Maybe Lamar will change his mind at the last minute."

Finally, as another hot summer descended on North Texas, the cold reality of the situation slapped him. Lamar wasn't going to change his mind. Stram's Dallas football champions would defend their title in Kansas City. He had to leave.

He and his wife packed up the house and shipped their belongings to Kansas City. The rest of the family went on vacation. Stram got in his car and started to drive. His emotions overtook him as he maneuvered the streets of North Dallas, heading for the highway that would take him north. He started to cry. He couldn't believe this was happening. Tears dripped down his cheeks. He bawled as he hit the highway, sped up, and looked in his rearview mirror at the Dallas skyline.

*Damn,* he thought, *we won the battle, but we still lost.*

# 19

---☆---

# "There's something I want to visit with you about"

T HE PEOPLE IN THE Cowboys' organization didn't exult when the
Texans left. They didn't break out champagne, stand on chairs,
and scream with joy. They just sighed. They hadn't won the battle
for Dallas, just survived it.

"This certainly presents a real challenge and responsibility," Tex
Schramm said. "We're now the sole representative of the entire Dallas–Fort Worth area in pro football, and the only major league sports
team in the area. We're looking forward to offering a team worthy of
the support of the entire community, and look forward to welcoming
all pro football fans to our games. We certainly wish Lamar and the
Texans the greatest of success in Kansas City. The competition of the
past three years, while not an artistic success for either team, certainly
made the area aware of pro football."

As always, the Texans found the Cowboys' superior attitude irritating. *Not an artistic success for either team? Who just won a championship?*

But the Texans' opinions were no longer an issue for the Cowboys.
With Dallas all to themselves, they believed they were poised to take
a gigantic leap forward, both on and off the field. Their attendance

was bound to rise, perhaps exponentially. And that rise would coincide, they believed, with major improvements on the field.

"We think we've made big strides in the past three years in building a team that can uphold the football tradition of the Southwest. We're quite optimistic about the coming season," Schramm said. "We think we're definitely in position to bid for a championship. We hope to bring an NFL title to Dallas, just as the Texans brought an AFL title."

Their boldness elicited snickers throughout the NFL. *The Cowboys think they can beat us? Win a title? What are they smoking?* But the Cowboys weren't the only ones who believed it. *Sports Illustrated*'s Tex Maule picked them to win the Eastern Division in the magazine's pro football preview.

Maule picked the Cowboys primarily because of Landry's multiple offense, which in 1962 had ranked second in the league in points scored and yardage gained. Their defense hadn't performed as well, but it figured to improve under Landry, the renowned defensive expert.

"If they can achieve even mediocrity on defense — and they should achieve more — they will win the first of their Eastern championships," Maule wrote.

It was heady stuff for a franchise that had won a grand total of nine games in three seasons.

The players and coaches knew something big was brewing when a *Sports Illustrated* photographer showed up at their training camp in July and snapped away during several practices. On the cover of the magazine's September 9 issue, linebacker Chuck Howley and defensive end George Andrie were pictured fending off a blocker under a bright blue sky. "Cowboys Can Ride High on Better Defense," blared the headline.

Maule's article was an ode to Murchison, Schramm, and Landry. He lauded the owner's patience, the general manager's sagacity, and the coach's brilliance. "If, as seems likely, the team wins the East this year, it will be the culmination of a remarkably swift rise to competence," Maule wrote. "Most of the credit goes to [Murchison, Schramm, and Landry] who make up the backbone of a smooth-running organization which rivals the Giants, operated by the Mara family, in closeness and efficiency."

Fearing the prediction would raise unrealistic expectations, Landry expressed doubt and suggested that the Giants, who had won the East the previous two years, still controlled the division. But it was too late. The nation's preeminent sports magazine had anointed his team as the Next Big Thing. A handful of lesser magazines also picked the Cowboys to rise up.

The widespread hopefulness was infectious. "With the personnel we have, I think we're one year ahead of our original five-year program [to contend]," Bedford Wynne crowed.

With optimism soaring, the Cowboys opened the 1963 season with a Saturday night game against the Cardinals before 36,432 at the Cotton Bowl — by far their best crowd for a home opener. When they took an early lead on a touchdown pass by Meredith, they seemed ready to fulfill the praise that had been heaped on them.

But in a stunning development, they stopped moving the ball and were pushed around by the Cardinals, deemed a playoff contender by few. The visitors pulled away to a 34–7 win.

It was a crushing disappointment, and another loss at the Cotton Bowl the next Sunday — 41–24 to Cleveland before 28,710 — darkened the gloom. By the end of the first month of their season of great expectations, the Cowboys had no wins and four losses. The fans booed Meredith, wrote critical letters about Landry to the papers, and in some cases whined about not having a winning AFL team to root for anymore. Abner Haynes had left and gone away.

The city's enduring doubts about pro football were plainly evident on a mid-October weekend. On Friday night a big noisy crowd filled the Cotton Bowl to watch SMU play Navy, the nation's fifth-ranked college team, led by quarterback Roger Staubach. Texas and Oklahoma packed the place again on Saturday afternoon. On Sunday, the Cowboys drew just 27,264 for a game against the Detroit Lions.

The Mustangs had fallen to the bottom of the Southwest Conference, winning just five of thirty-two games going back to 1960, and their attendance had fallen sharply. It was almost as if they had given up, expecting the pros to take over. But a new, young coach, Hayden Fry, was reviving the players' spirits, and on this Friday his team knocked Staubach out with an injured shoulder and beat the Midshipmen on a late touchdown. That drama was matched in Texas's victory over Oklahoma the next day. When the winless Cowboys kicked off before 45,000 empty seats, the atmosphere paled miserably.

After winning just one of their first seven games, the Cowboys drew 18,838 for a game against the Redskins in early November. It seemed the Texans' departure had not helped at all. The fans were all over them, Landry under intense pressure. If he was so darn smart, how come his team piled up losses year after year? Meanwhile, the Cotton Bowl filled again when the Longhorns defeated Navy (making a return trip) on New Year's Day.

On a Friday in November, the Cowboys had just started practicing when they learned that President John F. Kennedy had been assassinated on a downtown Dallas street, just a few miles from where they stood. As the nation mourned, Pete Rozelle made the dubious decision, which he later regretted, to play games that Sunday. The Cowboys flew to Cleveland, where some baggage handlers, angry at Dallas, refused to pick up their luggage. They took the field moments after watching Jack Ruby gun down Lee Harvey Oswald on national television and wondered if a sniper might take out the world's frustrations on them. In no mood to play, they lost.

This was a season that couldn't end soon enough. The Cowboys ended with four wins and ten losses, leaving Maule's prediction in tatters, a smoldering ruin.

There were a few bright spots. Don Perkins, continuing to pound away between the tackles, earned another Pro Bowl selection. Meredith, despite the fans' hounding, showed enough improvement that Landry ended his apprenticeship at midseason and named him the permanent starter. The quarterback shuttle was history, LeBaron relegated to the bench. That was fine with Eddie, who retired after the season to run a Nevada cement company for Murchison.

Also, in a seemingly minor move that would pay off later, Landry shifted Bob Lilly, the young defensive lineman, from end to tackle. Lilly had been a disappointment as an end, playing with such indifference that he lost confidence and wondered if he was even meant to play pro ball. Privately, he wished he had signed with the Texans. But stationed in the interior, he began to play better, his blend of size and agility giving him an advantage over less nimble guards and centers. A year later he would make the Pro Bowl for the first time, and two years later he earned the first of his seven All-NFL selections.

But other than the play of several of their young stars, it was an awful year for Dallas and the Cowboys. Landry's four-year record stood at 13-38-3. His reputation as a young whiz had given way to the consensus that he had his head in the clouds and talked a better game than he coached. Some fans called for Schramm to fire him.

Stepping in to calm the roiled waters after the season, Murchison gave the embattled coach a ten-year contract extension, the longest in pro sports history. The rest of the league was shocked, but for Murchison, it was a typically magisterial move. If you had the right guy for a job, let the world know. Murchison still believed in Landry, remembering the vision of him sitting under a tree in the Bahamas, focused intently on the playbook in his lap. That level of drive would pay off, Murchison believed. It was taking Landry longer than expected, but he would figure out how to win.

Once Lamar decided he was moving, he had to decide on a new name for the team. They couldn't still be the Texans when they played in Kansas City. Or could they? Lamar startled Steadman by saying that was precisely what he wanted to call them — the Kansas City Texans.

"Lamar, you can't do that!" Steadman exclaimed, wondering if his young boss had lost his mind.

Lamar argued that pro basketball's Lakers had kept their name when they moved from Minneapolis to Los Angeles, and that his franchise had won a championship as the Texans so it was almost heretical to discard it. Keeping the name also would honor Lamar's home state.

"Lamar," Steadman repeated, "you can't do that."

Knowing it was true, Lamar grudgingly relented. The *Kansas City Star* newspaper held a name-the-team contest, and thousands of respondents suggested ideas such as the Mules, the Stars, and the Royals. Lamar quickly settled on a favorite — Chiefs. It reflected the state's western heritage, connoted leadership and bravery, and paid homage to Chief Bartle, who had talked him into coming. Kansas City Chiefs, it was.

The team's colors, uniforms, and helmets would remain the same except for the white map of the state of Texas, which obviously had to come off the helmet. The team that took the field in 1963 also was mostly unchanged from the one that had won the title. Why tamper with success? The Chiefs were loaded. When they opened their first season in Kansas City with a 59–7 victory over the Broncos, it appeared they might be too good for the rest of the AFL.

But strange things soon started happening. They played to a tie in Buffalo as their defense allowed numerous big plays. They traveled to San Diego and lost to the Chargers, who had traded quarterback Jack Kemp, gone with young John Hadl, and recovered their winning touch.

After playing three away games to open the season (while trying to get their stadium ready), the Chiefs finally opened at home, drawing 27,801 fans — fewer than they had drawn for their opener in Dallas the year before, but still a decent crowd. When they won, beating the Oilers in a rematch of the overtime championship game, it appeared they were set to battle the Chargers for the division title.

But they lost again to Buffalo the next week, this time at home. The Chargers — on their way to the 1963 league title — came to Kansas City and blasted them. Dawson wasn't playing well, Haynes was fumbling, and the defense was soft. In early November, a depressing home loss to the Raiders ran the losing streak to five. Their season was in tatters.

Their last three games were at home, but most fans in their new hometown found plenty else to do besides watch meaningless contests. When just 12,202 watched them beat New York in the season finale, it seemed like they had never left Dallas.

After Landry's friend Vince Lombardi won a pair of NFL titles with the Green Bay Packers in 1961 and 1962, he wrote a book in 1963. *Run to Daylight* was an inside look at a team and the game it played. Lombardi detailed a single week with the Packers as they prepared to play the Detroit Lions. He explained strategies, revealed the intricacies of his relationships with his players, and gave readers a glimpse of life on the sidelines.

The book became a bestseller. When a television adaptation aired in prime time, it drew tens of millions of viewers. America's appetite for pro football was exploding. The nation could not get enough of the game and its stars and strategies. Baseball's long reign as the country's favorite sport was ending. In a cover story about pro football that ran as the 1964 season began, *Fortune* magazine called the sport "wonderfully attuned to the pace and style of American life in the 1960s."

It was a decade of turbulence, change, and extremes, a decade marked by the grimness of racial conflict, the onset of a puzzling war, the wonder of space exploration, and the rise of television as the centerpiece of family life. Baseball — a leisurely and pastoral summer game rooted in old traditions, best consumed on radio — suddenly seemed dull compared to the subtly intricate whir of violence, emotion, and raw athleticism in the sport that *Fortune* called "a spectacle."

In 1964, CBS landed the rights to broadcast NFL games by agreeing to pay a staggering $14 million per year; each team would receive $1 million annually. The AFL fared almost as well, agreeing to a five-year deal with NBC that gave each team slightly less than $1 million per year.

The teams in both leagues benefited as their sport took off. As President Kennedy had remarked, "A rising tide lifts all boats." Attendance at games soared in many cities in both leagues. Television made it easier to sell tickets.

Set against this backdrop of astounding growth, the Cowboys finally turned a corner in 1965. Opening the season with a pair of games at the Cotton Bowl, they pounded the Giants, 31–2, before 59,366 and defeated the Redskins, 27–7, before 61,577. Three years after the Texans' departure, they finally were winning Dallas over.

It was no coincidence that they also finally had a team worth watching. The small fortune they had spent on scouting and drafting since their inception was paying off. Gathering information on college players and gauging their relative merits was an inexact science to say the least — one might as well ask a fortuneteller at times — but Schramm, seeking clarity, had paid the Service Bureau Corporation, a subsidiary of IBM, to develop a computerized scouting system. Put to use for the first time at the draft in December 1963, it spit out a class that included Mel Renfro, a football and track star from Oregon; Bob Hayes, a receiver from Florida A&M who was an Olympic-caliber sprinter; and Roger Staubach, the star quarterback from Navy, who couldn't play pro football until he fulfilled his five-year military service commitment. All three would eventually gain induction into the Pro Football Hall of Fame — not a bad draft class.

The next year's rookie crop included Craig Morton, a quarterback expected to challenge Meredith for the starting job; Jethro Pugh, a mobile defensive tackle from tiny Elizabeth City (North Carolina) State, who would illustrate the Cowboys' ability to find talent where no one else was looking; and Ralph Neely, an offensive tackle who originally signed with Bud Adams and the AFL's Oilers but jumped to the Cowboys after they obtained his NFL rights from Baltimore, which had drafted him. Adams sued, and it took several years for the dispute to be resolved, but meanwhile, Neely became an anchor on the Cowboys' offensive line.

With all that young talent making plays, dressed in the sharp new uniforms Schramm had designed — white jerseys with dark blue numerals and shiny, metallic-blue pants and helmets — the Cowboys became a spectacle in their own right. Hayes, known as "the World's Fastest Human" after winning the gold medal in the 100-meter dash at the 1964 Olympics, caught a pair of long touchdown passes in his first two pro games in 1965. It was immediately clear that he was too fast for any defender in the league. Meanwhile, Perkins, ever reliable, churned for gains up the middle.

When Meredith slumped, generating a new round of boos and grumbles, Landry experimented with Morton. But after the Cowboys lost five games in a row, the coach announced in November that he was sticking with Meredith for the rest of the year. Coalescing, the Cowboys defeated the 49ers before 39,677, rallied to beat the Steelers before 57,293, and drew a sellout crowd to the Cotton Bowl — their first — for a game against the Browns on November 21. Schramm could not help smiling as he gazed down at the packed house from his seat in the press box before kickoff.

The Browns, the reigning NFL champs, built a two-touchdown lead, but Meredith led a rally, hitting Hayes on a long touchdown and driving the offense to the Cleveland 1-yard line late in the fourth quarter. But rather than hand to Perkins for the tying touchdown, he tried to throw for the score and was intercepted. The Browns ran out the clock for a 24–17 win, and Gary Cartwright's game story in the next day's *Morning News* began, "Outlined against the gray sky rode the Four Horsemen: Pestilence, Fame, Death, and Meredith."

But even in defeat the Cowboys had crossed an important threshold. Dallas had embraced them.

In early December, they took a 6-7 record into their season finale against the Giants in New York. A victory would qualify them for the Playoff Bowl, a game matching the runners-up in the NFL's two divisions. Veteran teams dubbed it the "losers' bowl," but the Cowboys, who had never had a winning season, desperately wanted in.

The Cowboys beat the Giants and traveled to Miami to play the Colts, who had lost the Western Division title in a bitter playoff with Lombardi's Packers. The young Cowboys partied on the beach all week, naively thinking they had arrived as major players, and the Colts punished them on Sunday, 35–3, before a sparse crowd at the Orange Bowl.

But far headier days lay just ahead.

Decades after they worked together, Mack Rankin smiled as he recalled Don Klosterman, who was Lamar's personnel expert from 1961 through 1965.

"Man, he was good," said Rankin, who left Hunt Oil and the Chiefs in 1967 and formed his own hugely successful oil company, McMoRan Oil and Gas, with two partners. "Don, he had a lot of bullshit. He could really talk to the black guys. Having lived out in California and played football with them, he could talk the lingo. When it came to signing time every year, I would take the white guys and Klosterman would take the black guys. That always worked out great."

Klosterman had worked for the Chargers in 1960, scouting for the AFL team that was the most progressive about suiting up African American players in the league's first years. He brought that open-mindedness to Lamar's franchise, especially after the move to Kansas City. Before Bud Adams hired him to run the Oilers in 1966, Klosterman put together pro football's most integrated lineup in Kansas City.

In 1963 he shocked the NFL when he used the first pick in the AFL draft (the one Lamar had obtained for Cotton Davidson) on Buck Buchanan, a mountainous defensive tackle from Grambling State, an all-black college in Louisiana. No NFL team had ever used a high pick on a player from the other side of college football's color line, having long disdained that brand of football. Most of the NFL's early black stars, such as Marion Motley, Ollie Matson, and Jim Brown, had all played major college ball. But the Chargers had struck gold with Ernie Ladd, a hulking defensive end from Grambling known as "Big Cat." Buchanan was even better.

As Klosterman built his national web of scouts, he included Lloyd Wells, an African American from Houston. Well known in that city's black community, Wells was a former Marine who worked as a photographer, writer, and editor for black newspapers. While breaking color lines in press boxes, he mentored young athletes and had gained insight into black college football by covering Prairie View and Texas Southern.

With Wells helping him identify talent, Klosterman dove repeatedly into the pool of black college football talent. In 1964 the Chiefs added Mack Lee Hill, a fullback from Southern who made the Pro Bowl as a rookie, and Willie Mitchell, a cornerback from Tennessee State. The next year they added a trio of receivers: Prairie View's Otis Taylor, who became one of pro football's top big-play threats; Southern's Frank Pitts; and Jackson State's Gloster Richardson. They also had black players from major schools, such as Bobby Bell, a linebacker from Minnesota, and Fred Williamson, a defensive back from Northwestern who had played for the Raiders.

"We never pretended we were making a conscious effort to open things up [racially]. We just made a conscious effort to find the best players anywhere we could," Lamar said later.

At first, their movement to integrate seemed almost ill fated. The same year they drafted Buchanan they took Stone Johnson, a running back from Grambling, but Johnson suffered a broken neck in a preseason game and died ten days later. Mack Lee Hill — a bowling ball of a ball-carrier who had become popular with fans — suffered an aneurysm while undergoing knee surgery and died on the operating table in December 1965. "The worst possible shock," Lamar called it.

With these tragedies hanging over them, the Chiefs continued to struggle to gain a foothold in Kansas City. In 1964 they were a .500 team (7-7) with an average home attendance of 18,126, second-lowest in the league. The next year they went 7-5-2 as their attendance rose slightly, to 21,493. The Bills, Patriots, and Chargers had surpassed them, winning division titles and battling for the league championship.

But as with the Cowboys, the Chiefs' years of accumulating superior talent were about to pay off.

Even though he had abandoned his hometown and his team now played in Kansas City, Lamar continued to live in Dallas. Memories of the Texans slowly faded around town, but not in his home. Divorced from his first wife, Lamar married the former Norma Lynn Knobel, a high school history teacher in Richardson, a Dallas suburb. They had first met in 1960 when the Texans hired thirty women to drive around town in red convertibles selling season tickets.

The one who sold the most was supposed to get to keep her car, but Norma wound up keeping the owner of the team.

Knowing that his admittedly over-the-top love of sports had contributed to the dissolution of his first marriage, Lamar tested Norma by taking her to five football games one weekend early in their courtship — a high school game, three college games, and a pro game.

"I think we went to five games," Norma exhaled after the last one.

"Isn't that great? A five-ple-header," Lamar exclaimed.

In a *Morning News* story announcing their engagement in January 1964, Norma, then twenty-five, said of her fiancé, "I love Lamar and football too."

Hank Stram was the best man at their wedding.

In the weeks before the 1965 AFL draft, the Chiefs felt great about their chances of signing Gale Sayers, the brilliant running back from Kansas. He went to college nearby, dated a girl from Kansas City, and had expressed interest in playing for the Chiefs. Then one day he just disappeared.

The Chiefs couldn't locate Sayers because Buddy Young, a former NFL player who now worked in Pete Rozelle's office, came to town and took him away. The next thing the Chiefs knew, George Halas had drafted Sayers and signed him. It turned out that Young had taken Sayers to Baltimore, where Young lived, and kept him squirreled away until his name was on an NFL contract.

Young's efforts were part of a new tactic the NFL had devised in its battle with the AFL to sign college talent. After seeing high picks such as USC quarterback Pete Beathard and Texas defensive tackle Scott Appleton sign with the AFL, the NFL had instituted a covert babysitting program. It paid operatives to take players away shortly before the draft and personally guard them until they signed. Rozelle himself signed off on the idea.

The Cowboys asked a stockbroker to go to Houston several days before the 1965 draft and bring back Otis Taylor, the superb receiver from Prairie View A&M whom the Chiefs had targeted. Taylor agreed to come with a teammate. The Cowboys put them up at the Continental Hotel in Richardson, a Dallas suburb, with the stockbroker situated in the hallway outside their room, prepared to stay until the Cowboys drafted Taylor and immediately signed him.

Before this hijacking, the Chiefs had felt confident about signing Taylor. Lloyd Wells had mentored him since Taylor was in high school. This was one player they couldn't lose, they felt. They were so confident that they assigned Wells to another player. But Klosterman became concerned when his calls to Taylor's dorm room repeatedly went unanswered. Finally, Klosterman called Wells, who hurried home to find the missing receiver.

From speaking to Taylor's mother, friends, and girlfriend, Wells ascertained that Taylor had been taken to Dallas. Wells traveled to Dallas, found the Continental Hotel, and tried to get to Taylor, but couldn't get past the Cowboys' babysitter. He went to the back of the motel, gained Taylor's attention, and motioned that he would return later. When things quieted down, the babysitter fell asleep, and Taylor quietly climbed out a back window, left with Wells, and signed with the Chiefs the next day.

The battle for talent was becoming absurd, and also expensive. Teams in the NFL had always had more money, but the playing field leveled after the AFL signed its lucrative TV contract with NBC. In 1965 the New York franchise, renamed the Jets, signed Alabama quarterback Joe Namath to a three-year contract worth $400,000, an unheard-of amount, overpaying to lure him from the St. Louis Cardinals.

A year later salaries escalated wildly, with teams from the two leagues combining to pay $7 million in bonuses to rookies. Vince Lombardi, known for being fiercely cheap, doled out $1 million for running backs Jim Grabowski and Donny Anderson, mostly because he feared the AFL might put a team in nearby Milwaukee.

Veteran players in both leagues complained bitterly about untested youngsters earning far more than they ever had, but their salaries rose too. Teams in both leagues were paying out more than they could earn. Even with the additional TV revenue and their sport's popularity skyrocketing, they were losing money.

The leagues had previously taken several stabs at seeing whether they could put an end to the nonsense and merge. Lamar and Halas had met a few times, getting nowhere. Colts owner Carroll Rosenbloom and Bills owner Ralph Wilson had gotten a little further, but eventually gave up. The situation was complex. Each league had some levelheaded owners willing to merge, but also some firebrands wanting to fight. The NFL wanted not only an indemnity payment but also the disbanding of several of the weaker AFL teams.

By 1966, Tex Schramm had seen enough. It was time for this to stop, he believed. No one in the NFL had fought harder to squash the AFL, but Schramm was a realist. The upstart league had issues, but it was going to survive. The NFL needed to deal with that.

Schramm confronted Rozelle with his opinion. The commissioner admired Schramm, who had brought him into football as a young publicist, and agreed with Schramm that a merger was the best course.

Rozelle knew he couldn't just get everyone in a room and hammer out a deal. There were too many agendas, too many opinions, too many voices. But a quiet conversation between two people who were levelheaded, open-minded, and discreet could get things going. The process needed to start with a one-on-one conversation, Rozelle believed.

Schramm agreed to represent the NFL, and after reviewing the possibilities on the other side, he concluded that only one person best fit the bill. He called Lamar.

"There's something I want to visit with you about. Would it be convenient to get together?" Schramm asked.

"Sure. Is there any urgency to it?" Lamar replied.

Schramm paused. "It's important," he finally said.

Lamar was in Kansas City, working on the Chiefs' season-ticket drive, but he had to fly to Houston for a league meeting and would be changing planes in Dallas. He told Schramm they could meet at Love Field during his layover.

On April 6, 1966, Schramm drove to Love Field, parked in the airport lot, and walked inside the terminal. He had arranged to meet Lamar at the statue of a Texas Ranger that loomed by the ticketing lounge.

Schramm waited several minutes, reading a paper, until Lamar walked up. They shook hands, and Schramm suggested they go out and talk in his car to avoid attracting attention.

Once they were in the car, Schramm said, "I think it's time to talk about a merger."

Lamar replied that he was interested.

They spent forty-five minutes discussing a possible framework. The NFL wanted an indemnity payment, wanted Rozelle to be commissioner, and, in a major concession, was willing to take all of the AFL franchises, although New York and Oakland would have to move. Lamar had problems with some of that, but he saw the outline of a potential agreement. Before he left for Houston, he agreed to talk with Schramm again soon.

Numerous obstacles arose in the coming months. Buffalo kicker Pete Gogolak signed with the Giants, leading to an aggressive AFL raid on NFL talent. The AFL owners fired Joe Foss as their commissioner and replaced him with Al Davis, the intensely competitive former Chargers scout who had taken over the Raiders; Davis wanted to kill the NFL, not merge with it. Meanwhile, owners in New York and the Bay Area opposed merging, not wanting to share their markets. Lamar could relate.

The relationship between Schramm and Lamar could easily have become another impediment. Lamar harbored no hard feelings from the years when their franchises had shared Dallas, but the feisty Schramm did.

"I see Lamar Hunt as one of the most selfish, commercial people I've ever met in sports," Schramm would state in his authorized biography published more than two decades later. "He created an image of himself as . . . a guy who only wanted to see pro football come to his hometown. That's a bunch of bull. He was scheming all along to start his own league, and when he saw a chance to get out of Dallas for a better deal, he cut and ran. So I hardly think he was all that interested in his hometown as he led people to believe. The truth, as I see it, was opposite of just about what everyone thought. It was Clint who was only interested in getting a pro team for his hometown and not Lamar."

Lamar never responded to those comments, as if he did not want to dignify the slights. His wife Norma said years later, "Lamar had no relationship with Tex. But he had no animosity toward Tex. Lamar was not an animosity guy. That's why he and Tex were able to work so closely when they needed to."

In the spring of 1966, Schramm put aside whatever bitterness he harbored and worked with Lamar to forge a pro football landscape each side could live with. Shepherding the process together, they calmly cleared hurdle after hurdle. The rival leagues settled on a $20 million indemnity payment, paid over time to ease the burden on the AFL owners. The NFL decided it was too thorny to try to move the Jets (probably to Memphis) and Raiders (probably to Portland, Oregon) and awarded the bulk of the indemnity payment to the Giants and 49ers for having to share their markets.

The merger was announced on June 6, 1966, at a press conference in New York. Rozelle sat in the middle, flanked by Lamar and Schramm. They outlined the agreement that would alter the course of American sports history. The leagues would merge into a single entity known as the National Football League beginning in 1970. They would share a common draft starting immediately, eliminating the bidding war. Rozelle would be the commissioner. Teams from the rival leagues could play exhibition games against each other starting immediately, and it was hoped that there would be a championship game pitting the winners of the two leagues.

Rozelle suggested that a committee made up of owners and/or GMs from both leagues finalize all details. Lamar and Schramm headed the committee. Their first piece of business was to arrange the championship game, which the public clearly wanted. During one of the committee's sessions, Lamar wondered aloud whether there needed to be an extra week before the "ultra" championship game. Some people in the room weren't sure which game he meant.

"You know," Lamar said, "the final game. The last game. The super bowl."

Postseason games in college football were called "bowls," so his instinct was to call this new pro game a bowl as well. And the word "super" was on his mind because he had recently watched his kids playing with a popular toy called a super ball, a tightly wound rubber ball that could bounce fifty feet high.

The committee settled on the Los Angeles Coliseum as the site for what it called the AFL-NFL World Championship Game, to be played in mid-January 1967, two weeks after the AFL and NFL titles were decided. But the bulky name never caught on. It was easier just to call the game what Lamar had casually labeled it — a name that rolled off the tongue and was quickly adopted by sports editors because it was short, punchy, and fit neatly in headlines:

The Super Bowl.

# 20

✦

# "Did Vince really say that?"

MEREDITH BROUGHT THE Cowboys' offense to the line of scrimmage. The Packers' defense dug in to try to make a stop. One yard was all the Cowboys needed to tie the score and send the 1966 NFL championship game into overtime, with the Cowboys owning the momentum. One yard would put them within reach of a stunning upset and a date with, of all teams, the Kansas City Chiefs in the inaugural AFL-NFL title game.

One yard could turn the first Super Bowl into the final chapter of the grim battle for Dallas that had been waged just a few years earlier.

Cowboys versus Chiefs. Murchison versus Hunt. They might get to play each other at last . . . if the Cowboys could gain just one more yard.

The date was January 1, 1967. The Cotton Bowl was crammed with more than 75,000 fans who sent up a howl as Meredith surveyed Green Bay's defense and prepared to take the snap.

Earlier that day the Chiefs had rolled over Buffalo, 31-7, in the AFL title game in Buffalo, easily capturing a contest that many experts had expected them to lose. The Bills were seeking a third straight league title and had the home-field edge at cold, muddy War Memorial Stadium, but a fumble on the opening kickoff had produced an early Kansas City touchdown, and the Chiefs never looked back.

After winning the game, the Chiefs tumbled into their cramped locker room, poured champagne on each other, and sat down to watch the CBS broadcast of the Packers-Cowboys game on a grainy black-and-white TV. Many players kept on their muddy white uniforms, wanting to preserve the glorious moment.

The fact that they would represent the AFL in the first Super Bowl began to sink in. It was a tremendous honor, but a heavy responsibility. Although the NFL and AFL had called a truce and joined hands, most people in the older league remained convinced that their brand of football was vastly superior. They had grudgingly conceded that the AFL could sign players, sell tickets, and generate TV audiences, but when it came to football, the game itself, the NFL wasn't granting its new partner the same respect.

Now it would be up to the Chiefs to earn that respect, which their league craved.

The Kansas City team that had knocked off the Bills was a blend of new and old talent, a mixture of young players who had arrived in the past few years and die-hards who dated to the Dallas days. Len Dawson, Curtis McClinton, Chris Burford, Jim Tyrer, and Fred Arbanas were still starters on offense, and Sherrill Headrick, E. J. Holub, Jerry Mays, and Johnny Robinson still played key roles on defense. Smokey Stover still played his share of snaps. (The Chiefs had traded Abner Haynes after the 1964 season to make room for the ill-fated Mack Lee Hill. The quintessential Dallas Texan, Haynes had amassed more than six thousand rushing and receiving yards and scored thirty-nine touchdowns in five years with the franchise.) Those players had combined with newer players such as Buck Buchanan, Bobby Bell, Otis Taylor, and Mike Garrett, a Heisman Trophy–winning halfback.

The generations had combined to pound the Bills. Dawson threw touchdowns to Arbanas and Taylor. Robinson set up a score with a long interception return, and Garrett set one up with a long punt return. The defense forced four turnovers and blunted Buffalo's ground game.

"Gentlemen, I would like to announce that I am very, very happy at this moment," Headrick shouted in the Chiefs' riotous postgame locker room, climbing on top of a trunk to be heard.

Dawson, speaking to reporters, called it "the second-most thrilling day of my life."

After what?

"The first-most thrilling," he said, "which is coming up on January 15."

That was the date of the inaugural "super" championship game in Los Angeles. The identity of the Chiefs' opponent was about to be determined, with the Cowboys and Packers kicking off in Dallas. Who did the Chiefs want to play? Opinion in the locker room was divided. Some wanted to take on the Packers because Vince Lombardi's team had lorded over the NFL, winning three titles since 1961, so beating them would be sweeter. But the older Chiefs, who had lived through the battle of Dallas, still burned at the memory of giving up their hometown.

"I'd be so high against Dallas that it might hurt me," said Mays, the Dallas native and former SMU star. "But the Packers are well established as the best in the NFL over a period of years. We want to play the best. If we had to play Dallas and we beat the Cowboys, people would say, 'Oh, well, the Cowboys were a fluke team, anyway.' This is not taking anything away from the Cowboys, but they have no more experience than we have. They started the same year we did."

Fans in Dallas knew the Cowboys had kicked off in the same year that the AFL began. In fact, the Cowboys had come into existence *because* Lamar brought an AFL team to Dallas, and the NFL didn't want to give up such a promising football market.

In their first six years, the Cowboys had elicited more groans than cheers, more catcalls than ovations, never finishing with a winning record. But like the Chiefs, they had blossomed in 1966 as years of clever talent evaluations and canny coaching finally paid off. The Cowboys had opened with four straight wins, averaging more than forty points per game, and remained atop the Eastern Division all season, winning enough to stay ahead of the Browns and Eagles and advance to the title game.

The Cowboys also featured a solid core of players tracing back to their early days — Bob Lilly, Chuck Howley, Don Perkins, Jerry Tubbs, Frank Clarke, and at the center of it all, Meredith, who had become an All-Pro quarterback in 1966 after battling injuries, failed expectations, and boos for years. Like the Chiefs, the Cowboys also had newer talent such as Bob Hayes, Mel Renfro, and Dan Reeves. A former college quarterback, Reeves had reinvented himself as a halfback who could run, catch, and throw.

To many fans across the country, the dazzling Cowboys, with their sophisticated multiple offense, breathtaking big plays, and stars from other sports, embodied what pro football was evolving into out of the simplistic, muddy scrums of the forties and fifties — a game for the space age, built on speed, trickery, and Landry's original thinking.

The Packers, of course, were a throwback to that era of simpler football. Whipped by the fanatical Lombardi, Landry's friend and former colleague, into a team of disciplined veterans who excelled at blocking, tackling, and straight-ahead play, they had come to Dallas seeking their fourth NFL title in six years.

The New Year's Day game was part of a two-day football doubleheader in Dallas. The day before, another sellout crowd had descended on Fair Park to root on SMU against the Georgia Bulldogs in the Cotton Bowl. The surprising Mustangs had won the Southwest Conference and were appearing in the holiday bowl game for the first time since Doak Walker's days, but interest in the college game paled next to the throbbing excitement generated in Dallas by the pending pro title game. After Georgia won, 24–9, many fans simply shrugged and counted the hours until the game they really cared about began.

A shattering cheer greeted the opening kickoff the next day; it was a certifiable pinch-me moment, the start of an NFL championship game *in Dallas.* The Cowboys had finally and definitively triumphed over what had been, in a way, their toughest opponent in their early years: college football's long-standing preeminence in Texas. Those days were over. Pro football ruled now.

But the Packers drove to a touchdown on their first possession, then picked up a fumble on the ensuing kickoff and returned it for another touchdown, putting them ahead, 14–0, before the Cowboys' first offensive snap. The Cotton Bowl fell silent. As the offensive players gathered in the huddle before their first play, Meredith drawled, "Well, boys, we're in a heap of shit." It lightened the mood, and the offense went to work. By the end of the first quarter, the Cowboys had driven to two touchdowns, tying the venerable Packers and sending the crowd into a frenzy.

The Packers, more accustomed to playing in big games, gradually regained control, expanding their lead to 34–20 on a touchdown pass from quarterback Bart Starr to Max McGee with five minutes to play. It appeared the Cowboys were beaten.

But Meredith rallied them again. With Green Bay's defense focused on Hayes, Clarke raced behind a safety into the clear and Meredith hit him with a perfect pass. Clarke raced untouched to the end zone to cut the lead to seven. When the Dallas defense rose up and forced a harried punt that traveled just sixteen yards, wobbling out of bounds near midfield, cheers shook the old stadium's concrete underpinnings.

With an eye on the clock, Meredith moved the offense toward the end zone, hitting Clarke again, for twenty-one yards. When Clarke raced into the clear yet again, Green Bay safety Tom Brown blatantly grabbed him near the goal line, taking the interference penalty to keep him from catching the tying touchdown. That put the ball on the Green Bay 2, and Dan Reeves rushed for a yard on first down, leaving the Cowboys one yard from the end zone with less than a minute to play.

One yard.

Millions of fans across the country stood in their living rooms, drawn to their feet by the drama. Lombardi and his Packers were teetering. The upstart Cowboys were about to bring them down.

Meredith put his hands under center and started barking signals. But before the ball could be snapped, a Dallas offensive lineman, tackle Jim Boeke, jumped prematurely. The crowd groaned and Landry grimaced on the sideline as the referee marked off a five-yard penalty. Now the Cowboys needed six yards, not one.

Meredith lobbed a pass to Reeves in the left flat, but the halfback's vision was blurred from getting his eye poked on a previous play, and he dropped the ball. On third down, Meredith threw low for tight end Pettis Norman, who grabbed the ball and fell out of bounds at the 2.

The game came down to a final play. Meredith took the snap and rolled to his right, but Hayes, mistakenly on the field in a goal-line situation, barely blocked Green Bay linebacker Dave Robinson, who rushed in and hit the quarterback before the play could develop. With

Robinson draped on him, Meredith was barely able to raise his right arm and fling a no-look prayer toward the end zone. The pass sailed to the Packers' Tom Brown, who grabbed the interception.

Landry turned away in frustration. The fans sat in their seats, stunned, as the final gun sounded. The Packers, not the Cowboys, would play the Chiefs in Los Angeles. The final chapter of the battle of Dallas would have to unfold at some other time, in some other place.

Landry and Lombardi met at midfield and shook hands. Lombardi congratulated his friend; the Cowboys were a hell of a team. As the players walked off the field, Clint Murchison Jr. spotted one of his favorite sportswriters heading for the locker rooms for interviews. "Well," Murchison said, managing a smile as he put his arm around the writer's shoulder, "I guess we don't want to give them too much too soon, do we?"

In Buffalo the Chiefs watched the ending, shouting at their set along with the rest of the country, then looked at each other and smiled as they finally peeled off their uniforms and showered. They would test themselves against pro football's consummate powerhouse in two weeks. The Cowboys would have to sit at home and watch, just like everyone else.

Many experts and most fans gave the Chiefs little chance against the Packers, believing that a lopsided mismatch was in the offing. Las Vegas originally favored the Packers by eight, but strong early betting on the Packers pushed the line to thirteen.

Stram tried an unusual motivational ploy as the Chiefs practiced in Los Angeles. Capitalizing on comments from NFL executives deriding the AFL as a "Mickey Mouse" league, he had the Chiefs' equipment manager and locker room attendants don Mickey Mouse hats.

Across town, Lombardi drilled his players with a grim purposefulness, fully aware that the Packers simply couldn't lose.

On the day of the game it was clear that the merger remained a work in progress. Both leagues' networks provided broadcasts, but Rozelle ordered CBS to handle the camera work for both, leaving NBC furious. More than 32,000 tickets went unsold. Two different balls were used — the NFL's brand when the Packers had the ball, the AFL's when the Chiefs had possession.

Many of the Chiefs had doubts about how well they could compete with a legendary opponent, but they held up well early. After Green Bay drove to an early touchdown, the Chiefs responded with a score of their own; Dawson hit Taylor for a thirty-one-yard gain and McClinton for a seven-yard touchdown. The Packers went back up on a fourteen-yard run by All-Pro fullback Jim Taylor, but the Chiefs countered with a field goal.

Trailing by just four points at halftime, the Chiefs were exuberant in their locker room; they were moving the ball and believed they had a chance to win. But Lombardi didn't rail at his slightly rattled players, just told them to bear down. Lombardi also ordered his defensive assistant, Phil Bengston, to ramp up the pressure on Dawson, who had plenty of time to throw in the first half. On a third down early in the third quarter, Green Bay's linebackers blitzed for the first time, and Dawson's arm was hit as he threw. The ball wobbled to Green Bay cornerback Willie Wood, who ran it back fifty yards to the Kansas City 5. The Packers quickly scored, and the mismatch finally was on. The Packers wound up winning, 35–10.

Lombardi had refrained from making disparaging comments about the Chiefs before the game, but reporters goaded him into assessing them in the winning locker room.

"I don't think they're as good as the top teams in the National Football League," he said. "They're a good team with fine speed, but I'd have to say NFL football is tougher. Dallas is a better team, and so are several others."

He paused and grumped, "That's what you've wanted me to say. Now I've said it."

Stram, who counted the Green Bay coach as a friend, was surprised by Lombardi's critique. "Did Vince really say we weren't that good? That we couldn't play at that level? Did Vince really say that?" he asked.

Despite the loss, the season was a rousing success for the Chiefs. Their attendance had soared thanks to an aggressive season-ticket drive and a championship season. They had finally caught on in Kansas City. Everyone loved a winner, it seemed.

They would never again play before a home crowd of fewer than 40,000 fans.

⋅ ⋅ ⋅

Seven months after the Super Bowl, the Chiefs exacted revenge. As stipulated in the merger agreement, AFL and NFL teams could now meet in exhibition games, and Lamar scheduled one with George Halas's Bears. It was played on August 23, 1967, before a record crowd for a preseason game in Kansas City. The Chiefs circled it on their calendars, eagerly anticipating it for months. They hadn't forgotten how it felt to get drubbed by the Packers and insulted by Lombardi.

Stram revisited those events in the locker room before the game, and the Chiefs came out in their red uniforms, snarling for revenge. The Bears, coming off a losing season, were a plodding, middle-of-the-pack team. After they opened with an early field goal, Dawson gathered the Chiefs' offense in the huddle. He had been out with the flu for a week but wasn't about to miss this shot at redemption. He flung a pass downfield to Otis Taylor, who had sprinted past the Bears' secondary. Taylor grabbed the ball and raced to the end zone to complete a seventy-yard scoring play.

A few minutes later, E. J. Holub intercepted a pass, and Dawson tossed a touchdown to Chris Burford as the crowd shrieked. Boy, this was fun. After another touchdown a few minutes later, Stram gave in to his emotions. Dawson knelt to hold for the extra point, but instead of putting the ball down when he caught it, he stood and threw to a wide-open Curtis McClinton, garnering two points instead of one. *Who plays in a Mickey Mouse league? Who isn't good enough?*

Before halftime Buck Buchanan grabbed Gale Sayers on a run, hurled the young runner to the ground, and snarled at him for turning down the Chiefs to play in Chicago. Soon after Bobby Bell leveled Sayers with a shot to the chest two plays later, Halas pulled "the Kansas Comet."

The Chiefs kept pouring it on — a double-reverse to Taylor, a long touchdown to Gloster Richardson. By halftime the score was 39–10. The Chiefs' starters pleaded to stay in, wanting to further the Bears' shame. Stram relented at first, but finally pulled them in favor of backups and rookies. Dawson's backup hurled an eighty-yard touchdown. A rookie ran ninety yards for a touchdown with a kickoff.

At the final gun, Fred Arbanas sought out Halas for a handshake. Arbanas had grown up in the Midwest and revered the legendary football man. He found Halas, grabbed his hand. Papa Bear's eyes were glassy, as if he could barely fathom what had just happened.

Years later Arbanas would not be able to recall the score of any game from his long career with the Chiefs except one — the score from that exhibition game in 1967 when the Chiefs unleashed an entire league's frustrations: Chiefs 66, Bears 24.

Mickey Mouse indeed.

The sting of their excruciating 1966 title-game loss to the Packers lingered with the Cowboys for months, but after living with small crowds and unfulfilled expectations for so long, they were happy just to be liked. They drew almost 70,000 fans to their season opener in 1967 and sold out their next game.

Not that long ago, they had practically begged people to come to their games. Now, with their speed, their shiny uniforms, and their computerized scouting system, they were regarded — by fans and industry experts across the country, not just in Dallas — as a progressive, cutting-edge team. Their fans waited in line for hours to get tickets to big games. Murchison's steady, hands-off ownership, Schramm's forward-thinking stewardship, and Landry's shrewd coaching had finally paid off.

But at the core of this now-rosy picture lay the troubled relationship between Landry and Meredith, best described as an unending truce. The coach, now beloved by fans for having produced a winner, still preached strict obedience to his blueprint, while the happy-go-lucky quarterback — beloved by his teammates more than the fans, who still chafed at his nonchalance — preferred to play instinctively, while humming a tune. Though the conflict was difficult to perceive from the outside, it endured. The Cowboys won five of six games to start the 1967 season, but when a hit left Meredith groggy one day and Landry was asked if he had noticed that his quarterback seemed out of it, he snapped in reply, "No, I'm used to seeing him that way."

After leading a late drive to beat the Redskins in October 1967, Meredith landed in the hospital with a broken rib, collapsed lung, and 105-degree fever. He had sacrificed his body to win, but instead of appreciating him for it, many fans were excited to see Craig Morton replace him. The experiment did not go well, and Meredith reclaimed the starting job when he was healthy. On Christmas Eve he gave one of his finest performances as the Cowboys pounded Cleveland at the Cotton Bowl in the Eastern Conference championship game, throwing an eighty-six-yard touchdown to Hayes to start the Cowboys on their way to a 52–14 win. That set up a rematch with the Packers in the NFL championship game.

The story line was the same — new against old, the Cowboys' dazzling swiftness against the Packers' punishing old-pro certitude — only this time the game was at Lambeau Field in Green Bay, where the temperature plummeted to thirteen below at kickoff, turning the field to ice and negating the Cowboys' speed. Green Bay jumped to a 14–0 lead, but the Cowboys rallied. On the first play of the fourth quarter, Meredith handed to Reeves, the former college quarterback, who threw a touchdown pass to flanker Lance Rentzel to give Dallas a 17–14 lead. With the Packers' offense stymied, the Cowboys seemed set to prevail.

But in the final minutes of what became a legendary game, the Packers' offense summoned a final surge and drove the length of the field. The Cowboys' defense dug in to make a stop at the goal line in the final seconds, but Green Bay quarterback Bart Starr sneaked over from the 1 for a touchdown. The Packers' fans flooded onto the field in celebration. The Cowboys had fallen again.

The Cowboy players sprawled in their locker room, numb and exhausted after an epic game played in bitter conditions; a few would battle frostbite. "It's most disappointing to have this happen twice in a row. I guess we can do everything except win the big one," said Meredith, who had not played well, completing just ten of twenty-five pass attempts.

Tears rolled down his cheeks as he stared out the window on the flight home. His body battered, his ego damaged, he almost retired before the next season. He had turned thirty, with kids to support. CBS had asked him to become a broadcaster, and with his quick wit and natural charm, he knew he would be good at it. That sounded like more fun than another year with the meticulous Landry. He came close to walking away.

But instead, Meredith signed a new three-year contract and landed on the cover of *Sports Illustrated*'s 1968 pro football preview issue, pledging to complete the task he had started and bring a title to Dallas. A fierce competitive streak burned inside his easygoing shell. He had unfinished business on the field.

He enjoyed one of his better seasons in 1968, but many fans still itched for Morton. When Meredith threw four interceptions in a pre-season game at the Cotton Bowl, he was booed ferociously. Meredith shrugged, saying he believed more fans were for him than against him. He wasn't as magnanimous after a regular-season game against the Redskins, during which he went out for a quarter with an injury and was booed upon returning. "I'm getting tired of it. The fun is about over," he said. His words would prove fateful.

In late December, the Cowboys were heavily favored to beat the Browns in the Eastern Conference championship game, played this time in Cleveland. But the game unfolded disastrously before a crowd of 81,000. The Cowboys took an early lead, but Meredith wasn't sharp, misfiring on many pass attempts. He threw an early interception, and then, just after halftime, with the teams tied, he tossed one into the flat that a Cleveland linebacker picked off and ran back for a touchdown.

Trying to lead a rally in the third quarter, Meredith threw a pass that bounced off Rentzel's hands and was intercepted. One play later, Browns halfback Leroy Kelly caught a short pass in the left flat, broke into the clear along the sideline, and raced to the end zone to complete a thirty-six-yard scoring play. The crowd went delirious. The Browns had a 24–10 lead.

On the sideline, Landry summoned Morton and sent the young quarterback onto the field. "I think we ought to go with Craig," he told Meredith, who nodded and moved away.

The coach explained later that he was simply trying to give the team a lift, but Cleveland held on to win, 31–20. As the final seconds ticked off the clock, Tex Schramm came down from the press box, stood for-lornly by Meredith, and finally buried his head tearfully in the quarter-back's chest. Meredith gently patted the general manager on the back.

The Cowboys regrouped to beat the Vikings in the Playoff Bowl in Miami the next week, but before training camp began the following summer, Meredith called a press conference and announced that he was retiring from football. He simply had lost the desire to play, he said.

Years later, some of his teammates said that the final loss to Cleveland pushed him over the brink — or not the loss so much as its aftermath, when Landry failed to explain that Meredith had been following orders on the interceptions that lost the game. He had read the coach's beloved "keys" and made the throws they suggested, but the Browns adjusted, trumping Landry's offensive design. That never came up after the game, leaving Meredith looking like the goat.

He was thirty-one, tired of the whole scene, and ready to do something else.

With Morton at quarterback, the Cowboys rolled to yet another division title in 1969, winning twelve of fourteen games, but the season ended with another shocking playoff debacle, a 38–14 loss to Cleveland in the Eastern Conference title game at the Cotton Bowl.

The Cowboys had come unimaginably far in a decade, surviving the Texans and luring Dallas's fans away from the grasp of the college game, but after so many playoff losses the *Times Herald*'s wry Steve Perkins wrote a book about them titled *Next Year's Champions* — as in never this year's. Snickers were audible as far away as Kansas City.

Lamar's original expectations for the AFL had been exceeded by 1969, the final year before the merger took effect and the AFL vanished. All eight of the league's original franchises had survived; they would become part of the NFL in 1970 along with the league's add-on franchises in Miami and Cincinnati. It was one of the great upsets in American sports history. Lamar had taken on the pro football establishment and won.

Most doubts about the AFL's legitimacy disappeared when Joe Namath and the New York Jets defeated the Baltimore Colts, 16–7, in Super Bowl III in Miami, Florida, on January 12, 1969, leaving NFL officials pale with shock. Most experts had deemed the Colts worthy successors to Lombardi's Packers, who had easily won the first two Super Bowls. Las Vegas favored Baltimore by sixteen points, showing little faith in the AFL's ability to compete. But Namath, whose brazen attitude and long hair enraged the NFL's old guard, guaranteed an upset several days before kickoff and backed up his pledge, leading the Jets to a convincing victory.

In one afternoon the AFL achieved the credibility it had sought for a decade. But as the next season — the last before the merger — unfolded, many fans across the country continued to believe that NFL teams were across-the-board superior, reasoning that the Jets' victory had been a fluke, a one-in-a-million accident of the football fates. Surely normalcy would return at Super Bowl IV in New Orleans on January 11, 1970.

As had happened the year before, the NFL produced a champion it believed was unbeatable. The Minnesota Vikings, in their ninth year of existence, dominated with a hard-edged authority reminiscent of the Packers, strutting through a series of lopsided victories. Led by blue-collar quarterback Joe Kapp and a swarming defense nicknamed "the Purple People Eaters," the Vikings rooted for the Jets to make it to the Super Bowl out of the AFL; certain they could set the record straight, they desperately wanted a crack at the cocky Namath. But Lamar's Chiefs upset the Jets in a playoff game and took down the favored Raiders in the AFL title game to advance to the Super Bowl.

Las Vegas gave the Chiefs little chance, favoring the Vikings by thirteen. Many fans and sportswriters bought into the notion, predicting a long day for the Chiefs.

But the more the Chiefs studied film of the Vikings, the more they believed they should win. The game was perceived as a mismatch, but they actually were the better team, with more size and speed. Their defense was a punishing unit that represented what the AFL had stood for — eight of its eleven starters were African Americans, the majority from all-black colleges such as Grambling, Prairie View, and Morgan State. Its rivals in the AFL had been unable to crack it.

Several days before the game, Stram received a call from Walt Corey, who had played linebacker for the Texans and Chiefs and was now a college assistant coach.

"Let me be the first to congratulate you on winning the Super Bowl," Corey said.

"What you mean, Walt? We haven't even played the game," Stram replied.

"Well, you're going to win," Corey said.

"How do you know?" Stram asked.

The Chiefs' defensive front was too big and quick, Corey said, with noseguard Curley Culp positioned right over center, where the Vikings liked to run, and Buck Buchanan alongside him. The Chiefs favored a three-four alignment, which most NFL coaches disdained.

"They've never gone up against anything like that," Corey said. "It's not going to go well for them."

Stram laughed. "I hope you're right," he said.

It was fitting that the team owned by the AFL's founder represented the league in its final game, and to Lamar, it was also fitting that the Vikings were the opponent. Lamar would never forget Minnesota's owners, led by Max Winter, signing on with the AFL only to jump to the NFL when Halas offered them a franchise. Their about-face had devastated the AFL, leaving bitter feelings. A matchup between the Chiefs and Vikings was a fitting conclusion to the AFL-NFL war.

Lamar and his wife Norma flew to New Orleans for the game from their home in Dallas. Rain fell on the morning of the game, then stopped. As Lamar and Norma left for the game, they stepped into an elevator at the Royal Sonesta Hotel to find two other people in it — Max Winter and his wife. The men sputtered through a few moments of awkward small talk before the elevator reached the ground floor and the couples parted.

As the Winters walked away, Lamar smiled and told Norma, "You know what? They're more scared than we are."

The Vikings, wearing all-white uniforms with purple trim and purple helmets, drove into Kansas City territory on their first possession, but the Chiefs, wearing red jerseys, red helmets, and white pants, finally stopped them, forcing a punt. Len Dawson, still the quarterback, led a drive that produced a field goal by Jan Stenerud.

As the teams settled in, the Vikings' running game couldn't get untracked; as Corey had predicted, the Vikings' 235-pound All-Pro center, Mick Tinglehoff, couldn't budge the bigger Culp and Buchanan. Meanwhile, Dawson had success passing to Taylor and Frank Pitts, and two more field goals by Stenerud gave the Chiefs a 9–0 lead.

Late in the second quarter, the Vikings fumbled a kickoff return, and the Chiefs recovered and scored a touchdown to take a 16–0 lead as the teams headed to their locker rooms for halftime. Across the nation, fans of the NFL, watching on CBS, could barely believe what they were seeing.

Kapp finally led a touchdown drive early in the second half, but the rally ended quickly. The Chiefs came right back and scored on a forty-six-yard pass from Dawson to Taylor. The receiver ran a short sideline route, reeled in the catch, shed his defender, raced down the sideline, juked a tackler, and crossed the goal line. The Vikings were sunk.

The fourth quarter was a rousing valedictory. The Chiefs knocked Kapp out of the game and intercepted three passes. The final score was 23–7. No one would dare say it was a fluke. The Chiefs had manhandled the Vikings. The NFL's reigning superpower had been squashed.

Lamar had never felt happier. The lowly franchise he had started a decade ago was about to reign over pro football. In the beginning, he had stuffed free tickets into packages of Fritos to get people to come see the Dallas Texans. Now the whole world was watching his team.

As the clock wound down, a lone fan in the stands at the Sugar Bowl raised a handwritten sign near midfield: DALLAS TEXANS, COME HOME. Lamar smiled, thinking about his hometown.

"I am in no way saying he didn't want to succeed in Dallas and remain in Dallas. Definitely, that was what he wanted," Norma said years later. "So of course, it was hard when you see you have to move. But I suppose it couldn't have happened to a better guy as far as personality, because he had the ability to handle it. Of course he wanted to remain. But he didn't live with acrimony and recriminations."

In the locker room after the game, Lamar stood on a podium with Pete Rozelle and CBS broadcaster Frank Gifford for the trophy presentation.

"Lamar, as you look back over those other years, some ten years ago, there must be quite a feeling," Gifford said.

"It's pretty fantastic," Lamar said. "This is a beautiful trophy, and it really is a satisfying conclusion to the ten years of the American Football League."

An inveterate scorekeeper, he had feared losing to the Vikings because he knew that would leave the AFL, after its final game, with just one win in four Super Bowls, a record that connoted inferiority and would exist permanently, leaving all future generations of sports fans to contemplate the AFL's second-class status.

Now, though, the final score was AFL 2, NFL 2. The upstarts had tied their haughty older brothers.

And though he would never share this statistic with the public, he also thought of another score: Texans 1, Cowboys 0.

Yes, he had ceded his hometown to his rivals, but he had prevailed in their race to pro football glory.

# EPILOGUE

**E**IGHT MONTHS AFTER their Super Bowl triumph, the Chiefs played a game that, while far less important, carried its own unique significance. They took on the Cowboys in an exhibition game at the Cotton Bowl on September 5, 1970.

"The once-inconceivable will happen," Clint Murchison Jr. wrote before the game in his weekly column for the *Dallas Cowboys Insiders Newsletter*. "Lamar and I will meet in the press box, shake hands and make some small talk. Then we will see a great battle on the field, one that everybody has been anticipating for ten years. But it won't be a fight like in the good, old days."

The game drew a near-sellout crowd of 69,000. Had it taken place a decade earlier, the atmosphere would have been rowdy, some fans cheering for Murchison's team, others for Lamar's. But Lamar and his team were just visitors now. The Cowboys owned Dallas.

On this night, more than a few Dallas fans wondered if the wrong team had left. The Chiefs, led by their Super Bowl–winning defense, completely smothered the Cowboys, 13–0.

Fans in Dallas had already discovered, to their dismay, that Don Meredith's departure, long awaited by some, hadn't enabled their team to get over its playoff "issue." With Craig Morton under center, the Cowboys had lost again in the postseason the year before, absorbing a drubbing from Cleveland. Now, months later, as Morton struggled in an exhibition game against the team formerly known as the Dallas Texans, he heard the same boos that had serenaded Meredith for years.

The victory was enormously satisfying for Lamar, Jack Steadman, and Chiefs such as Len Dawson and Johnny Robinson, who dated back to the franchise's days in Dallas. But the Cowboys gained revenge seven weeks later, winning a regular-season game in Kansas City. Murchison and Tex Schramm wore broad smiles as Morton sealed the 27–16 victory with an eighty-nine-yard touchdown pass to Bob Hayes.

As that season — the first year of the merger — played out, the Chiefs wound up missing the playoffs, while the Cowboys finally overcame their hex, winning a pair of postseason games to advance to Super Bowl V against the Baltimore Colts. They were favored and led at halftime, but blew the lead and lost on a last-second field goal. Yet again, they were "Next Year's Champions."

The following year, the Chiefs and Cowboys both qualified for the postseason as favorites to reach the Super Bowl. The Chiefs had their marauding defense, and the Cowboys had gone on a roll after Roger Staubach replaced Morton at midseason and provided the playmaking agility and psychological ballast the team had lacked.

The Cowboys made it to the Super Bowl, but the Chiefs fell short, losing to the Miami Dolphins in an epic double-overtime playoff game at Municipal Stadium. It was the longest pro football game ever — some five minutes beyond the 1962 AFL championship game between the Texans and Oilers.

The Cowboys' presence in Super Bowl VI, played at the Sugar Bowl in New Orleans on January 16, 1972, meant that four of the first six Super Bowls had featured either the Cowboys or the former Dallas Texans. The Chiefs had won the big game two years earlier, and now the Cowboys matched that "ultimate" victory, defeating the Dolphins, 24–3.

Twelve years after their unceremonious birth as a winless expansion team, they were the champions of pro football. "It's the successful completion of our twelve-year plan," Murchison said.

One year after his retirement, Don Meredith joined the broadcasting crew of ABC's *Monday Night Football*, a new prime-time NFL broadcast. Mixing glitz and sports as never before, the show became enormously popular, owing in no small part to Meredith's on-air sparring with Howard Cosell, a bombastic New York lawyer turned sportscaster.

Meredith's homespun personality made him a bigger star in broadcasting than he ever was in football. Millions of fans tuned in every week to hear him joke, sing, and occasionally analyze the game. His signature call was singing the refrain from a classic Willie Nelson song when a game's outcome had been determined.

"Turn out the liiights, the party's over," he would warble.

In a 1972 Monday night game at Houston's Astrodome, the Oakland Raiders were on their way to a 34–0 victory over the Oilers when an ABC cameraman zeroed in on a disgruntled Houston fan, who made an obscene gesture with his middle finger.

"He thinks they're number one in the nation," Meredith drawled.

As laughter rang out in living rooms across America, Meredith's former teammates smiled and nodded. That was the "Dandy Don" they knew.

By the early seventies, the difficulties the Cowboys and Texans had experienced in their early years seemed like ancient history. A decade after many speculated that the battle for Dallas's football future would produce two losers, it was clear that both teams had won. They were successful not only on the field but also off the field.

In 1971 the Cowboys left the Cotton Bowl for Texas Stadium, a gleaming, futuristic facility with an artificial-turf field and partial dome that kept fans dry when it rained. Located in suburban Irving — Murchison and the city of Dallas had been unable to agree on a site for a new home — the stadium had been financed by construction bonds that season-ticket holders purchased, giving them the right to buy their tickets. With its large scoreboards, carpeted luxury suites, and wide corridors, the stadium attracted the cream of Dallas society and transformed the Cowboys into an elite franchise.

A year later, the Chiefs completed a similar move. After the city of Kansas City failed to determine a suitable location for a replacement for Municipal Stadium, voters in suburban Jackson County approved a bond issue to pay for adjacent football and baseball stadiums. As the Chiefs moved into Arrowhead Stadium on Kansas City's outskirts, George Halas, around since the twenties, called the twin-stadium site "the most revolutionary, futuristic sports complex I have ever seen."

After losing the double-overtime playoff game in 1971, the Chiefs fell into a decline, failing to return to the playoffs until the mid-1980s. The slump cost Hank Stram his job after the team posted a 5-9 record in 1974. Lamar hated to fire the best man at his wedding and only coach in the franchise's history, but he believed that a change was needed.

After Stram departed, the Chiefs posted a winning record just once in the next eleven years.

The Cowboys fared far better. With Landry coolly pacing the sidelines in his fedora and Staubach working miracles under center, they matured into football royalty. Over the twenty-year period that began in 1966, they won two Super Bowls, five NFC titles, and fourteen division titles without once posting a losing record in a season. Schramm's original vision of a successful franchise was realized and surpassed. The Cowboys' home games were social events, their players as famous as any pro athletes in America thanks to frequent national TV broadcasts.

Although two Super Bowl losses to the Pittsburgh Steelers kept them from achieving an absolute dynasty on the field, their popularity was so widespread that an NFL Films producer labeled them "America's Team" in 1978. The nickname stuck to them like the stars on the sides of their helmets. The Cowboys were more than just a sports team. They were cultural icons, dashing symbols of modern Texas.

During a game at RFK Stadium in Washington in 1981, a Washington fan threw ice into Murchison's box and hit his wife in the eye. A security officer gave the fan a stern rebuke: "Do you realize you have hit the wife of the Cowboys' owner, Mrs. Murchison, in the eye?"

The fan responded, "I thought Tex Schramm owned the Cowboys."

Outside of Dallas, few fans knew who actually owned the country's favorite football team. Although Murchison's vast financial empire stretched around the globe, he remained a low-key presence in football, letting his general manager and coach take the spotlight.

"The Cowboys were pretty much always a minuscule part of what he was doing," his son Robert said in 2011. "They got more valuable with time, but what made them so important was just the high profile. You read about them every day in the paper. They were good for his other businesses as far as his image as a winner. It helped him a lot. He capitalized on it."

Behind the scenes, Murchison relished the high life, playing the role of Texas royalty — overplaying it, actually. His womanizing and drug use, chronicled in several books about the team and his family, cost Murchison his marriage; his first wife divorced him in 1972. Three years later, he married the ex-wife of Gil Brandt, his team's personnel director. A devout Christian, his new wife convinced him to change his lifestyle.

In the early eighties, Murchison experienced the onset of a degenerative nerve disease related to Parkinson's and also experienced a severe financial reversal as some of his investments soured and oil prices dropped. His practice of trusting the people he had hired backfired in several cases.

"As time went on, he had some financial issues that began to back up on him," his son Burk said in 2011. "But I don't think it ever impacted what the Cowboys did. Dad was always overleveraged, but he kept the Cowboys on an island, never pledged them as collateral, that kind of stuff. He kept them segregated, really protected them as a kind of a jewel."

He remained friendly with Lamar, able to joke about the years they fought over Dallas. In 1982 Lamar's friends threw a surprise fiftieth birthday party for him and asked Murchison to help with a video they filmed as a tribute. Murchison — by now relegated to a wheelchair because of his illness — participated in a re-creation of the 1960 episode in which Lamar popped out of a birthday cake, surprising Murchison.

"We had Clint pop out of the cake this time. He was sick as hell, but he was game and determined to do it," said Lamar's friend Buzz Kemble, the Fort Worth lawyer, who filmed the video. "He popped out of the cake and shouted, 'Happy birthday, Lamar! Go Cowboys!'"

It was a sad statement on the decline in Murchison's fortunes when his mounting debts forced him to put the Cowboys up for sale in

1983. A Dallas banker, H. R. "Bum" Bright, bought the team the next year.

Murchison died in 1987.

On Thanksgiving morning in 1995, Lamar left his house on Preston Road in Dallas and went to Texas Stadium to watch his team play. The Chiefs were taking on the Cowboys that afternoon.

He had long ago come to terms with the fact that his hometown belonged to someone else. He was popular and immensely respected in Kansas City. The man who had been nicknamed "Games" as a boy had become involved in other sports as well as pro football over the years, starting a pro tennis tour and helping bring pro soccer to America. The Chiefs were just one of his interests, and although they had never won another Super Bowl, they were obviously far better off for having left Dallas all those years ago.

When the Chiefs played at home, Lamar usually flew up the day before, traveling commercial, and spent the night at his Arrowhead Stadium suite. On Sunday mornings he went for a jog around the stadium, mingling with the fans before settling in for the game. Known for his hands-off ownership style, he let his football decision-makers run the team, figuring they were the experts.

In 1995 the Cowboys were now in the hands of an owner with a decidedly different approach. Jerry Jones, an aggressive Arkansas oilman, had bought the team in 1989 from Bum Bright. Jones was "hands-on," to say the least, overseeing personnel decisions, stalking the sidelines during games, and giving daily interviews to reporters.

His first move upon taking over the team had been to fire Landry, earning him widespread enmity among the team's fans even though Landry had lost his winning touch in the late eighties. But Jones had prevailed over his detractors, directing the revamped Cowboys to a pair of Super Bowl victories in the early nineties. In five years as an owner, he had won as many Super Bowls as Murchison, Landry, and Schramm did in almost three decades.

Lamar liked Jones, a relentless businessman always looking for new revenue streams to boost the Cowboys' bottom line. Having started a league from scratch years ago, Lamar admired that. The two got along well. In fact, Jones lived near Lamar, and as the 1995 game approached they joked about holding the pregame coin flip in the middle of Preston Road.

But while Lamar was fine with someone else owning the team in his hometown, he still wanted to beat the Cowboys. "It's very important to him. There's no question anytime Lamar Hunt's Chiefs play the Dallas Cowboys, it's a big game," Carl Peterson, the Chiefs' general manager, told the *Morning News* that week. Ralph Wilson, who still owned the Buffalo franchise Lamar had recruited him to run thirty-five years earlier, told the paper, "He's never said anything, but I'm sure it bothered Lamar. He wanted to stay in Dallas. The NFL came in and forced him out. We were just a little fledgling league. The whole thing was very tough on him."

All Lamar would say before the Thanksgiving game was, "I have been looking forward to it." The Chiefs had an NFL-best 10-1 record. They had made the playoffs for five straight seasons, energizing Kansas City's fans, who filled Arrowhead Stadium on Sundays. The Cowboys were also on a high with a 9-2 record heading into the Thanksgiving game.

But if Lamar sought a pound of Cowboy flesh that afternoon, he went home disappointed. The Cowboys won, 24–12.

The Chiefs bounced back to end the regular season with a 13-3 record, earning the number-one seed in the AFC playoff field; with a first-round bye and home-field advantage throughout the postseason, they were positioned perfectly to make a Super Bowl run. Maybe they would face the Cowboys, the top seed in the NFC, in the big game.

A howling crowd filled Arrowhead Stadium on January 7, 1996, as the Chiefs began their anticipated playoff run. They hadn't lost at home all season and were heavily favored to defeat the Indianapolis Colts, a wild-card playoff qualifier. But the Colts surprised them, 10–7, bitterly disappointing Lamar.

Three weeks later, the Cowboys won another Super Bowl, their third in four years and fifth overall.

In 1996 I interviewed Landry for a book I was writing about having grown up in Dallas as a Cowboy fan. We met at his North Dallas home on a winter afternoon and spent several hours in his den. He had been out of football for seven years and was clearly happy to be retired. He told funny stories and took on all topics.

When the Cowboys' battle with the Texans came up, we discussed the possibility that the Texans might have won if the teams had played.

"Oh, I think so," Landry said quickly. "They surely would have had a chance. I suspect they were the better team. They never had a chance to prove it, but they were assembling some pretty good personnel that wound up giving the Packers a pretty good game in the [first] Super Bowl. And we had castoffs."

When I repeated his comments to Wes Wise, a former Dallas sportscaster who had broadcast the Cowboys' games in 1960 and later served as Dallas's mayor in the seventies, he said, "I'm surprised to hear Tom admit that. I suspect that he's right — the Texans probably did have a better team at first. But that would have raised a ruckus back then."

On February 6, 2011, America stopped to watch the Super Bowl, as it always does. The championship game spawned by the AFL-NFL merger — and named by Lamar — was now the country's premier sports spectacle, a de facto national holiday that drew TV audiences of more than 100 million and dwarfed the World Series in interest and buzz.

For the first time, the game was being played in Dallas. Fifty-one years after the Cowboys and Texans kicked off before sparse crowds at the Cotton Bowl, the city they had fought over was hosting the NFL's biggest party. Jerry Jones had lured it by building a spectacular new home for the Cowboys, a massive Taj Mahal of a stadium in suburban Arlington that seated over 100,000 and had cost $1.2 billion to build.

In the year leading up to the game, the local host committee — the group charged with staging the event — commemorated the history of football in North Texas with a contest titled "A Century in the Making." Fans were asked to pick the region's one hundred greatest football moments from a larger list of suggestions going back to 1913, when high school football dominated the scene. To promote the contest, the committee brought together a group of local high school, college, and pro legends at Dallas's Woodrow Wilson High School on January 12, 2010.

Several rows of chairs were arranged on the stage in the school's auditorium. Former Cowboy quarterbacks Roger Staubach and Troy Aikman, winners of five Super Bowls between them, sat up front. Other football icons with local roots, such as Tony Dorsett, Michael Irvin, "Mean" Joe Greene, Tim Brown, and Billy Sims, were also on the stage.

As the event began, people in the packed auditorium wondered about the guy seated in the back row all the way to the right. Who was that smallish African American gentleman with a close crop of white hair and a full white Santa beard? He wasn't a former Cowboy, was he?

The moderator introduced him: "Ladies and gentlemen, please welcome South Dallas's original legend, from Lincoln High School, North Texas, and the AFL's Dallas Texans . . . Abner Haynes!"

Some people in the crowd had never heard of him and didn't even know Dallas had once cheered for two pro teams. The Texans had officially faded into the mists of distant history. But Haynes — now seventy-three, raising goats on a farm south of Dallas — was living proof that the Texans did exist and gave the Cowboys a battle before packing up and leaving.

Just as he had at the Cotton Bowl a half-century earlier, Haynes stole the show in the auditorium, recalling his days as a barrier-busting black athlete at segregated North Texas.

"I was scared to death. We were shot at, almost assassinated," he said in a gravelly baritone. "My teammates had no idea what they were getting into. They didn't know I was coming to the school. But we became a family. Fifty years later, I'm very proud of them."

The crowd applauded, and after the event reporters went to Haynes to get more from him.

"It's a great story," he said. "But honestly, I don't like talking about race. It just dominates everything."

He paused and smiled, his eyes crinkling.

"Just once," he said, "I would love someone to ask if I could play football."

He certainly could.

# AUTHOR'S NOTE ON SOURCES

⎯⎯⎯ ★ ⎯⎯⎯

THIS NARRATIVE WAS constructed from original interviews with almost sixty sources, as well as information gleaned from newspapers, books, magazines, films, and websites.

The following sources were interviewed specifically for this book: Fred Arbanas, May 5, 2010, in Kansas City; Dick Bielski, April 28, 2010, in Baltimore; Sam Blair, February 16, 2010, in Dallas; Tom Braatz, April 2, 2010, by phone; Gil Brandt, January 6, 2010, in Dallas; Tommy Brooker, June 28, 2011, by phone; Chris Burford, March 24, 2010, by phone; Walt Corey, May 4, 2010, in Kansas City; Jerry Cornelison, May 5, 2010, in Kansas City; Gene Cronin; April 2, 2010, by phone; Cotton Davidson, March 29, 2010, by phone; Len Dawson, May 5, 2010, in Kansas City; Fred Dugan, April 2, 2010, by phone; Sissy Dupre, March 31, 2010, by phone; Abner Haynes, January 5, 2010, in Dallas; Clark Hunt, May 17, 2010, by phone; Norma Hunt, May 17, 2010, by phone; Ed Husmann, March 31, 2010, by phone; Buzz Kemble, July 7, 2011, in Fort Worth; Walt Kowalczyk, March 25, 2010, by phone; Bill Livingston, April 1, 2010, by phone; Buddy Macatee, September 17, 2011, by phone; Curtis McClinton, May 4, 2010, in Kansas City; Don McIlhenny, March 31, 2010, by phone; Burk Murchison, July 7, 2011, in Dallas; Clint Murchison III, July 8, 2011, in Dallas; Robert Murchison, July 7, 2011, in Dallas; Nancy Nichols, January 21,

2011, by phone; Jack Patera, March 31, 2010, by phone; Mack Rankin, January 6, 2012, by phone; Al Reynolds, May 10, 2010, by phone; Mike Rhyner, January 6, 2011, by phone; Jack Spikes, February 15, 2010, in Dallas; Jack Steadman, March 24, 2010, by phone; Smokey Stover, April 7, 2010, by phone; Jerry Tubbs, January 8, 2010, in Dallas; Wes Wise, February 17, 2010, in Dallas.

I also relied on interviews conducted more than a decade earlier for *Cotton Bowl Days: Growing Up with Dallas and the Cowboys in the 1960s,* my 1997 memoir about being a young fan, which included a chapter about the Cowboys-Texans battle. In that earlier round of interviews, I spoke at length with many of the characters in this book who have since passed away, including Lamar Hunt, Tom Landry, and Hank Stram. For *Cotton Bowl Days* I interviewed: Walt Garrison, February 7, 1996, in Lewisville, Texas; E. J. Holub, January 17, 1996, by phone; Lamar Hunt, December 13, 1995, by phone; Tom Landry, January 13, 1996, in Dallas; Eddie LeBaron, January 17, 1996, by phone; Bob Lilly, February 5, 1996, in Graham, Texas; Don McIlhenny, January 11, 1996, in Dallas; Don Perkins, February 9, 1996, in Albuquerque, New Mexico; Tex Schramm, February 11, 1996, by phone; Hank Stram, December 9, 1995, by phone; Jerry Tubbs, January 10, 1996, in Dallas; Wes Wise, January 12, 1996, in Dallas.

I read old issues of the *Dallas Morning News* on microfilm at the Library of Congress in Washington, DC. Old issues of the *Dallas Times Herald* were scanned for me at SMU's Fondren Library in Dallas and then e-mailed to me. Ashley Krone, a freelance researcher, performed the scanning and e-mailing. Thanks, Ashley, for a job well done.

I was helped immensely by the work of journalists who have previously covered aspects of this story. Sam Blair's *Dallas Cowboys: Pro or Con?* (1970) offers a detailed rendering of the franchise's first decade. Michael MacCambridge's *America's Game: The Epic Story of How Pro Football Captured a Nation* (2004) is, in my opinion, the definitive study of the NFL as it evolved into the nation's number-one sport. It helped me depict the machinations that led to Dallas landing a pair of franchises in 1960.

Jeff Miller's oral history *Going Long: The Wild 10-Year Saga of the Renegade American Football League in the Words of Those Who Lived It* (2003) enabled me to hear from sources I couldn't reach. Bryan Burrough's *The Big Rich* (2009) reports on the rising and falling fortunes of several Texas oil families, including the Hunts and Murchisons. *Tex!: The Man Who Built the Dallas Cowboys* (1988) by Bob St. John contains Tex Schramm's pointed views on the battle with the Texans. Burk Murchison gave me a copy of *The Island Remembered*, his book about life on his father's private island in the Bahamas, which included several wonderful remembrances.

Other books I found helpful included *The Murchisons: The Rise and Fall of a Texas Dynasty* (1989) by Jane Wolfe; *Next Year's Champions* (1969) by Steve Perkins; *Classic Clint: The Laughs and Times of Clint Murchison Jr.* (1992) by Dick Hitt; *The Landry Legend* (2000) by Bob St. John; *The Dallas Cowboys and the NFL* (1970) by Donald Chipman, Randolph Campbell, and Robert Calvert; *75 Seasons: The Complete Story of the National Football League* (1994) by Peter King; *God's Coach: The Hymns, Hype, and Hypocrisy of Tom Landry's Cowboys* (1990) by Skip Bayless; *Lamar Hunt: The Gentle Giant Who Revolutionized Pro Sports* (2010) by David Sweet; *Lamar Hunt and the Founding of the American Football League* (2009) by Tom Richey; and *They're Playing My Game* (2006) by Hank Stram with Lou Sahadi.

Pete Moris, then of the Kansas City Chiefs, took a keen interest in the project and helped me line up interviews. Bill Nichols of the *Dallas Morning News* gave me some contact information to help me get started. Abner Haynes was an enthusiastic subject and generous with his amazing contact information. Thom Meredith gave me insight into Lamar Hunt, as did *Games,* an NFL Films–produced biographical video. *Full Color Football,* Showtime's history of the AFL, paints a vivid portrait of the league. The website pro-football-reference.com was my go-to place on the Internet for factual information about the early 1960s.

Creating a narrative that utilizes many voices and sources, I have strived to avoid error and also to convey quotes, thoughts, and intentions exactly as they were conveyed to me, but three decades as a sports journalist have taught me that perfection is a difficult standard to attain. Any mistakes are mine.

It was only after I appeared on *Full Color Football,* interviewed about the Cowboys-Texans war because of the chapter I wrote in *Cot-*

*ton Bowl Days,* that I realized the subject was worthy of an entire book. My agent, Scott Waxman, agreed wholeheartedly and quickly found a home for the project at Houghton Mifflin Harcourt. Susan Canavan was an editor who never failed to take the draft of my manuscript and make it infinitely better. My thanks to Scott and Susan for making this book happen.

# INDEX

10/12